THE PATHFINDER
DIARIES

TALES SCULPTED BY SEA

CORY BELYEA

ISBN: 978-1-7168-9300-1 (sc)
ISBN: 978-1-7168-9299-8 (e)

Library of Congress Control Number: 2020907932

Map Illustration by Matt Munz

Lulu Publishing Services rev. date: 10/07/2020

Author's Notes: On Sucking

I was going to change the world, expose government corruption, and activate consciousness around the globe while honoring the people of Latin America as well as my fallen friend, Mike, and the ocean. Sounds like a mouthful. It was. After several of my friends failed to provide feedback, an experienced editor stepped in to deliver the truth: there were too many stories, themes, and people. The 135,000-word manuscript, like my life, resembled a mental pinball machine, and it sucked. Forget about changing the world; in order to serve it, I knew I was the one who needed to change. As my friend Nate said, "Don't go right when the wave is going left."

So it was time to dig deep. Where were the roots? What was the common thread that bound these stories? The love for Mike, the ocean, and Latin American adventures. Now, twenty-nine sea-centric tales remain.

I have reconstructed the experiences to the best of my memory. To improve comprehension, I have translated my answers in conversations to English. Some names have been changed to protect identities.

It's very important to have people in your life who believe in you, encourage you, and inspire you to go after your dreams. Mike was one of those people. His support for his friends was unwavering and eternal. And eternal he will remain.

A diary is a living expression. By reading *The Pathfinder Diaries*, you are bringing life to these experiences and people. For this, I thank you.

*Map of American Continent with labeled
stops and cities tracing the journey*

Contents

Part I

Growing Pains

"We can't get to the center without going through the heart of the storm."
–Mark Nepo

Foreword

To my older brother,
My best friend,
My words of wisdom,
I love you more…..
–Jackie Brant

The hole in my heart will not mend.

My first born, my son, the joy of my life, an enigma, a total fuck-up by conventional standards, a kind gentle soul, too soft for the harsh reality of our world, slipped beneath the surface of life into the immortality of the sea. Impossible not to love; impossible not to miss; forever engrained in our hearts, minds and souls.

Be at peace my son, the demons, the man-made demons of drugs and alcohol no longer tear at your mind, body and soul. You are free to be reborn if God sees fit from the endless sea. Be patient. Rise again and be free.

Reading *The Pathfinder Diaries* on the long flight to China, brought a lot of crying and laughter.

This was a very good read even if you don't know us, and if you read it, you soon will.

A bitter sweet story of freedom and death, and if you think about the Pathfinder, we are all on the road. All we can do is ENJOY the JOURNEY.

If the lessons taught from these stories save one life, then Mike's life and legacy lives on.

If you are reading this, if you knew and loved Mike, you carry him in your heart.

Love life,

Wes Brant
November, 2019

Good friends come and go, but the greatest friends never leave the heart.

In Loving Memory of Michael Cole Brant

Bajan Baptism

Everyone has a Mike Brant story. Mike had just received a healthy-sized check from his grandmother. With his immoderate ways, I knew he would be broke soon. I asked him if he wanted to go to Barbados for spring break. He looked at me with his newly purchased giant black bubble North Face jacket and said, "Fuckin-A Sauce, let's do this, mon!"

I'd say Mike had been surfing for a total of five months, and by surfing, I mean nothing over waist high, O' Hawaiian. When we got to Bathsheba, we were greeted by a solid 8-10' swell that was lighting up the famed right-hander Soup Bowls. A break known for its power and shallow, razor-sharp, urchin-covered reef. Basically, it could really fuck you up if you fell in the wrong spot. Most people would be shitting a brick. I was. Mike handed me the camera and said, "Watch this, mon." As he paddled out, an ominous set stretched across the darkening horizon. I lost sight of him in the wild and angry ocean. Less than fifteen minutes later, half a board fluttered in the fresh trade winds as the whitewater steam rolled in. I zoomed in. I could see a little piece of red that resembled Mike's new, unridden 6'3 Byrne thumb tail[1].

Where was Mike?

The second half of the board washed in with half of a leash dragging behind. Now, Mike found himself without a board, his lifeline, in the biggest waves of his inexperienced surfing life. He surfaced from the frothing sea and began swimming for his life. Struggling against the infinite power of the sea, he stroked and stroked. He paused to take a

---

[1] At least our friend Shane gave him a killer deal on his new board. Within our clan, Shane is known as the Big Kahuna; watch him surf-wake board, snowboard or listen to him spin a yarn and you will learn. Greatness deserves a title, and within our group of surfers, that's the BIG KAHUNA.

breath as the ocean ripped him back out to sea, and then he stroked some more. His head was down; he was making it. Eventually, the surge washed him ashore like some used toilet paper. SPENT. His face was flushed like he had just seen a ghost. He struggled to pack air into his oxygen-starved lungs.

I looked into his awe-struck eyes and said, "Hey, Mike, I'm still watching."

A serrated leash clung to his fat ankle[2]. His feet were sliced to ribbons, and I could see the black dots peppering them: sea urchin spines. He was flat on his belly with his chin hovering just over the coarse sand, mouth agape, as he issued two words, "Dom, mon!" He rolled over on his back and looked into the tropical blue sky. No doubt, it was the beat-down of his life. He shook his head in disbelief.

"Dude, are you OK?"

Mike froze, listening to the thundering surf. Life swelled in his eyes as a savage smile tugged at his face. He threw his hands in the air, rolling around in the sand in a fit of laughter. From that day on, I knew he was a surfer.

---

[2] I would later find out that his ankles were not swollen, just fat, naturally fat.

Preface

Clouds of white dust and negativity swirled in my rearview as the path snaked its way through the cactus-covered hills. The ocean hid behind a thick wall of fog. I knew the break was there; my nostrils stretched to meet the salty breeze. The sandy trail dissolved into a bluff that towered over waves echoing from beyond an impenetrable gloom. I pulled over. My head throbbed, the product of last night's farewell fiesta. In the middle of nowhere, I asked myself, *what am I doing here?*

I was alone. My existence was reduced to an abundance of question marks. I decided to keep myself busy and set up camp. As I opened the back hatch of the Pathfinder, my life's possessions lunged out at me, a disheveled mess coated in Mexican dust. I reminded myself that I was here because of a dream. A dream spawned from a nightmare, a series of nightmares. Crossing over at San Ysidro, I had passed the point of no return; the iron curtain had closed behind me. I was on a one-way trip, destination south. What I had to do was simple: I had to act. My pulsating temples demanded action. As I searched for water, my heart sank like a stone. A motionless vial rested in a cup holder, its presence haunting. The cremated remains of one of my best friends, Mike Brant, a wild and restless soul, were now peering up at me from behind transparent glass. I took a deep breath; the salty air cooled my lungs.

Mike's day of redemption would come.

In my daydreaming, the fog had loosened its grip on the coastline. The Mexican sun torched the sky. Vultures were first to appear, looping eagerly overhead. Hope materialized behind the fading marine layer in the form of corduroy lines stretching out to infinity. Energized saltwater marched upon the breathless sea. My mouth dropped: hurricane-swell waves that had traveled hundreds of miles across the Pacific had arrived at their final destination, a place somewhere in Baja.

The desert sand shimmered with the return of the sun to its fiery zenith. My shattered heart pumped joy and adrenaline back into my veins as the first set uncoiled on the shallow rock bottom. The ocean-sea sparkled. I was on the right path. The spirit of Mike was going to guide me out of my darkest hour. I felt it. I did what any surfer would have done: I howled and frantically pulled at my wet, sandy wetsuit. The tent would have to wait.

I ran along the sheer cliffs, past the dormant fishing outpost, and down the boat ramp. I slipped into the surging sea and paddled out. *Solo.*

It was firing[3]!

---

[3] Going off, mental, *buenaso—epico—otro nivel*, really good.

San Diego Extreme

"You are lost the instant you know what the result will be."
–Juan Gris

"Pacific Beach (San Diego) is like Wrightsville Beach times ten. You guys are going to love it!"

Gushing enthusiasm, a small man draped in a denim suit stood before us. His name was Stay-up-Player, proud owner of white-frosted tips and energetic eyes. He obviously knew the deal. Taking Player's advice, we loaded up Munz's Forerunner and charged west on I-40[4]. We had it all: bachelor's degrees from University of North Carolina at Wilmington fresh in hand[5], 21 years old, an upcoming Halloween party, and we were moving to a place that was WB times ten! Pacific Beach, here we come. It felt like we were surfing's version of *Aspen Extreme,* a movie about young skiers who left crappy jobs in Detroit to chase down the dream of skiing the Rocky Mountains. We too were in search of adventure and looked to push our limits in the mighty Pacific Ocean. In that painfully long car ride, Munz looked over at me, wearing an oversized Whalers hockey jersey with his big blue eyes brimming with wonderment. His casual yet strange smoothness in and out of the water made me think that he was to play TJ Burke, the star of our movie, *San Diego Extreme.* I, being the extraverted loose cannon of immoderation, was left with the role of Dexter Rutecki,

---

[4] Full name Matt Munz aka Rictore, Minghy, Fats, Yao Ming Fat, Fathew, Fatrick, Whale, and Lard Hamilton. The funny thing is that he's not even fat. He just has robust ribs.

[5] Munz had a degree in communications, and I had one in criminal justice. Look out, world!

who died skiing out of bounds in a class five slide, avalanche. I hoped I wouldn't share his fate surfing[6].

After three months of attending job fairs and corporate interviews, our California Dream consisted of a one-bedroom studio, sharing a porch with gay neighbors whose place smelled like cat piss, poop, and cigarettes. Munz landed a bussing job at PF Changs, and I found work at Equity 1 Lenders Group, making hundreds of unwanted calls from an automatic dialer. We sucked. But the waves did not. There were waves every day. We raved to all our boyz back East about the glory of the Pacific. Our lives had become a living surf video.

Well, if there was one guy who loves surf videos, it was Mike Brant. Mike had heard enough and booked his flight seventeen months later. Picking him up at the train station at Solana Beach, we barely recognized him. Like Medusa, his blonde, dirty dreads slithered around his shoulders as he moved. He still had the same expressive eyes as he toted a hemorrhaging board bag with perfect posture.

Munz and I had been anxiously monitoring a giant storm brewing in the North Pacific, the biggest swell of the year. We were sure that Mike hadn't done any training. Getting back to our place, we told him of the swell about to hammer the coast. Mike was more concerned about showing us his secret weapon.

"Check this out, boys. Kahuna[7] hooked it up!"

The brand new Orion surfboard (squash tail) had a ton of volume, like it was made for a really fat guy or some beginner. Mike was neither. Reading my dubious look, he turned it over to reveal the deck.

"Nah, dude, the thing is bodass, mon."

Munz exploded in high-pitched laughter. Tears edged his eyes as he laughed uncontrollably. Mike's board was by far the ugliest surfboard we had ever seen. It looked like a smurf had vomited and then someone swirled it into camouflage. Mike loved it, in fact, it was his custom order. His unbridled energy bounced him all over the apartment as he

---

[6] TJ Burke honored his fallen friend by winning the powder eight and skiing out of bounds. If you watch this, be sure to keep some tissues close by, especially if you watch it with an emotional person like my mother, aka the faucet. Epic film!

[7] Shane, revisit the first footnote to refresh your memory.

inspected/fondled our possessions; his dreads followed, writhing like agitated eels.

I had to ask, "What's with the hair, dude? You look like Rising Lion[8]."

Munz unleashed another hearty laugh. "Whatever, mon. Rising Lion doesn't have this." He worked his hands through his crusty dreads. "It's a Dready Graham[9]."

Sure enough, Mike had grown a dread that looked exactly like the cereal Golden Grahams[10]. Munz doubled over, gripping his gut in a laughing-seizure. We asked no further questions. Mike had a long list of unequaled exploits. We added the Dready Graham to the list and moved along.

When Munz collected himself, he looked at me with a nervous smirk. "So you're driving to Mex, right?" His stress filled our cramped apartment. His first trip to Mexico resulted in him being pulled over and extorted in Tijuana[11].

I ended up driving Munz's car, and we stumbled upon some good right-hand point breaks. The highlight of the trip was not the waves, but the border. The Tijuana border, San Ysidro, over-heated, hellish conditions? We decided to haze Mike by locking his window down. This attracted all the vendors on the street. With Mike being incapable of saying no, vendors swarmed him. "Very funny. Come on, mon."

Munz's laugh-cry ensured that the window remained down. You could feel their pressure and Mike's growing anxiety. For hours, they pestered him. "Screw you guys," was his response to our incessant laughter.

I can still hear Munz's ear-busting wail.

---

[8] White Rastaman and lead singer of a reggae group called the Rising Lion around Wilmington.

[9] We got a package the following year from Kahuna. It read, "I think you know what or who this is." It was a bag full of Mike's dreads. Munz held onto it for over ten years, much to the chagrin of his long-time partner, Cameron. Yeah, we are a bunch of weirdos.

[10] Cereal that looks like a small teddy bear. If you haven't tried it, you haven't lived. Make sure to drink the milk afterward.

[11] He was with Forest Richardson and Katie Mitchel. They had planned to walk across the border but missed the last exit, which includes a sign saying, "Last U.S. Exit." Oops.

When we returned to San Diego, we headed to a spot that nearly had me join Dexter in the afterlife. After almost being buried alive in an aquatic avalanche, I quit smoking cigarettes. Even at the tail end of a big swell, the wave is intimidating. The place is notorious for sneaker sets, canyon sets that pummel everyone in their path. On those bigger days, many claim that the experience will show you either heaven or hell. That morning, my gut churned as I walked along the cold, abrasive pavement. We snuck around the black gate and descended down the damp road. Torrey pines and shrubs punctuated the sheer cliffs. The unstable, loose landscape plummeted to meet the infinite blue.

As we looked upon the vast seascape, a huge set of stacked lefts mowed over the sand. Paralyzed, Munz watched giant blue cylinders grinding across the shore. His eyes were as wide as saucers. I glimpsed over at Mike, who bit down on his lip and started banging his head to his internal soundtrack. His dreads thrashed as he strummed his hideous smurf board[12]. I had to laugh at Mike being Mike.

We were greeted by a thick smell of kelp as we charged down the cliff and entered the mix. I can still hear Mike's howl as he flew down the line in his backhand bliss. People don't scream like that at Blacks—that place is an intense gladiator pit of aggressive surfers. Mike did. Munz sat way south and deep. He knew the wave he wanted. He also really didn't want to get caught by the rolling avalanches. When that wall of indigo-blue perfection roped his way, there was no doubt he was going, in the perfect spot, with the perfect board, drop, and style. Maybe he was TJ Burke after all?

The session melted into California's golden sun. In the shadows of the towering bluff, we floated our way back up the trail. Never before had we seen such a display of size, power, and beauty. Mind-shattering surf. Munz and I attributed it to Mike's swell magnetism. It was sad to see him go.

"Fucking-A, you dudes are in the zone." His voice swelled with pride.

"Don't worry, Mike. We'll keep living it up and catch as many waves as we can for you surf-starved bros back East."

"Damn right!"

---

[12] He left the board behind and months later his brother Jason destroyed it going left onto the rocks of a notorious right point break in Mexico. He then purchased a Dallas Cowboys poncho. Solid trip.

It was a vow I took seriously. I still do. There's a part of me that thinks that had we taken Mike to the nude beach just to the north, maybe he would have moved to San Diego. We didn't, and unfortunately, Mike never returned.

Legend

"Caught on the inside of despair."
−Mike Brant

On a cool California gray morning, the campground shined with the spirit of Chris and Lori. These sea lovers, who sailed over 10,000 miles of the South Pacific and lived to tell about it, had recently eloped and been married on surfboards in a kelp forest off the coast of San Diego[13]. Now, we all gathered at Refugio State Park in Santa Barbara to celebrate their inspirational union. People rejoiced in the flow of yoga. Stand-up paddle boarders (sea janitors) dropped into little dribbling rights of delight. Spearfishers (*spearos*) stalked the edges of the kelp forest looking to feed the barbeque. Others lounged in beach chairs wrapped in colorful Baja blankets, mimosas in hand. We all knew the party was going to end but stayed anchored in the present.

My phone rang from inside my tent. The screen on my electronic tether read one missed call: a voicemail from Da Don, Victor Oyola.

His words shattered my soul, like I had just swallowed a pin-less grenade.

"Mike Brant didn't make it. He passed away early this morning in David, Panama."

The cheerful chatter vanished.

I walked to the ocean's edge. Santa Cruz Island rose out of the deep Pacific. I tried to find peace among the passive waters, but storm clouds

---

[13] A ceremony conducted by Megan Shuck, a world-traveling ordained minister who happens to wed people in the most unique and fabulous ways. Yes, Chris and Lori wore fancy wedding-esque attire over their wetsuits.

loomed. Here we were just finishing a glorious celebration of two great souls. Everyone was overflowing with life, after several days filled with salsa dancing, boating, free diving, hiking, and camping.

Now this.

My thoughts shifted to the Brant family: Wes, Lisa, Jason, Jackie, and Sasha. It wasn't just their loss; it was ours, complete devastation for anyone who had the pleasure of knowing Mike Brant, McSauce.

Life didn't make sense. People aren't supposed to die at the age of thirty-one, especially not someone of Mike's ilk.

I bottled my raging emotions. I didn't want to ruin everyone's good time. Besides, they couldn't comprehend the loss because they didn't know Mike. I wanted space. My body went into autopilot as I returned to breaking down the tent. Only a three-hour car ride to San Diego stood before me and my solitude.

We said our goodbyes, and I crawled into the back of my friend Trisha's car. I struggled to put the pieces together. All I could come up with was, *what the FUCK?*

I knew Mike had some sort of "illness" that forced him to go to a Panamanian hospital. The report was that he was getting better. Mike was a survivor. What he survived in and out of the water had made me confident that he was going to pull through, like that 15-foot clean-up set he took on the head at Sunset Cliffs in San Diego and laughed about. How could this "God," this "Universe" take someone like that from us? I felt Empty-GUTTED-and pissed off. With the loss of Mike Brant, never again would we witness a dude singing Disney princess songs, never again see those dramatic hair flips as he kicked off the wave, never again hear the epic "yeah, mon"[14], never again "Who's that friend of yours with the heavy surfer accent?", never again the Dready Graham, never again the biggest-flaming-homosexual/straight-dude-I've-ever-met, never again the epic surf trips and swells of the year...

---

[14] Jason does a pretty good one too, but Mike's earned top honors. And no, he wasn't Jamaican, although I think his accent and excessive use of the word was inspired by the Disney film *Cool Runnings* about the Jamaican bobsled team.

Never again to infinity, fucking sauce[15].

We merged onto Highway 5 and an endless sea of cars. *Where are all these people racing to? Do they even know?* The expressionless faces raced to get ahead. Poor souls. They had no idea what—who—the universe lost today.

Visions of Mike and Shane smiling from our last Skype conversation surfaced. They were running a hostel called Casa Del Toro in some Caribbean tropical paradise, an archipelago known as Bocas Del Toro. Shane and I blabbed about waves and hurricanes and how I was going to visit them in the fall. Mike seemed quieter than normal. He stood behind Shane with a light shining just above his head. His face seemed more like a smiling silhouette.

That was the last time I saw Mike.

I couldn't hold back any longer, and unleashed a torrent of tears. My body shook, and my lip quivered. Why now?

Trish and Crystal couldn't ignore me balling my eyes out.

"Do you want to talk about it?"

I didn't. They knew I had lost a good friend, but *how do I describe Mike Brant to sane people?* They decided it was best to have me drive. I got behind the wheel and focused. I shifted my thoughts from his loss to who he was.

Who is—was—Mike Brant[16]?

Mike had no shame. His aim was to always stretch social boundaries. If it was weirdly unthinkable, had never been done before, creepy, and fun,

---

[15] Sauce-noun-1.of or relating to the male genitalia-phallus 2. A sausage 3. An unknown male, a dude 4. A friend
Sauce-verb-1.adding more males to an environment 2. The act of adding masculinity to an environment, making your presence felt often in an obnoxious-disorderly-destructive way 3. to get intoxicated
Saucy-adjective-1. An area that has a high concentration of males 2. Extremely masculine person, action, or place 3. intoxicated 4. destructive-messy-disorderly conduct
McSauce-noun-1-of or relating to Mike Brant, may also include the male genitalia-phallus
[16] I could easily write a book solely on the specimen that is Mike Brant. It would be a sketchy shock to the senses.

he was doing it, no questions asked. His brother, Jason, *Mongenie*[17], once said, "He was ahead of his time. He was Jackass before Jackass was Jackass." Others referred to him as a true pioneer, a visionary. For me, coming from the upper-middle-class suburbs of New Jersey, I was blown away by Mike's unorthodox approach to life. He was groomed in the backwoods of Wake Forrest, North Carolina, by a group known as the Dark Squad. They were really into fucked-up shit like dark satanic magic and shrunken baby heads. He was a freak. He was both their protégé and their demi-god.

My initial impression was, *who is this psychotic gay guy living next to me at The Mandolin Townhomes in Wilmington, North Carolina, and should I really be hanging out with him? What would my "normal" parents or my All-American-lacrosse-playing high school classmates/stockbrokers think?*

I came to my own conclusion: being around Mike was refreshing. I respected a person who wasn't afraid to be himself, even if it meant creeping people out.

My greatest gift to him was surfing. Mike was a yes guy. So when I said, "Let's go surfing at Carolina Beach tomorrow at 6 am. The water is the color of poop, and the temp is about 50 degrees," an emphatic, "Fuck yeah, mon!" was what I got.

His eyes bursting with energy telegraphed, *why the fuck wouldn't I go?* From what I experienced, there was never a suggestion or an offering that Mike declined. When Mike embraced surfing, he instantly became one of my closest friends.

Meeting McButt[18] made me feel extremely sane and normal. His approach to life was inspirational. After hanging with him throughout the years, it made me pose the questions: *Why are so many of us so concerned about what others think? Why are we always trying to promote ourselves in socially accepted ways when that isn't who we truly are?* As Mike would say, "Fuck that shit, mon! Want to see me light this match with my dick?"

Passing under the Encinitas sign meant our ride from Santa Barbara

---

[17] Yes, this originates from the Brant brothers' excessive use of the word "mon." Jason is also extremely smart, especially when it comes to board sports; a genius, hence the name Mongenie.

[18] "McButt" evolved from "Mike Brant" to "McBrant" to "McButtcut" (middle hair part) to "McButt."

was over. While at the helm driving back, I didn't shed another tear. The driving therapy worked[19]!

My mind returned to the living, *where the hell was Shane? How is he handling this?* I later reached out to some of Mike's close friends. The more I talked about it, the worse it got. The pieces weren't coming together. *What the hell happened?* Shane had sent out the message that Mike was hospitalized and recovering. When he recovered, he was going to be sent back to the States with a valuable lesson learned: respect your body, right?

Wrong. He never got another chance. He died a few days later.

Lao Tzu once said, "The flame that burns twice as bright, burns half as long." Well, Mike loved flames, and his flame burned with blinding brightness.

I was at a loss of what to do and where to go, so like the rest of the world, I logged into Facebook. People were speaking directly to Mike and god.

"Rest in peace, Mike."

"May god be with you, Mike."

Did they really think he was checking his Facebook account from heaven? He never did it while he was alive, why now? When I saw Mike's family get involved, I warmed up to the idea. Wes, Mike's father, and Jackie, his sister, were appreciating the outpouring of electronic love. In this virtual world, his memory and legacy thrived. For those who didn't know Mike, they would get a heavy dose of his photos and quotes for many months, actually years, to come. Mike Brant, in his passing, was indirectly fucking saucing the shit out of the internet and Facebook. The postings were relentless. People desperately clung to his memory.

Wes later shared a poem by Sasha, Mike's twelve-year-old sister:

---

[19] Thanks, ladies!

<u>I AM</u>
I am a sister and a best friend
I wonder if he looks down on me
I hear his voice still
I see his blonde hair
I want to have him here again
I am a sister and a best friend
I pretend to not think about it
I feel fine
I touch the sadness and grief
I cry about his absence
I am a sister and a best friend
I understand I will never see him again
I say to myself it's OK
I dream about the past memories
I try to think about other subjects
I hope to somehow be OK with it
I am a sister and a best friend

A service was going be held in Wrightsville Beach, North Carolina. *What would result from a gathering of Mike's people?* It seemed like an explosion of sauce waiting to happen, a Mal-sauce-cocktail. Did I really want to spend that kind of money on a last-minute flight for the impending insanity? Weirdos, drunken surfers, the Dark Squad converging at a dive bar; I felt something or someone was going to be sacrificed. Mike evoked that kind of emotion in people. He put his heart and soul into the people he loved.

For those who were fortunate enough to have known Mike, they were drawn to the magnetism of his soul. He put his friends on a pedestal of praise and kept himself below. A selfless human, Mike didn't have personal possessions; his things were for everyone. His positive energy, coupled with the fact that he was up for anything, made him the life of the party. This was a blessing and a curse: one of the reasons he was loved, and one of the reasons he passed. Everyone wanted a piece of the action, Mike Brant.

I thought about a few of the offers Mike had accepted over the years:

"Mike, I want to go to Mase (a twenty-minute paddle across a shark-infested inlet with strong currents), but I don't know how to surf or have a surfboard."

"Shit yeah. Take my board. I'll swim."

"Mike, this girl wants to hook up with me, but I have nowhere to stay."

"Use my bed, mon. If you need 'em, condoms are in the top drawer."

"Mike, we'd like you to be a DJ at our new restaurant called Pig Out. We won't pay you, but you and your friends can drink for free."

"Fuck yeah, mon!"

"Mike, can you help me move back to DC (a six-hour drive)? I have a U-Haul but the radio is broken."

"Damn right. I got this. I know all the Disney Princess songs that have ever been made."

McButt gave and gave until there was nothing left. For the thirteen years I knew him, the partying never ceased. There was never moderation in his life. When he wasn't full throttle, he was unconscious. Ultimately, his body could not keep up. The main cause of death was acute liver failure; the weapon booze and pills, like oxycodone. Legal pills, *pharmies,* have been stealing thousands of lives around the globe. One of our heroes, the late great Andy Irons, three time world surfing champ, lost his life to such a battle. *When will people start to take this threat seriously? How many more greats do we have to lose?*

The sand felt cold as we gathered on the north end of Wrightsville Beach that morning. With the sun creeping out of the sea, the clouds glowed with a surreal fusion of orangish-pink. Gazing out into the Atlantic, we saw that the water was flat like a rippleless tropical lake, a reminder of how difficult it is to be a surfer on the East Coast. Maybe Mike was resting after all? Beautiful and deeply touching words rained down on us from Joel, Ru, and Vic, some of Mike's closest friends, as the ceremony began. The beach continued to fill up with people lining the shore in board shorts and leis, determined to paddle out. This was Michael Cole Brant's day, August 22, 2014.

The magnitude of the moment hit me like a sledgehammer as I entered the water. *We were actually paddling out to an aquatic funeral for Mike Fucking Brant.* My lungs constricted. I had difficulty breathing. A duck dive into the salty opaque-turquoise water, 80-degree bath-water, calmed my nerves. The cattail in my mouth went flaccid. Several hundred yards offshore, we joined hands in a circle, totaling close to fifty, around Jason, Mallorie, Jess, and Mike's sister Jackie in a motor boat. Mike's dad, Wes, wobbled on a surfboard, determined to stay afloat. A cluster of non-surfers, aquaphobes, stood watching from the shoreline. They served as a testament to Mike's inclusiveness. He reached out to everyone and anyone who was in need of a friend. Tara, one of Mike's childhood friends, once said, "Mike made you confident to be a human being."

Jason rose from the boat. Here was one of Mike's biggest heroes. Mike's face lit up when he told stories of his younger brother winning dirt bike competitions or getting shots in skate magazines in Bama. His legendary stories of his brother are why Jason got the nickname "Lord," as in "Lord of Shredding."

Jason's voice broke the silence,

"We really appreciate everyone coming out."

He looked around, removed Mike's remains (in a white porcelain container),and returned them to the Atlantic. Silence fell over the crowd. Vic's eyes grew as he looked to me to say something. I didn't have anything planned. The only thing I knew was that someone had just peed[20]. Apart from a few cackles in the crowd, all went quiet. The silence began to build.

"Errr, uhh."

I looked into a sea of sad faces. I felt a concoction of love, sorrow, despair, and confused energy. My mind went blank. I closed my eyes. Here we were together, all of the people that Mike loved, at one of his favorite places. This was Mike's moment; I felt Mike's presence. Words filled the vacuum.

"I had the privilege of mentoring Mike through his early days of surfing down at Carolina Beach. I've never seen someone who was so quickly enamored and hooked on surfing. I've taken a lot of people out surfing, but none of them had the enthusiasm and love for the ocean like Mike. In the early days, we set out to do two things: First, to get barreled in the water, and second, to get laid (land barreled). Most of the time, we did neither, but we sure had a damn good time trying. To Mike!"

---

[20] Mike loved the peeing experience almost as much as the surfing. He was often wet before entering the water. Yes, this creeped people out. And yes, Mike giggled while doing it.

I threw water up to the sky; the rest of the circle followed. The sea boiled with Mike's energy. With all of our strength, we heaved buckets of saltwater to the heavens. Like a set in the ocean, the splashing came in waves and then faded away. Once again, silence touched down over the calm water. And with it, we made our way back to shore.

I wanted to speak more about his early days surfing, but the weight of the moment told me more words weren't necessary. I thought about the hundreds of times I saw Mike get into his little crouched position to fit inside the wave, looking for the tube, only to be guillotined by the lip. He was relentless in his quest to get pitted. The warming memory brought a smile to my face as we prepared for the evening celebration at one of Mike's favorite dive bars, the Palm Room.

That night in Wrightsville Beach, we continued honoring Mike. Drunken bodies covered in glitter spilled out of the bar, beers in hand. We flooded the chunk of sand below Johnny Mercers Pier. I wasn't sure who brought the giant sparklers (three feet in length), but the entire crowd of about eighty people lit up and screamed out, "Mike Brant!"

"McBrant!"

We stood on the beach for the cherry on the top, the cock rocket.

There stood Ole Man Wells, one of Mike's biggest fans, in all his glory. His belly bulged from his large frame while his long hair undulated from under a top hat in the freshening northeast wind. He looked out at the crowd and then glanced down to admire his DC Capitals jersey. Below, a three-foot cylindrical mount extended from his genitals. Things were about to get saucy! Everyone knew and had heard the legend of the cock rocket. It was Mike and Ole Man Wells' Fourth of July tradition and included the movie *Independence Day*, a plethora of dudes, and a fiery sauce.

The crowd ignited the tropical night with more chanting.

"Cock rocket! Cock rocket! Cock rocket!"

Jason Brant provided a light. Like a skilled ninja, Ole Man Wells jumped around to the roar of the crowd. Flames ejaculated from his top hat and crotch. His movements were suspended in time as the beach erupted with energy. It was truly amazing the cops didn't come, and no one was arrested.

Mike's flame burned bright.

Through the night, the northeast winds continued blowing. We awoke the next day to rideable waves, a Wrightsville Beach miracle! We knew we needed to paddle across a sharky inlet. The reward, an uninhabited island where magical waves wedged upon its mystical shores. *Did the surfing gods and Mike deliver us really good swell?* Hell no. It was chest-high, windswept slop-the kind of shitty conditions Mike loved!

It was the perfect ending to the story, so I thought. My flight was the next day. Just as Vic and I were about to leave, Jason stopped us.

"Hold on, boys."

He returned holding two vials. His deep blue eyes peered out from below the brim of a beaten-up, black Thrasher hat. In his low, manly voice he said, "We wanted to give these to you guys. I'm sure Mike would have wanted this."

I looked at the clear container; Mike's remains looked back.

I found no words. We said our good-byes, and I headed off to the airport.

On my flight back to the West Coast, my gaze stretched across the rolling field of clouds. What was my reality? Where was all this heading? What do I do with this? I pulled Mike's ashes from my backpack and took a painful look within. There was a part of me that wanted to crawl into a hole and mourn, but there was a reason some of his remains rested in my hands. There was destiny in that bottle, and I needed to figure out what the hell it was. Maybe I could put Mike in a pretty container and rest him on a mantel? Would resting speak to Mike's soul?

Fuck no. After witnessing Mike's appetite for surfing, the sky was the limit. I envisioned his tall, lanky frame weaving through huge, tropical barrels with perfect posture and his bleached-blond hair proudly parted down the middle. Unfortunately, I never experienced such a moment, nor did he ever tell me of such a day. Despite being a good surfer, Mike spent most of his time talking up his friends and their epic rides.

What would Mike have wanted?

It didn't take long to determine that one last surf trip was in order. The objective, like days of yore: get Mike barreled!

From the beginning, this was what we were chasing: the eternal moment of bliss where time ceases to exist.

I began to dream. What an ending that would be, releasing Mike's ashes inside of a wave, a brilliant blue cavern.

For a surfer, there would be no higher honor.

With the El Niño year being forecast[21], I envisioned giant waves of perfection sweeping across the Pacific. It was all a matter of being in the right place in time. In order to take such a trip, I knew what I had to do. I had to quit my teaching jobs (English as a Second Language) in San Diego and then sell my soul. I had to sell my beloved twenty-seven-foot sloop, *Mañana*.

It surprised me little that my return to California with Mike's remains coincided with the largest hurricane of the Pacific season, Hurricane Marie, a Category 5 storm with 160-mph winds. The search had begun.

---

[21] El Niño (the boy) refers the climatic changes that usually occurs every ten years. The result is above average water temperatures in the Pacific. Theses warmer waters fuel massive storms and unleash heavy rains. The event usually peaks around late December(Christmas), which is where it got its name after the birth of Jesus.

Part II

Dusty Roads

"*The more you are motivated by love, the more fearless and free your actions will be.*"
–Dalai Lama

UNDERWAY. A GRINGO with nothing to lose slipped past Mexican inspection, undetected. I had been here before. The view and feel hadn't changed. Tijuana's urgent desperation and frantic energy engulfs the road south to *Playas* (beaches). Concrete drainage filled with sewage and trash pile up against a tin fence. This fence with broken patches of rusty barbed wire divides our two worlds. Only a small, flat patch of dirt lies between Mexico and the United States and its clean, orderly suburban sprawl.

On the south side, it's a far different story. Meager palm trees shoot up from putrid waste that reeks of dead fish. The stench causes many to simply roll the windows up as they accelerate faster to the beach. A concrete-coated cliff leans into the road while police helicopters circle overhead. The broken-down yellow median attempts to separate traffic while shrubs, fed by a cesspool, sparsely populate the rain-starved earth. Glass shards run along the tops of brick walls—Mexican residential security. The Tijuana wheel arches over dilapidated buildings and humans drowning in poverty. The merciless Mexican sun fires down upon the weathered beggars ambling toward San Ysidro and their day of panhandling hell at the border. Traffic bulges from the northbound border line, sitting targets for jugglers, beggars, window washers, amputees, Jesus lovers, and vendors mostly pushing Chinese-made products. It is impossible to ignore the human suffering.

Many ask, why would an "American" go down there? For surfers, the answer is simple: space. For many years, Baja[22] has been synonymous with surf exploration. Maybe it's the adventure with its wild lawlessness or the less-crowded point breaks? To me, it always felt like I was tapping into the true spirit of surfing, the unknown.

Despite the squalor, poverty, danger, and hassle, each year the number of surfers heading south grows. Each year, the breaks attract more people and more crowds, resulting in more frustration. If you surf enough spots along the peninsula, you will inevitably come across people who feel that they are more entitled to the waves than you. Like the resource grab of the modern era, people feel the need to claim their "break." I've learned that instead of fighting and resenting the crowded lineups, it's better to focus on what you can control, yourself. If it is crowded, don't paddle out. Keep searching.

Following Highway 1, the road banked around Playa Tijuana. Looking beyond the infamous bullring, growing lines swept across the ocean. Hurricane swell! I knew my saltwater salvation was not going to be found at a popular point break underneath an eighty-foot Jesus statue. My vision extended beyond Ensenada, a mere hour and half drive from San Diego. In this day and age, if you want to really score and find space, you have to be willing to push farther.

The ribboning road south vanished behind the swirling dustbowl.

---

[22] In Spanish, Baja means "nub," "short," or "lower." Baja California got its name to indicate lower California, belonging to Mexico.

Farting Back to Life

"The more you know, the less you need."
–Yvon Chouinard

On Sunday October 12, 2014, I farted. As they say in Spanish, *tiré un pedo,* I threw a fart. So what? For me, this meant everything. I was back. It made me laugh. I thought of my coworker who divided the world into two types of families, fart families and non-fart families. She continued, "You know, there are families that think farts are funny and acceptable. My boyfriend comes from a fart family; I don't." I thought about my family and chuckled. Surely someone would have laughed when they heard the seam-stretching-fart ignite the tent. As my father says, "There was a little back-talk."

Enough about farts, I was there to surf.

The ocean boomed, hurling melon-sized cobblestones like insignificant ping-pong balls. The sea hissed while ripping them back down the embankment. Endless stacks of whitewater methodically rolled down the point. The view inspired action.

Seven suns had set since I drove under the *Bienvenidos a México* sign. I was rewarded with a week straight of solid surf and great fishing; I could do no wrong. Scoring familiar surf spots of northern Baja and making connections charged my blood with confidence. I was "in the zone." The momentum came to an abrupt halt when I awoke one night in a deserted *palapa.* My insides gurgled. I tried my best to ignore them. I laid my head back down. The gnawing continued. It felt like Mexican piranhas were trying to eat their way out. They demanded an exit. I answered the call. Gastric missiles fired from my *culo.* With the orange morning glow upon the hills, I looked to the sea, dormant and swell-less.

A purple blob, swells in excess of thirty feet, had formed thousands of miles away from a monstrous storm in the north Pacific; the first proper northwest ground swell of the season was en route. Time to move!

After thirty hours of runs and feverish sweats, I collected myself and headed south; the images of long blue walls kept me going in my weakened state. I was told that it was faster to follow the beach road from the north. The Pathfinder[23] and I confronted myriad dirt roads riddled with giant mud craters and questionable passibility. Busted-up lobster traps littered the coast. Rocky, rolling hills bloomed with yellow agaves, their green spikes sharper than swords. Cutting along the coastline, I kept the heading south, pressing on through the sloppy remains of tropical system Odile. The formerly rain-starved *arroyos* had mutated into some sort of treacherous Pathfinder-consuming mud pits, forcing me to make frequent stops, probing the depths of the trenches. *When in doubt, walk it out.* Keep in mind, I was a fraction of myself, having been drained of my vigor; I viewed getting stuck as potentially fatal. My head spun. I needed rest. I cursed myself for even being in this position—the surfing mind can be a hasty, dangerous beast when chasing swells. Precarious predicaments have been a reoccurring theme in my life. *Would I ever learn?*

The cobblestone minefield indicated I had arrived. Heavy onshores whitecapped the ocean as far as the eye could see. My feeble frame was almost flattened in the howling winds. I was relieved. No surfing. Rest.

Transient surfers and fishermen constructed bunkers, piles of cobblestones in an attempt to hide from the relentless harsh desert winds known as the *El Norte*, comparable to the Santa Ana winds of California. I continued down the *arroyo* 100 yards south of the river mouth passing pickleweeds and scattered brush before claiming a spot. I wrestled with my tent, which was wildly blowing in the landward wind. Once it was erect, I collapsed. Spent. Laying dazed in my tent, I wondered, *what went wrong? Maybe it was the sheepshead ceviche I had over at George and Sandra's place?* It was the biggest sheepshead I had ever caught. Maybe it was contaminated?

---

[23] Yes, the Pathfinder had over 240,000 miles; yes, she needed a new catalytic converter to pass the smog check, which is why my California registration was expired. And yes, she was a long way from where she had started: the smooth, congested highways of New Jersey. But I believed in her.

Big, reef-eating fish can often have a high concentration of toxins from human-caused runoff and waste.

Whatever it was, my stomach abhorred me. It became harder and harder to answer the call. One more round. With shaky legs I made my way to the nearby pickleweeds as another flood exploded out of me. The wind pelted me with sand daggers. To keep myself upright, I grabbed a hold of the brush. *When would it end?* All I wanted to do was hold something down. My joints ached. I limped back to my tent. I felt fortunate that there was a bunker blocking the wind from completely flattening my $17, shitty Coleman tent I'd bought at Walmart. *Maybe next time I would get proper gear(or maybe I just like suffering?)?*

Late in the day, the wind withdrew its heavy hand from the sea. Good news for surfing, but then the man-eating horseflies swarmed in. I dove back into the tent. Of course, a few found their way in. Yes, the zipper was busted. The flies buzzed overhead waiting to strike while I hurled profanities at them. After a few ineffective kill swipes, I surrender to the torment.

Under the dying wind, coyotes cried. People told stories of them luring male dogs in camp with a lone female, often in heat. Her intoxicating invitation drew the aroused males into the *arroyos* where the other coyotes waited, ready to kill. Their seductive howling continued deep into the night. Hopefully, everyone had their dogs locked up. The relentless surf echoed in the charged air. In my current state, I couldn't fathom the idea of getting slammed by one of those waves. I took a big swig of water and prayed it would stay down.

In the golden orange twilight, my time had come. I graduated from water to stale bread. A weaker version of me ambled toward the ocean's edge. This break isn't known for its power but for its long, rolling rights and has been compared to the famous break Trestles in California but with a quarter of the guys[24]. The bathymetry is quite similar, with cobblestone bottom creating consistent and evenly paced waves. As we say in surfing, super *rippable*[25].

---

[24] I initially found this spot from word-of-mouth and then verified its location on Google Maps.

[25] I would say the wave is like two legendary waves, Bells Beach and Trestles, had mated.

The swell was peaking, and the waves were pumping. Three-foot overhead mounds of water met stiff *El Nortes,* offshore wind, resulting in ruler-edged perfection. After stumbling several times over the slime-covered cobblestones, I dove in. Swept southward, I dug into the water to meet the incoming stacks of whitewater. I got pummeled. *Was I about to shit myself?* Clinging to my surfboard underwater, I couldn't believe I was in boardies. The water was balmy, about 74 degrees. The ocean took its foot off the gas as I surfaced; a lull gave me a window to make it out. Like an injured, soggy rodent, I reached the take-off zone.

I was received by welcoming faces. *Maybe this was because I was alone?* A Baja maxim, the more males you bring, the worse you are going to be received[26].

Encouraged, I paddled over. *"Está caliente el agua."*

I knew this white-haired, white-skinned man was from the States, but I enjoy leading with Spanish. I mean we're in México, *güey*[27]!

"Sí. The water is warm."

Harry had the body of an ancient man. Deep lines of experience radiated out from his blue eyes like rays of sun. They enlarged when he spoke. "It's great isn't it? I've been coming here for over thirty years and have never seen it this warm."

His eyes held the brightness of an enthusiastic child.

"Yeah, all the fisherman around Ensenada have been saying the same thing."

Normally, there's a great deal of upwelling and a convergence of colder water currents in northern Baja. Not this season. Warm water was the precursor, the fuel, to a strong El Niño, one for the record books.

The lineup of around ten guys stirred as a large set lumbered in with Harry to my inside. Respect told me to let this wave go. Harry's eyes shined with life as he stroked with all his essence to drop in. From the top, I could

---

[26] My first international surf trip was to Playa Hermosa, Costa Rica, with five other sausages: Munz-Minghy, Josh-DJ God, Shane-Kahuna, J Reece-Dos metros, Jason-the DUDE (my nickname was 'Sauce'). We all learned a valuable lesson: never travel in a group of six dudes. Traveling places, making decisions, and getting meaningful cross-cultural exchanges wasn't possible in such a saucy environment.

[27] Pronounced "{way}," meaning "guy-dude." In Mexico, there are infinite opportunities to say *guey.* Don't know what to say? Say *guey* (way).

barely see the bottom. He hung on the lip and then disappeared from sight. A rainbow arched off the back of the wave with saltwater showers fanning in the wind. I turned my head from the blinding spray.

The following wave, I scratched into position. Riding a 5'8 Lost quad, I was slightly undergunned. I told myself, *the drop is all that matters. Focus.* The wave rose quickly in front of me. Like Harry, I felt myself right on the lip, hanging with the offshore *Norte* winds blowing me off the face. With an adrenaline-filled kick and paddle, I felt myself falling. Weightlessness, just for a moment, sent a shot of serotonin through my veins. The fins cut into the building wall. The section stood up like a closeout on the inside. I contemplated kicking out of the wave. My body refused to listen. I pumped and weaved up and down the large blue wall hoping for enough speed to make it around. Midway through the section, the wave hit the brakes and began to slow down. My fins hummed underneath me as a long overhead wall lay before me like liquid ice cream. An open canvas of boundless opportunities, the first section, I opted to carve down the face putting the board on rail. The board dug in as I heard a hoot from down the line. Dropping back down into the wave, I saw Harry paddling back out. My mouth was wide open with amazement. My frailty from the previous days was a thing of the past. Saltwater pumped vigor through my body. Three sections and 150 yards later, I kicked out. I couldn't get back out there fast enough.

The next wave, a long-haired guy swooped in on a short, round fish surfboard. His hair streaked behind him as he flew down the wave. His graceful movements were as effortless as a pelican gliding over an unbroken ocean crest. The session was in full swing. It was the perfect group that shared the ocean with respect while trading waves. Days disappeared in a sea of stoke.

Darkness once again fell over the campground. As the stars rolled out, fires dotted the coastline. Still riding an oceanic high, I felt compelled to share my newly found life force. I first met Kyle and Jim, optimistic owners of an Orange County marijuana dispensary. They sported the nicest gear known to man: new Al Merrick surfboards, a camera with telescopic lens, a GoPro camera with every mounting option under the sun, and a souped-up Land Rover. Their profession also afforded them time to take a week off for any given swell. This impressed me more than their assortment of modern gadgetry. Before Hurricane Odile came, they had heard reports of whale sharks being spotted around Los Angeles Bay. Were they still there? Were the roads even accessible? Some claimed that the roads had been washed out. No one knew for sure the extent of the damage. The fact that LA Bay was five hours away mattered little, the mental splinter had been planted: WHALE SHARKS.

The essence of surfing and traveling boils down to talking story. Harry sat in his chair wearing an eternal smile as I approached. After sharing the ocean, it felt like we had known each other for years. He was the oldest guy in camp, but his internal glow shined brightest. Although I placed him well into his sixties, I didn't catch a hint of dwelling in his past glories; it appeared his entire life was his golden years. He exuded genuine contentment and life satisfaction. I had much to learn.

Harry's knowledge and love for this rugged strip of coastline stretched across three generations. Baja adventures were his religion, his culture, and his passion for life. Harry picked up a small child waddling toward the fire. "And this guy!" He showed me Jacob, who grabbed a hold of his grandfather's collar and looked away. "I remember taking your daddy down here when he was your age."

Jacob stared at his grandfather in wide-eyed wonder. Imagine being a little grommet gazing upon the wild seascape, then seeing your white-haired grandpa gliding down the face of a huge waterfall.

Harry's eyes returned to the fire.

"This is why I love coming down here." He paused, his face gleamed in the firelight. "You hear that?"

The booming surf eclipsed the distant human chatter. "That's why."

He swept his free hand to the surroundings. "There's no distractions. No nonsense. This is what life is all about, sharing these experiences with friends and family. Can I get you another beer?"

I nodded. He headed for his camper.

It was great to feel so comfortable among "strangers." I thought about modern society, and how it can make us feel so isolated and behind. Life runs so fast with its rigid institutions and regulations, forever pulling us into the future. *But what is the future if we don't have the present?* Staring into the fire, life slowed down. It felt like a portal through time, back to the lives that our ancestors led, 100,000 years ago as hunter-gathers before the Industrial Revolution and technology.

I was happy that my phone read, *fuera de servicio* (out of service).

Harry returned with a Tecate. "Come meet my son. I was telling him about your trip."

John extended his hand. John, in his thirties, had already done a great deal of traveling with his wife. They, of course, both surfed and shared some of Harry's passion for life. One of their favorite trips was their drive down to Panama. They told me of the wonders of places like Lake Atitlan in Guatemala and Chinandega in Nicaragua. He shared a tip: "When in a bind, you can always spend the night at the Pemex's gas stations. They are safe."

When I heard the word "Panama," I immediately thought of Mike. I told them his story, and how I was taking him on his last surf trip. A quest for waves, adventure, and some sort of closure.

Of all the stories they told me, what stood out was John's biggest regret, not continuing on to South America. I hadn't thought beyond Mexico. *Panama? South America?* It all seemed so distant, another hemisphere, another world.

Like a nimble cat, Harry sprang to the top of his camper and asked, "Which one is yours?"

He shined his floodlight out across the blackness.

"It's that silver Pathfinder to the south."

His light landed on the Pathfinder hiding behind the rock bunker. The top of my cheap tent flagged in the wind. His eyes and expression said it all: *You're going in that?* He paused, searching for the right words.

"When I was younger, I used to rough it like that, but the ole lady stopped coming down. I wanted my family to be comfortable and get excited about coming down. He sighed as he slid down the ladder. His eyes brightened once again as he leaned against his RV, "So I had to upgrade to this ole camper."

"Maybe one day I'll make it to your realm, Harry?"

He threw his hand down as if embarrassed by my comment.

"You're on the right track."

I could see that everyone was getting ready to crash, so we parted ways. *"Buenas noches. Hasta mañana!"*

As I laid my head to rest, the wind lightly tugged at the tent. The oceanic thunder now sounded like a faint whisper. Tomorrow it would be time to move. I thought about Harry's wisdom. It coincided with the book *Sapiens*, where the author Harari mentions, "The industrial revolution has condemned us to living unnatural lives that can't give full expression to our inherent inclinations and instincts, and therefore can't satisfy our deepest yearnings." Despite all the waves and fish, I continued yearning. My thoughts migrated to a reoccurring dream of a massive shadow, a tail gliding through the depths. The ominous figure drifted further and further away. My subconscious was calling me below the surface.

Whale Sharks y Beheadings

*"Freedom is an adventure with no end, in which we risk
our lives and much more for a few moments of something
beyond words, beyond thoughts or feelings."*
–Don Juan Matus, Yaqui Sorcerer

"Did you hear about the beheadings in La Paz?"

Sara's eyes flooded with fear.

I shook my head.

"There are reports of people being beheaded in broad daylight in the middle of the city. Apparently, it is some turf war between the drug cartels."

My dream was now taking us straight into a nightmare.

You might be asking, who is Sara, and how did I get myself into this mess?

It began with the dropping swell, and my surf-beaten body begging for a break, my instincts (yearnings) told me it was time to harvest. Time to spearfish[28]. Finding an empty point and anchoring myself in desolation, I embraced the solitude. The sandy point wrapped into a well-defined hook. At the top, a few prominent boulders stuck up, indicating a potential drop-off. The sun bounced off the sand below, penetrating through the invisible

---

[28] My first attempt at spearfishing was with Adam Lyliston in Encinitas, San Diego, using a Hawaiian sling I got from Play-It-Again-Sports for $15. We were shocked when we speared a small perch. I then progressed to get a single-band rail gun and fished a lot with Nate Graham. We were lucky that we didn't spear one another in those murky, trigger-happy times. Eventually, I learned about restraint and the importance of taking safe, selective shots. Throughout, Chris Thompson has been a great mentor and underwater sage of the deep.

water. Warm water slowed my heart rate as I entered the ocean. Empty shells rolled in the gentle currents. As I swam out to the point, schools of nervous baitfish darted by. I scanned to see if anything was chasing them. *Nada.* I swam onward to the dark patch of water. I found a few land markers–the Pathfinder, the tip of the point, and the end of the rolling sand dunes—and then dropped below. Large, urchin-covered rocks with kelp anchored to their roofs sat fifteen feet below. Despite the decline in swell, the ocean surged. The undulating kelp glistening in the pure sunlight was beyond seductive; it was hypnotic. Tentacles of lucid brown algae swirled before me, igniting my imagination. The kelp had magnificently morphed into some sort of hula grass. Hula grass upon a nice round brown… My diaphragm squeezed. The aquatic daydream-turned-fantasy was over.

Air!

I packed a few deep breaths and reconnected with my senses. I was there to find dinner, not to drown fantasizing. A few inquisitive calico bass came over to greet me. It told me that the area saw very few human predators. These little 10-12" bass were completely oblivious to the 4' double-banded spear just a finger squeeze away from their annihilation. I enjoyed their company. I felt that if I had small, relaxed fish around me, maybe I was blending in. *Maybe the creatures of the sea were accepting me into their world?* A few sheepshead disagreed and fled for the rocks. They seemed to be wary of my company and rightfully so. I was casting a large shadow with the sun beating down overhead.

Breathe.

The dives would eventually lead me to a flash of yellow. The tail disappeared under a little ledge about twenty feet down. I dove away from the opening and snuck around the corner. Sure enough, there it was, giving me a broad side shot, a good-sized *pargo* (snapper), the perfect guest for dinner. We made eye contact. For a moment, we both froze. He was assessing the threat. His pectoral fins swirled. He looked me up and down. I floated motionless before him. He twitched as if his instincts were about to tell him, *FLIGHT!* I pulled the trigger, and the *pargo* spiraled violently out of its dwelling. I swam over and wrestled it to the surface. The wild-eyed *pargo* stared into my eyes. I grabbed my dive knife and ended its suffering. I brained[29] the *pargo*, and swam its lifeless, bloody body back to shore. In doing so, I kept a constant eye on my surroundings. The hunter, being well aware that with blood in the water, he could soon become the hunted.

In Spanish, they differentiate a fish in the water from when it is caught. Five minutes ago, this had been *un pez*; now it was *un pescado*. I secured my gear before making my way clumsily through the shore break. Yes, walking with large dive fins, a gun, and a fish across an uneven bottom is awkward. Once on land, I marveled at this beautiful fish glistening in the afternoon light. Thank you!

A distant figure approached along the shore. A skinny brown mutt led the way, happily sniffing the sand and chasing crabs. Detecting my presence, the dog came running. Its master, a young female, followed behind with her wavy, sandy-blond hair blowing in the breeze. Her sun-glazed skin glinted around a black bikini. I saluted. She waved back.

We exchanged hellos. And then I hoisted the fish, "Are you hungry?"

"Wow, that thing is huge. What is it?"

"*Es un pargo, muy rico.*"

"What? I don't speak Spanish."

"Oh," I said. "It's a snapper, delicious."

I figured her boyfriend was waiting for her back in town but asked the question anyway.

"Are you camping in town?"

"Yes, just Coco and I."

She pointed to her dog prancing up and down the beach. Wow, she was alone and knew no Spanish. What female travels *sola* down in Mexico?

SARA.

I offered the dinner invitation again. "Well, I'm definitely going to need some help with this guy."

The fish swayed from my waistline.

"Sounds good. Where should I park? I don't have four-wheel drive."

I pointed behind the sand dunes to a dirt track. She continued walking down the point, and I stripped off my dive gear and filleted the fish. Several hours later, Sara and Coco returned in her golden '90s Astro van.

---

[29] Inserting the dive knife into the fish's brain. It kills them instantly. Sharks sense the electromagnetic waves of a dying fish often faster than detecting blood.

We began working on a fire for the fish feast. With the *fogata* ablaze, it was time for her story. Sara, an intrepid firefighting smoke-jumping thrill-seeking Canadian, was on her way to Los Cabos with her little pooch, Coco, to work as a whale-watching dive guide studying their migratory patterns. *Que Chingona! How cool!* Although her van didn't have four-wheel drive, she put me and my Pathfinder to shame with her mindful packing and supplies. As I listened to her story, I wondered if she had a death wish.

Willfully jumping out of a plane into the flames of forest fires takes a lot of guts. When she wasn't risking her life putting out deadly fires, she traveled the world diving, hiking, surfing, or whatever else seemed dangerously fun. She had been frost bitten, burnt, bruised, broken, bitten again, and then put back together. She lived her mantra, "It's never too late to beef up your obituary," to the fullest.

Our conversation had an easy flow, flavored by cold Tecates while watching another perfect Mexican sunset plunge into the Pacific. We were living a Tecate-Pacifico commercial. As the night consumed the day, we continued to stoke the fire. She rolled a joint from her own supply. The evening was filled with more stories, more Tecates, more wood, and more joy. Her coconut oil added a sweet savory taste to the *pargo*, complemented by foil-wrapped potatoes, carrots, and caramelized onions roasted on the coals. The meat melted off the bone. Our feast was bountiful and unequaled, especially considering our surroundings.

As we eased into the warming sand and gazed at the stars, reflection time was upon us. Our world drifted off into the stillness of the night. AHHH. The crackling fire blended with the soft-crashing waves. A light, cool breeze caressed the sand dunes. The embers glowed with an array of eternal blues, reds, yellows, and purples. We had seen this earlier among the sky and the sea. Looking deeper into the fire, it was as if we were looking into ourselves, following a magnetic attraction.

It was that pull of the ocean that led Sara to walk along that beach. It was that pull that had her look up at the stars. It was that pull that led her to the fire beside me.

"How good is this?!"

She nodded. She didn't have to say anything. We felt it. I looked into her inviting eyes from across the flickering flame. We started inching toward one another. Then, our moment was lost in Coco's cacophony. She erupted out of the sand announcing intruders. *Damn!* She most certainly hadn't neglected her duties and continued her sonorous bark. Lights appeared out of the night, bouncing over the dunes. *What the hell?* Whoever it was, they were coming in hot. My mind flashed to the worst-case scenario: *Mexican banditos.* We were in the middle of nowhere with a large fire and two cars. There was no way we were hiding. With the Tecates, *mota,* and tequila pulsating through my veins, I climbed atop the dunes. Two separate sets of headlights were fast approaching. Bikers. Coco's continuous yapping was overpowered by the two *motos.* As soon as I saw them, I knew they were *extranjeros* (foreigners); they looked like they were biking through Mars in uncomfortable spacesuits.

"Howz zee fiea?" one asked through his helmet.

"What?"

They removed their huge helmets and bounded over. Coco continued to blitz them with barks. Sara was eventually able to subdue her little enraged beast. They said they were doing some scouting for the upcoming Baja 1,000[30]. They were Germans. One was named Lars and the other sounded something similar to "Lars," maybe Larsen? This would have been a classic Mike Brant moment. I figured it was a sign from Mike, sending us some weird random dudes to add to the romance of the evening.

Small talk ensued, mainly them talking about themselves. They would eventually realize the situation: a male and a female, a fire, the remains of dinner, and a bunch of empty beer cans. I mean this was our first date, and the Universe had brought us together. Hello? Finally reading the signals, party of two, not four, they bid us *"Buenas niches"* and continued. If Mike had been here in the flesh, there was no way those dudes were leaving. He would have given them everything, even his tent to "party." Mike was inclusive. Me, I was selfish and very content with my company. *Lo siento,* Lars and Larsen.

The engines faded and silence returned. I shared with Sara one of my favorite quotes from the blind Argentinian writer Jorge Borges[31]:

"No hables a menos que puedas mejorar el silencio."

---

[30] An off-road race where people of all skills charge the 1,000+ miles of Baja. Some make it, others learn a lesson. Everyone leaves with a story.

[31] His ideas inspired the movie *Inception*, a dream within a dream. *Are we awake or are we still dreaming?*

Don't speak unless you can better the silence.

So we didn't.

The following morning, the once-swirling tail of smoke stood tall and gray. Not a breath of wind, things were heating up fast in the desert. Time to move. Next stop, Mulege. Like a lot of Baja, the town had been ravaged by Odile, which had destroyed not only the boardwalk and many homes, but also left the majority of the population without provisions and water. It truly seemed like a Mexican *pesadilla* (nightmare). In Mulege, Sara stopped at an internet café to check a Baja travelers' discussion forum. It turned into a good news-bad news scenario. Her flush face let me know that she was leading with the bad.

"Have you heard anything about the beheadings in La Paz?"

I shook my head.

"Beheadings? Who? Lars?"

She didn't acknowledge my stupidity. She then told me about the beheadings and the drug cartels' turf war in *El Centro* of La Paz.

"La Paz already has enough problems," I retorted. I wondered if Sara knew about the stifling heat, aggressive drivers, and twisted street signs. The intersections there are like a four-way game of chicken. Now, add beheadings in the plaza in broad daylight, which I thought happened only in the distant lands of mainland Mexico, Chiapas, or Sinaloa[32]. Like any threatened animal, I weighed my options: fight or flight? Was I really about to stick my neck out there for some elusive shadow of a dream? Skepticism and rationality became my defense. I mean, how was that possible anyway? Wouldn't they need a guillotine, or were they dumping headless bodies in the center? Maybe a video showing the execution in the town square? No way was this going down in the middle of town, *El Centro*. I imagined these stories were concocted by gringos tweaked out on peyote. Further investigation was in order. When in doubt, ask it out.

"And what about the good news?"

"My boss, the owner of the dive shop in Cabo, told me that there are whale sharks being spotted in La Paz." A smile crept up her face.

"A lot of them?"

"Every dive last week had sightings."

---

[32] The previous year in 2013, two Aussies surfers had been shot and killed there, and their van was burned.

Six fully armed marines stood waiting in line at a grocery store in Mulege.

"*Hola, Buenas tardes.*"

"*Buenas.*"

He looked over at me with his gun dangling from his shoulder. Noticing that the barrel of his gun had a slight tilt in my direction,

I stepped back and asked, "Is the safety on?"

He examined his AK-47 like a foreign object. Then he cast a wide grin. "*Sí, claro.*"

The rest of his squad laughed. They became intrigued and walked over. I had six armed men surrounding me, probably thinking, *Who is this gringo with a dirty mustache speaking our language? Shouldn't he be scared of us?* The expression on their faces read harmless and inquisitive. I got right to the point.

"So what's happening right now in La Paz?"

"*Oh no pasa nada en La Paz?*"

His comrades nodded.

"My friend just told me that people were being killed in the middle of the day in *El Centro.*"

"*Oh, eso fue antes ahora está tranquila, ándale. No pasa nada.*"

The conversation was slightly comforting, *no pasa nada* (nothing bad is happening). Of course they were a reliable source. The words of men toting guns have a tendency to be quite compelling. They all assured me that the killings were something of the past.

But similar to asking for directions, I kept asking until I got the answer I was looking for. In hotels and restaurants, I encountered evasive eyes. Many faces read, "*De qué hablas?*" I don't know what you are talking about, gringo. It seemed like they were hiding something. *Why wouldn't they acknowledge something of that magnitude occurring just a few hours south?* Come on, Latinos love to gossip about their neighbors[33]. After enough prodding, one old man lowered his paper. His sharp black eyes drilled into me.

"Yes, there's violence between the narcos, but they don't care about you. Just enjoy your trip."

---

[33] Due to the excessive gossiping, they have a common saying in Latin America, "Pueblo pequeño, infierno grande." Small town, big hell.

He returned to his paper. I respected his directness. Maybe the others had tried to deny the massacres because they didn't want to scare the scant number of tourists? After the area had been hammered by hurricanes and the spread of dengue fever[34], every cent of commerce was desperately needed. For most people in Baja, tourism and gringos represented hope.

We stopped in Loreto to see if we could find whale sharks instead of driving into the cartel war zone. All the park officials had different answers. Some said we should go to Los Angeles Bay; others said La Paz. What they did agree on was that there were no whale shark sightings in Loreto.

Decision time. Backtrack ten hours to a potentially impassable roadway or proceed south? In case I didn't make it, I made one last call to the States. With my predicament unknown to my friend Victor, he proceeded to give me an in-depth rundown of his healthcare job, which he hated, and females. The dude loves to talk; we both do. Eventually, I let him know what I was about to drive into. His response, "Sketch!"

I explained that nothing had been confirmed, but I agreed that daytime beheadings were indeed, "SKETCH."

He wished me luck.

My mind was made up—I was going. I assured myself that I wasn't the target: I wasn't a *narco*, I wasn't in politics, and I didn't work for Monsanto or other Mexican-exploiting conglomerates. I was just a gringo who was taking his deceased friend's remains to get barreled. Somewhere. Who would want to sever my big-ass head anyway? *Mike, if you're up there watching this shit, now would be a good time to … I don't know, save my neck-head*[35].

A checkpoint was set up in Constitucion, an hour and a half south of Mulege. I assumed it to be a military inspection. The standard interrogation and search generally goes as follows:

De dónde vienes? Where are you coming from?

Adónde vas? Where are you going?

---

[34] Again, with climate change, we have warmer water, which fuels bigger storms. In the wake of these storms is lack of power, and water, which causes people to store more water. This stagnant water from flooding and poor storage serves as a breeding ground for mosquitos and related infectious diseases.

[35] Bad humor is a family defense mechanism. I blame my father and the people who encourage his "humor."

En qué te dedicas? What do you do?

Llevas armas o drogas adentro? Are you carrying any weapons or drugs?

Permítanos revisar tu carro. Puedes bajar?

Allow us to search your vehicle. Can you get out of the vehicle?

A search then ensues. They have their hands full when searching the Pathfinder: camping gear, cookware, dive gear, wetsuits, boards, cooler, and dusty clumps of clothes. If I have any drinks in the cooler, I offer it to them. October, like most months in Southern Baja, is usually 100+ degrees, and these guys are standing on asphalt overloaded with artillery while their brains broil in their helmets. They check under the seats and the glove compartment. They eventually make their way to the cup holder. They are drawn to it. Could it be *drogas?* You never know with these stupid gringos.

"*Mira esta.*" Often they call to their associates.

A camouflage beer cozie around a mysterious vial rests before them. As the bottle from within is fondled with great and meticulous care, their eyes grow with bewilderment. Holding the container, one usually says, "*Qué tiene acá?*"

"That's my friend Mike."

Often they look at it carefully from different angles and finish with the question, "*Y el resto?*"

Responding to the question "Where is the rest of him?" could take a really long time, so I usually paint Mike's story with broad strokes. I let them know that I am on a mission: taking him on his final surf trip. Most are touched by the story, and the search ends with a nod and the delightful words, "*Buen viaje, pásale.*"

With each checkpoint passed, I give a quick thanks to Mike for watching out for me. He would be delighted knowing that he was still creeping out dudes in the afterlife.

The checkpoint in Constitucion, a solid seventeen hours south of the border, was different. This was not a military checkpoint but *la policía.*

I approached a very stern-faced cop.

"*Adónde vas?*"

"I'm going to La Paz."

"*Ahora La Paz es bien peligroso.*"

I could feel the tension in his words. In fact, they terrified me.

"No pares para nadie!"

He pointed to his black boots.

He paused, *"Solo si ves estas."*

After scaring me and telling me not to stop for anyone unless they were wearing black boots like his, he gave me the *pásale* to continue southward.

Sara followed close behind.

This was a far different picture than the jovial *ejército* (military) that the people in Mulege had painted. This was real. It was no longer some paranoid gringo talking shit on an untrustworthy forum, this was straight from the horse's mouth: *la policía, el jefe.*

I spared Sara the troubling news. She didn't need anything else to exacerbate her situation. She was without air-conditioning while the Pathfinder kicked up 103-degree clouds of searing white dust. Baking in that metal box, she and her pooch had no option but to drive with the windows down. I could see Coco's flaccid tongue drooping to the floor. I couldn't imagine the heat inside her fur coat.

Road construction was underway for many miles leading into La Paz. Both the north-and south-bound lanes of the Mexico's Highway 1 merged into a single lane. Men stood on the side of the road, not working, but waving a flag—a black shirt on a stick. Each time I passed, they wildly waved their flags. Were they telling me to slow down or speed up? I decided to reduce my speed. They waved with even more intensity. I sped up, and it caused more frantic waving. I raised my hands in consternation. All that could be seen from the dust-covered figures were their eyes. Faces hidden behind soiled t-shirts shouted, *"Dale. Ándale. Órale!"* Which is the equivalent of saying, "Go, carry onward, hurry up."

So one of the great mysteries of the world continues as to just what the fuck these men do all day under the blazing Mexican sun.

My thoughts returned to the task at hand: we were driving straight into a fiery pit of violence.

When we got to La Paz, my music shuffled to "Keep Your Eyes Peeled" by Queens of the Stone Age, with the lyrics, "Don't look/just keep your eyes peeled." The sounds of broken glass and destruction rattled the cage of the Pathfinder as the song synchronized with my clenched nerves. Entering the city, we followed six Hummers, each carrying five armed soldiers. *What were we getting ourselves into?*

The sign read *Bienvenidos a La Paz*; alongside it, a colossal cement whale tail fluked out of the earth. I imagined it was once white, now the fluke wore a coat of polluted dust. I tried to go to my happy place, my dream state, the underwater kingdom swimming next to pre-historic giants.

No turning back now.

We followed signs toward the *malecón* (boardwalk) the tourist side of town. Fear loomed at every intersection. There were more police in sight than pedestrians. Their eyes darted from the cars to the boardwalk. I was more scared for them than myself. The tension, along with the heat, made the city feel like a sausage, a sausage over an open flame, a sausage that was ready burst. All we had to do was survive the night. We booked the whale shark tour for mañana, and escaped to camp in Pachilingue, ten miles outside of the city.

Our provisions for the following day included beer, water, and bread. At *la panadería*, I asked the vendor about the killings.

His face awoke. His bushy eyebrows raised, and he offered a toothless smile. *"El número es vienticinco y creciendo."*

Twenty-five and growing is not what I wanted to hear.

"Is it only the *narcos* being killed? Have any civilians or tourists been killed?"

"Todavía no."

He started laughing with a creepy gleam in his eyes.

Was this guy insane?

I understand through the use of *muñecos* and the Day of the Dead that the Mexican culture does not fear death, like gringos. They embrace it as a part of life. They joke about it:

Los muertos al cajón y los vivos al fiestón.

"Put the dead in the coffin and let the living party!"

But these horrific killings in the middle of town were a different story, right? Surely, this couldn't be celebrated and laughed at? I placed myself in the man's rotted shoes. What could he do? This was his home. He couldn't flee the city. We could.

The *panga* was set to leave at ten the next day. In the rising morning sun, in the absence of police, the *malecón* seemed eerily tranquil and safe. We loaded onto a twenty-four-foot skiff with six other *pasajeros*. Before firing up the engine, our guide, Arturo, began his lecture. "There are four basic rules." He held his fingers high.

"One, keep at least a two-meter distance from the shark, the world's largest fish. Two, no more than six people in the water. Three, no splashing. Four, no touching the shark." He concluded that we must strictly adhere to the rules in order to not disturb the whale sharks in their "natural habitat."

"Understand?"

He looked at the Mexican passengers. *"Entienden?"*

Everyone nodded. The captain fired up the fifty-horsepower Yamaha outboard engine, and away we went.

Just a quarter mile out, three boats clustered together. As we drew near, a dark stain whirled just below the surface. *Could this be what I think it is?* Were they that easy to find? Could I have just paddled my 8'4 board out here and saved some *plata*? A large fin broke the surface and answered my question. The captain pointed with self-satisfaction, "Whale eShark! *Tiburón ballena*!"

After all the fantasizing and dreaming about this magical creature, the moment was finally here, a conscious dream. Taking into account all the effort and risk, I should have felt fulfilled and content.

Negativo.

Everything about it looked and felt wrong. At least a dozen reckless swimmers transformed the placid gulf into a boiling cauldron of agitated kook-water. I saw a fat man reach over to grab the shark's tremendous tale. What happened to the rules that we were "to strictly adhere to"? I was disgusted by my fellow man. The juvenile whale shark, about three meters, quickened its pace to distance itself from its attackers. Due to the abundance of plankton in the area, the visibility was reduced to fifteen feet. It was obvious that the poor whale shark just wanted to be left alone to feast on the plankton.

Knowing that I was adding to the problem, after a few quick dives with this agitated fish, I was done. It felt like a cramped zoo, the exact opposite of what I had dreamt about. It was apparent that these people were more concerned about getting the shot for social media than the animal's well-being. Returning to the boat, I strongly suggested to the guide that we look for another whale shark. Arturo contested, *"Allí está."* but when we sat back and watched the aggressiveness of the tourists, completely disrespecting the guidelines and the whale shark, we both reached the same conclusion: better to run the risk of not seeing another whale shark than continue in the aggressive swarm.

We corralled the *pasajeros* and continued our sea search. As we left the disturbance in our wake, the serene sea once again looked inviting. The sheer beauty of the shimmering green water, the surrounding islands, and dramatic bluffs seized my breath. Arturo pinned the throttle. The others wrapped themselves in towels. I stayed in my wetsuit jacket, *LISTO*. With the whale shark variable in the equation, the atmosphere was once again electric. Off in the distance, I spotted some turbulent, discolored water. I screamed to the captain, "What's that over there?!" and pointed to the large, dark stain below the milky green water.

His response, "*Híjole! Una mancha grande.*"

The shadow was gargantuan, longer than our twenty-plus foot panga. I looked around, not a boat in sight, and then at Arturo.

"*Dale. Ándale!*" he yelled as he motioned his hands overboard.

We were still in gear. I envisioned my friend John Cotner[36] calling me "an abundance of caution" as I waited for Arturo to kick the boat in neutral, not wanting to be sliced to bits by the prop. Once we were in neutral, I dove in. An ominous presence approached from behind. A dark figure bigger than the Pathfinder rose upward to the surface with his mouth wide open. He was coming right for me. I floated motionless. *Was I dreaming?* The beauty. The size. The grace. His mouth stretched wider. My senses sharpened as I dug my fins into water and darted out of the way like a frightened bait fish. I yelled over to Sara, "He almost just swallowed me!"

She laughed and pulled out her snorkel.

"No way. At worst, you would have just gotten stuck in his mouth."

Tangling with a fish as long as the *panga* was not a good idea. We kept a respectful distance. The gentle giant just carried on binging on plankton with complete indifference to our presence. A thick cloud of sardines hovered skittishly around his colossal dorsal fin. His huge gill slits opened and closed like large air-conditioning vents. He made slow but extremely powerful movements.

---

[36] Also known as 'Dealyo.' I had an entire chapter dedicated to our sailing adventures and his wild, "go for it" attitude, his Dealyo. In the stories, he referred to me as "an abundance of caution." They didn't make the cut, so he will now live on as a footnote.

On the surface, one of the Mexican women diving with us cried, *"El tiburón está chido!"*

The shark is so cool!

Her mask fogged as her eyes flooded with joy. Arturo informed us his name was Flavio, a large male, eight meters (about twenty-four feet) long, that frequents the area. The hands of man had left a large white gash upon his great back, most likely the result of a reckless *panguero*.

Pilot and feeder fish schooled below. With the plankton compromising the visibility, I couldn't even see the shark in his entirety. After being in the vertical position inhaling plankton for almost an hour, he fluked and then his enormous shadow vanished.

On the boat, beyond the astonishment of our watery world, I couldn't help but think about the future. How much longer will these sea behemoths be around? Over the last 60 years, the number of phytoplankton has decreased by 40%. A total 70% of the oxygen we breathe comes from ocean algae. *Will we even have enough oxygen left to breathe*[37]*?*

My thoughts were interrupted by something ice-cold on my skin. Sara stood pressing a handful of Tecates against my arm. We passed them around to the rest of the passengers. They were much appreciated. Under the midday sun, we raised them skyward.

"Salud!"

What an experience!

I sat beside Sara, and cheersed her one last time.

"What a life!"

Snarling the engine, Arturo told us it was time to go.

As we headed in, I couldn't wipe the smile off my face. The entire experience was everything I could have hoped for, and it came with a natural flow. Nothing was forced; everything came into place. *Maybe someone was looking out for me from above?* I knew I hadn't yet found Mike's barrel, but had the trip ended that day, I would have still deemed it a complete success. Over a month of incessant waves from both the Northern and Southern Hemispheres with obscenely warm waters, plenty

---

[37] Information cited from the book, *Deep.*

of fish, good people, good vibes, and to finish up with an unforgettable swim with a whale shark[38]...my mind was blown.

Then it began to drift, shift, and flutter to the future.

I asked Arturo about what was happening in La Paz. He responded, *"Quién sabe?"*

He saw the concern on my face. He continued, *"No te precupes es entre los narcos."* This is what I had heard before: "It's between the drug dealers."

The previous night, a guy offering marijuana at the campsite in Pichilingue said the violence was due to the government backing one of the cartels attempting to wipe out the competition. La Paz, representing an essential port in the drug trade, had a long history of violence. Most of the drugs pass through Sonora (mainland Mexico) and are ferried to La Paz en route to the United States. The dealer joked, "Don't worry. You are fine as long as you were supporting the right side." He ensured that his chilling laugh was heard beyond our conversation.

I would later read that my encounters with a few locals did not reflect the collective Mexican sentiment. Many people were worried and scared. *La gente* eventually marched in the streets for peace in La Paz (which, ironically, means "peace"). More than forty people had been killed, "disappeared." There were no credible reports of any beheadings. Stories of other violent clashes between the state and its people swept across the nation. It seemed like Mexico was on the verge of combustion. *Was it time to turn back?*

The surfer within countered with, *What other mind-altering experiences await down the road?* I had been following the surfers' creed: chasing highs and aquatic thrills. Once the mission was completed or a wave surfed, the inevitable question arose: what next? Halloween in Puerto Escondido seemed like a good start. After hearing an earful from Jon *"Dealyo"* about the raw power of the surf there and the feel of getting spat out of truck-sized tubes, how could I not go and take a little look? *When would I ever have a vehicle at the tip of Baja with a non-existent schedule?* Probably never again.

Dale!

Ándale!

Órale!

---

[38] The best time to see whale sharks is between October and March, where they migrate to the Gulf of California in search of plankton.

Llévame a la Cárcel

"When everything goes wrong, that's when the adventure starts."
–Yvon Chouinard

I wish I could begin with a ruby-red sunset bleeding into the Gulf of California, Sea of Cortez, with the refreshing taste of a margarita mixed with new adventures. I could almost hear the mariachis serenading me and the Pathfinder. Unfortunately, life doesn't always pan out the way you want.

The story of Sara, Coco, and I had come to an end. They were off to Los Cabos, and I had a date with Puerto Escondido, the *hidden port*. I fished for the right words. Her smile read: words aren't necessary. We embraced. Her tan skin pressed against my damp body. Our breath synchronized. Once again, the infinite moment was ours… then it wasn't. Blaring horns and sizzling clouds of dust delivered the message: Go! With a farewell wave and a "ciao" from her legendary van, they puttered down the dusty Mexican road.

As the dust settled, my mind shifted gears to the distant sands of Puerto Escondido. Before getting nervous about the bone-crushing waves of Puerto, first I had to get there. Having driven the Baja peninsula several times, I was still in somewhat familiar territory. I had heard about the thirteen-hour ferry from La Paz to Mazatlan (250 miles), and with the current events in La Paz, I was beyond ready to move on. As I approached the ferry line, an authoritative crew member stopped me.

"Dónde están tus papeles?"

I handed him the documents: my insurance, driver's license, and my expired registration. Still high from the whale shark experience, I was confident things were going to work out.

"Tu E-st-ee-ker? E-st-ee-ker?"

I felt a sudden stab in my gut like I had been caught running a red light.

"What sticker? What are you talking about?"

As he continued, my dreams of seeing a whale shark and catching the afternoon-overnight ferry to Mazatlan vaporized. There was no sweet-talking my way out of this one.

Ten years of being a Baja-head had given me the false sense of security about documentation, or lack thereof. Never had there been any mention of import permits or E-st-ee-ckers. I thought back to when I had left San Diego, relieved to escape and giddy with the anticipation of swell. It never even crossed my mind.

Calm; there was a solution. I would have to return to La Paz, the war zone, and get the paperwork from *aduanas* (customs). A mere inconvenience-assuming I wasn't killed. After several frantic loops around the city, I arrived at *aduanas*. The sign read, "*Cerrado.*" It was 3pm. Banging away, I took my frustrations out on the door. *HOLA!* A señora finally answered, opening the door. She said there was nothing she could do for me because it was a Friday afternoon, and the office was closed. She mentioned that someone had gotten the import permit and e-stickers issued here a few months back. I also needed a signed form from Banjercito. There was hope!

That following Monday, after fleeing the city to Todos Santos, I returned to La Paz determined to keep the dream alive. Entering the *aduanas* office, I was overwhelmed by the oppressive heat. The atmosphere was gloomy and stagnant. Behind the counter sat a globular-shaped man. His eyes were dull and lifeless. He repeated the words while flapping his flaccid face:

"*La otra oficina le puede ayudar. Aquí, no. No podemos hacer nada.*"

He pointed out the door in the direction of Banjercito. So there I went. When I got to Banjercito, their finger pointed back to *aduanas*. It turned into a finger-pointing game between Banjercito and *aduanas*. What made matters worse was that as I got volleyed back and forth between this dangerous *Dante's Inferno*, I was told again the paperwork had been issued in La Paz before. The day disappeared in that dreadful dustbowl.

Each encounter, I was given a new wrinkle of hope. If I wrote this letter or filled out this form, I might have a chance. That night I returned to Pichilingue to camp. I had trouble sleeping, not knowing if there would be a shakedown, or where I was heading. With the rising of the sun, I returned to La Paz with new optimism.

Nothing changed. Each side continued to blame the other department while trying to appear sympathetic. My body was bathed in sweat as my internal system overheated. **The suffocating heat combined with the nervous energy of potentially getting hit by a stray bullet made La Paz unbearable.** I felt for the people whose daily lives had become this constant hyperalert existence.

The tension built along with the pile of documentation. I felt like a pawn between battling offices. I was hit with a barrage of NO, but, Yes, No. No. No. That one "yes" kept me going another day.

Tired of the contradicting banter and beating my head against the wall, I accepted defeat. *Que chingada!* (Fuck, how shitty!) Storming out of the *aduanas* office for the final time, the whale of a man called me back with a friendly tone. I ran back to the counter, thinking he'd had a change of heart. *Negativo.* He wanted me to translate to this Canadian girl that she too would not be issued this import E-sticker for her motorbike. If she wanted it, she would have to return to Tijuana. Misery loves company, but in this case, I was over it. *No más.* The morale-destroying heat along with the political violence telegraphed the message: leave immediately. I listened.

The time had come to pay for the "just wing it" attitude. I tried to console myself by replaying images of the whale shark and peeling waves. A perfect start to the trip, now hit the reset button. How would I begin this new phase of the trip? By driving all the way back up to Tijuana to get those *malditos tramites* papers and the E-st-ee-cker!

Adversity is where you find yourself. Bullshit. What an epic fuck-up. I cranked up some NOFX (punk rock), *The Decline* and began the long ascent up Baja. It was during these lonely times that the question surfaced, *what am I doing this all for?* This trip isn't going to bring Mike back. He's gone. I took a deep breath and looked down at his remains. And if I went back, just what would I do with Mike? I thought about a comment Wes made when seeing Mike in the camouflage cozie resting on my dashboard, "Mike's Endless Summer continues." Who was I to end Mike's Endless

Summer? With that, my mind returned to the dream. Visions of empty gaping barrels swept across my neurons. My mind softened, and my mouth stretched wide. The view was coming as the Pacific stretched out across the reef. I waited for it to throw over its radiant indigo waterfall, and then a light appeared at the end of the tunnel. The wave looked like it was going to have an exit with a big giant…. *Beep!* Oh shit. I guess the truck driver behind me didn't like my mind surfing. I returned my focus to the rugged and unruly roads of Baja. I knew I was in for one hell of a ride.

I pushed on through the dark. I told the "never drive at night" rule of Latin America to *bésame el culo* (kiss my ass). Bad call. Next thing I knew, Highway 1 dissolved into the night. I was super lost. My brooding anger quickly transformed to fear. Somehow in Baja, one of the driest places on Earth, I had found a dark, dense jungle. A looming jungle where a gringo and his Pathfinder could easily disappear. The tense atmosphere made me feel like I was being watched. Headlights up ahead cut through the night. It was 2am. My eyes burned. Armed men stood on the dirt road in front of a school.

Checkpoint.

Exhausted, I said, "Mulege?"

"*Está lejos.*"

When asking directions at two in the morning, *lejos* is the last word you want to hear. I asked for clarification.

"How far?"

"100K."

You might think 100 kilometers isn't far, but given the fact that I would need to drive on goat trails along ravines and rivers to get back to the main highway, it was indeed *lejos,* hours away *lejos.* I wanted to cry. Then I cursed myself for driving at night.

There were eight *ejércitos* (military), and two Hummers all stationed around the school, standing guard along the entrance archway. I asked what they were doing in such a remote outpost. Maybe some drug education program for the kids? *Negativo.* They said that the area saw heavy drug trafficking, and it was best that I spend the night close to them, only a few meters away from their roadblock, parked on a slightly inclined patch of dirt. *Peligroso,* guns, drugs, and frightening looks of concern made the severity of the situation very clear. If that wasn't enough, I continued to beat myself up.

There should be a photo of me next to the phrase "blowing it," but I probably would have blown the photo too. I felt like I was letting Mike down; this was supposed to be his glorious trip. Someone was indeed testing me. I felt the weight of the world upon my ignorant shoulders.

I woke up a few hours later in a cold sweat, an eerie chill creeping along my spine. Condensation fogged the windows. It was quiet outside, disturbingly quiet. Eight young militant men, quiet? No way. This didn't make sense. I cautiously cleared the fog from the window. Peering out, *nada*. Gone. They had left me in the middle of the night sleeping along a drug trafficking route. *Gracias amigos!*

The following day, my plan was simplified: Stop sucking! I looked into the mirror; my eyes were bloody red. It didn't matter. I had some serious ground to cover. Just south of the small, dusty pueblo of Constitucion, a cop leaned against his car. He had been waiting all morning for such an opportunity, a gringo. He stood in the middle of the road looking to secure his fortune. I stopped. With the thought of adding thousands of miles to an already absurdly long drive to Puerto Escondido, I was not in the mood to be fucked with. Yes, I knew I had expired tags from California, so what? This was Mexico.

He came to the window and dove right in. He pointed to the expired tags, *"Estas placas están vencidas."* He stood erect awaiting my response.

"Yes, they are expired." I paused, then said, "In my country..."

He dropped his head and continued playing his hand, *"Yo soy el jefe de la calle y digo lo que pasa acá."*

"I respect that you are taking care of the streets and the town."

"La multa por esa infracción es 1,800 pesos."

I looked at him and smiled. No way in hell was I paying a *multa* of 1,800 pesos, over $100, for expired tags. All 300 muscles in my face tightened.

"OK, I understand, but I don't have that amount of money right now." My blood simmered. "In fact, I'd rather go to jail. Take me to jail. *Llévame a la cárcel!* Because I'm quite tired after driving for days without sleep."

I lifted my sunglasses to show him my fiery red eyes. Then I explained my situation and my mission with Mike.

He nodded along in approval.

"*Bueno, tú puedes pasar.*"

I thanked him for his understanding and letting me pass. I said, "At the very least, I could give you 50 pesos for your time."

"*Ándate , no te quiero quitar la plata.*"

After all that, he didn't even want my money. I was free to go. Later, I called my dad, using up all of my Telcel credit, telling him that was the dumbest, ballsiest hand I had ever played. You can't plan how you will react when your back is against the wall. I was pissed off, courage and stupidity under fire. It was a huge turning point.

I knew I could overcome all obstacles in front of me, even *el jefe* (the boss).

I thought I was prepared for Puerto Escondido.

Por Eso Se Llama Puerto Escondido

*"Man cannot discover new oceans unless he has
the courage to lose sight of the shore."*
–Andre Gide

Puerto Escondido, my new object of fixation, was deemed my thirty-third birthday present to myself. The carrot emerged in a medium-sized southwest swell of five-to-seven foot and clean conditions hitting Puerto in a week. Anyone who knows me knows that when I get focused on something, it becomes all consuming, a fixation for my one-track mind. Whale sharks faded from my imagination as barrels began to spin out of control. *Puerto. Puerto. Barrels. Puerto. Tropical water. Puerto.* All of the enigmatic questions and tribulations of life could now be understood by a single word: Puerto.

The excessive time driving alone, three straight twelve-hour days, plowing over large chunks of asphalt and dry dirt, combined with barely any sleep was warping my mind. As night blanketed the road, I once again veered off when I saw the bright lights of Pemex. I remembered the words of Harry's son, "When in a bind, stay at the Pemex. They're safe." After the financial dent the toll roads and gas stations had made, frugality became a necessity. I figured, if I were to be a true vagrant dirt bag in the ensuing months, I better harden up and get even more familiar with sleeping in the Pathfinder.

Approaching a few parked trucks on the outer periphery of Pemex, I embraced my fellow trucking brethren. As the Pathfinder drew closer, the trucks awoke. They growled and their running lights pulsed with blinding orbs. Too tired to worry, I inserted the Pathfinder among the slightly agitated truck drivers, *matadores*-killers. I didn't give a shit.

I began to set up for another luxuriant night aboard the Pathfinder. First, I needed to move the cardboard boxes and the dusty cooler. Then I inched my way past the five stacked surfboards, spear guns, ropes, bungees, fins, and tent that all shared a fresh coat of dirt, mud, and sand. What a dream! I thought of Sara all snuggled up in her van with Coco in their nice, clean, cozy, well-organized bed. What was I doing? I was blowing it. Again!

Hoping to ease my discomfort, I inched over to my box of goodies and took a swig of tequila, Tequila from Jalisco, and assumed my position contorted around the wheel well.

The sharp pain in my neck, bent at a ninety-degree angle, announced the arrival of a fresh day. Time to move! And, yes I know what you're thinking. *Aduanas*, Tijuana, import paperwork. I decided to get my sticker and import papers in Otay Mesa, thirty minutes inland from San Ysidro, a slightly less intense experience.

Driving through mainland Mexico via Mexicali along *Carretera* 15 felt like I was driving through Texas with its industrialized plateaus of production: warehouses, farms, banks, outlet stores, billboards, and truck stops. Robust mustaches donning cowboy hats loitered out front of the steakhouses. I was a long way from the little *cantinas* and taco stands of Baja. Everything seemed grotesquely large and over-abundant. The highways offered two spacious lanes, with a well-defined median. With minimal to no risk of head-on collisions came a feeling of comfort and safety. The Highway 1 of Baja, lined with crucifixes and tombstones winding along precipitous cliffs, never affords comfort.

But this comfort came at a price, with tolls between Guadalajara and Distrito Federal (DF) exceeding 300 pesos, at the time $20. *How can they get away with that?* It seemed like an offensive joke. Pulling up to another quota, I asked.

A friendly woman working the toll booth informed me that the pricing was based on the population and distance traveled on the highway. The larger the population and longer the distances equated to higher fees. That made sense. She added that the number of *cuotas*-tolls and the prices had increased since President Nieto came to power. I had also heard people mention there were ties to Sr. Nieto and his government officials supporting one of the drug cartels in La Paz. The more I learned about him, the more I could understand the growing opposition.

Frugality mixed with curiosity made La Libre look more and more enticing. It spoke to me. Try me. I am free. So when the road split offering a choice between La Cuota and La Libre, I veered right. I should have known better.

Taking the La Libre ramp, I was greeted with a quick bang-bang combination, a nice one-two jab to the Pathfinder's suspension. Not even 100 yards later, the Pathfinder launched herself out of another roadside ditch. The flat, easy driving of La Cuota was a thing of the past. The acne-faced road coiled around the mountain. Climbing the hill and rounding a sharp bend in the cliff, I was forced off the road by an oncoming pickup truck. I found myself stopped on the side of a cliff. On that *curva* stood a small cross, not a guardrail. *What goes on in a person's mind when they pass on a blind turn going downhill?* I held my breath with each curve. The suspension-pounding ruts were incessant. My average speed dropped from around 150km per hour on La Cuota to around 70km per hour on La Libre.

After taking flight off another unmarked *tope* (speed bump), I passed a sign: "*mécanico 100 metros.*" I pose the question, who might benefit from these random archaic mounds of demonic cement? If risking a head-on collision with another car and driving a third of the speed while beating the shit out of your vehicle weren't enough reasons to avoid La Libre, then you have *la policía* in the *pueblitos*. What do you think popped into their corrupt, opportunistic minds when they saw a dusty old Pathfinder approach with California tags? Right after one of the *malditos topes*, three policemen waited resting on a parked cop car. As I approached, their eyes stretched open. One of *la policía* almost fell over with excitement to stop me. They readied themselves for the big gringo jackpot. I heard, "*Ya viene,*" as I pulled off the road.

"*Buenas tardes.*"

He leaned into the vehicle and firmly shook my hand. His dark-eyed stare was as cold as an Arctic winter.

"*Adónde vas?*"

"I'm going to Puerto Escondido."

Then a pause, an uncomfortably long pause….

In most situations, many would scramble to say something; something that often worsens the situation. I breathed deep and remained calm. These verbal volleys were becoming second nature. I waited for him to take the lead. I was in no rush. I had done nothing wrong, and most importantly, I was in a public area in broad daylight[39]. Finally, a wide grin stretched his thick black mustache to his ears. He looked back at his cohorts as if to say, "Watch this."

"*Invítanos a tomar.*"

This could be taken a few different ways. The translations would be: take us out for drinks, give us a drink, or give us money, so that we can go out drinking.

It was open to interpretation. I had options.

"*Claro,* I'd love to help you." Wedged under the passenger seat, I fished up a half-crushed, dusty plastic bottle filled with warm water, the Poland Spring variety. I lifted up the half-drunk bottle and shook it.

"It's a little hot, but it's still drinkable." I showed the others. They all started laughing.

"*Jajaja* (hahaha). *Pásale.*"

And the wheels rolled on.

I did my best to keep a straight face, but on the inside, it felt as if I had cheated death. I had survived another extortion attempt. After being searched and stopped so many times, I can relate *la policía* to a shark. The shark often circles its prey looking for a weakness, looking for an opportunity to strike. If vigor and life is detected, the shark (hopefully) moves on, and in this case, so too does the prey, the Pathfinder. Each encounter is different, but usually there arrives a moment to say something absurd, not showing fear, or a joke, which increases the likelihood of a blessed "*pásale.*" That being said, I took La Cuota for the remainder of the trip. I truly feel for the Mexicans who can't afford La Cuota and risk their lives daily on La Libre.

Well-lit signs led the way to Puebla.

The sun rose over the mountains as the cross cast its shadow upon the land below. The ruins of former Aztec temples were now the site of churches. In the presence of such spiritual ground, I couldn't help but think back to the Mexican Revolution. The people keep hold of the memory of revolutionary leaders such as Pancho Villa and Emiliano Zapata. Just a

---

[39] I would later learn that this means nothing if they really want to kidnap you—make you disappear.

century ago, these lands were stained red with their struggle. Faith was outlawed. Why? The movement saw wealthy priests fattening themselves while the people starved. Priests were hunted down in large numbers and exterminated. In the eyes of the revolutionaries, the church represented imperialism of the mind and spirit. Looking up at the cross towering over me, I felt the culmination of conquest, faith, fear, and a fiery future. There was a building groundswell of indignation; this time it was not aimed at the church but at President Enrique Peña Nieto and his henchmen.

But what could I do?

My focus returned to Puerto. I was getting close. I was told, "*Siete horas a Puerto.*"

Seven hours later, I pulled over in Oaxaca. "Am I close to Puerto Escondido?"

"*Sí, tres horas.*" He *Latinoed* me with a series of animated gestures supplemented with inexact directions.

Que bueno! Three hours away. I wanted to believe him. But my experience in Latin American told me otherwise. Asking directions has turned into a game to see how far off the estimated drive time is from the actual time. It keeps me entertained, so I continue to play.

Winding through the mountainous road, the first sign read, "Puerto Escondido 300 km." Looking at my speed and the terrain, I knew that *tres horas* was out of the question. It was 3pm. Now it became a race against the dying day. A reasonable person might see this, turn around, and spend the night in Oaxaca.

Not me. My brain wouldn't allow it. I smelled the finish line: PUERTO.

The air cooled as the road snaked through the mountains presenting a vista of the hills and valleys. Never had I seen cactus among verdant forests, a stark contrast to the dry, arid cactus in Baja. The road continued to weave up, down, and around *curvas*. Here in this land, the big tour buses rule the roadways. Clinging to the edge of the road, I made room for another torpedoing flash of Oaxaca-Puerto. The serpentine road coiled tighter. Rounding another corner, the road dipped into a valley and *wham*! The boards jumped up to the ceiling. My spine cracked. I felt for the Pathfinder. She was taking another beating. I dropped my speed to below 60 km per hour.

Another turn and… *wham*! This time it was a *tope* right after a turn, a blind *tope*. Once again, there was a sign: *taller mécanico*. Coming into a small patch of tin-roofed houses, *un pueblito,* set in the mountains, my speed dropped. A teenage girl sat looking through vacant eyes toward the canyon below. She cradled a baby in her right arm while the baby choked on a large chunk of dark purple flesh. Our eyes met in a passing glance. A *gallo* (rooster) came running around the corner squawking with his outstretched wings, ending our moment. The girl returned her gaze into the abyss. To me, she represented something I had seen so many times in Latin America. A young girl who had her dreams snatched away in that one night of unprotected sex with the local *macho,* her life changed forever.

The punishing *topes* demanded my concentration. The Pathfinder's beating continued until finally she burst. An explosion from the underbelly sent sparks firing astern. I pulled over. A sign read, *"mécanico 100 metros."* I took a look at a mangled piece of metal that had once resembled a muffler. Now a scalding-hot carcass of rusty metal lay limp and lifeless against the road.

Think.

I grabbed a wire coat hanger and suspended the muffler to the axel. It was by no means a permanent solution, but I figured it would be enough to get me to Puerto. The end was near.

With each passing minute, dusk crept further over the hills. The temperature dropped. A tour bus with blinding headlights was coming up fast. The pace quickened. Accelerating around a turn, *wham!* Should have known, *tope*. A steady stream of sparks rocketed out from below.

Stopping was not an option, even though I was dragging the corpse of a muffler. I was making it to Puerto. Tonight! Puerto! Rounding yet another turn, the valley opened up to the sea. Thick strokes of ruby red and indigo orange painted the sky. Its rich glow radiated off the mountainous terrain and the ocean below, the most beautiful sunset I had ever seen.

It was *Día de los Muertos.* Was this a sign from the dead?

A calm sedation filled the *Pathfinder.* The clouds resting atop the mountains gave the illusion of a distant island resting high above the ocean. Hidden way beneath the sea of clouds was Puerto Escondido. No way was I making it there before dark, but it was all downhill from here! The race was over. Accepting the day's victory, I let go of urgency.

To celebrate the end of the journey, *chelas* (beers) from the local *mercado* were in order.

Loosening my grip on the wheel, the *Pathfinder* and I descended. The road corkscrewed its way down the mountainside to the foothills, where a crowd of cowboy hats gathered around a ring. People sat in stands; others stood along the road. I had stumbled upon a rodeo-in the middle of nowhere. Bulls and horses stood motionlessly incarcerated in their holding pens. A running of the bulls, perhaps? As I drove along, my muffler grinded away, throwing sparkling flames into the Mexican night. The ceremony came to a screeching halt. The stands, cowboys, *viejos, tamale* vendors, children, even the animals stopped. All eyes were upon me. Nobody moved. Nobody said anything. They just stared.

I broke the silence: *"Hola! Buenas noches! Qué tal?"*
Nada.

They held a stare like an alien invader had descended upon them.

Feeling like a rodeo-stopping alien, I pressed onward. The Pathfinder could sense the sea. Driving beneath the sign *"Bienvenidos a Puerto Escondido,"* it came to me, *por eso se llama Puerto Escondido.* On the journey, I had just experienced why it is called the hidden port. It was 10 pm; only a seven-hour drive from Oaxaca, total drive from Puebla fourteen hours, drive time estimate only seven hours off. I followed signs to Playa Zicatela.

I rounded the corner passing the harbor and was emptied onto the palm-studded strip. The main drag consisted of hostels, thatched-roofed restaurants, and an iridescent Oxxo sign. So this was it? Ground Zero. This was where the big-wave legends came to get their saltwater fix. Where the dragon slayers came to slay dragons. There was a lot of commotion on the streets, much busier than I would have imagined. Once again, the noise of dragging oxidized metal across asphalt grabbed people's attention. I stopped at the first hostel I saw. Seven bucks a night, private room with a fridge, and an ocean view. Sold.

The wave at Puerto has gained its fame as being somewhat of a freak of nature. A beach break that can hold size in excess of thirty feet. Due to its positioning, it gobbles up most fetches sent from the Southern Hemisphere. Often these storms travel all the way from New Zealand or Antarctica sending swells like a freight train up the American continent. Whatever swell heads to Puerto Escondido is magnified by the Mesoamerica Trench offshore, which drops off thousands of feet, making it one of the deepest in the Americas. The power of the Pacific slams into these shores completely unobstructed by the ocean floor, resulting in the Mexican Pipeline.

The following morning, I awoke to clean conditions groomed by a light offshore breeze. Coffee in hand, it was time to get a feel for the area. I wanted to see where the take-off points were and observe the crowd. Walking down the strip, I saw that the swell continued to grow. A solid wave reared to life and collapsed. The beach trembled from a 100-yard closeout that was unrideable. There was no one surfing here, and for good reason. To the east, about a dozen guys bobbed in the water. Waves approached. The peak was split, one guy went right and the other left. Both guys pulled in with the guy on the right completely disappearing and coming out with the spray. It was slightly overhead, and I had seen enough. I sprinted back to the room. Forget the coffee[40]. Like an excited kid getting called out of school, I frantically gathered my belongings. Board shorts? I was already wearing a pair. Board: 5'8, 5'10, 6'0, 6'9, or 8'4? Based on the fast hollow conditions, I grabbed my florescent green 5'10 Stretch epoxy quad known as Slimmer[41].

Upon entering the water, I was grabbed by the river-like rapid. It was easy to see how people panic and drown here. For its size, maybe four to six feet, there was a ton of water moving around. The feeling in the crowd was intense and aggressive. Walls of water stormed in. With a rider screaming, "*Oye!*" everyone knew to stay out of his way.

I moved out and away from the crowd and lined one up. The water quickly went vertical. I sprang to my feet, and looked down. All I could see was the bottom approaching fast. I was already disconnected from my board. *How did that happen?* This was not how I envisioned my first wave at Puerto. After four straight days and more than fifty hours of driving and dreaming, this was my reward. Within seconds, I was spun around and firmly planted on the sand. The sand felt like cement, the result of thousands of years, millions of pulverizing waves grinding away. Luckily, I fell feet first and was able to push off the bottom. Within ten minutes, I'd had my first Puerto baptism.

Tiene power!

---

[40] It was going mental, going off, berserker, looney tunes, off its face, cooking bru!
[41] Yes, the name was inspired by the movie *Ghostbusters*. I ain't afraid of no ghosts.

Chingón

"It's important to be surrounded by good energy. When you are younger you do everything by the heart because you feel good. You need to keep that."
–Nomme

Crowds. Intensity. Every session. I found myself just getting smaller close-outs. Eventually, frustration kicked in and drew me into the pack. There was a lot of jockeying and calling people off. You could feel the *machismo. Los Mexicanos* were dominating. Boogie boarders, surfers, and this one guy riding a stand-up with a Nacho Libre mask on, a true hellman.

Like anywhere around the world, if you are respectful and patient, your time will come. A large set rushed in. My heart raced. I sprint-paddled for the horizon. The first wave a guy fell out of the sky, stuck the drop, and stood tall in the belly of the beast. Just ducking under, the heavy lip came booming down. I breathed a sigh of relief, a near escape. Most of the other guys wore its power on their heads. The second wave lurched to life. The peak was coming right for me. My eyes widened. My heart hammered into the board. I looked to my inside as a boogie boarder was kicking hard into position.

My excitement deflated. I was going to have to let this one go. I started to slow my paddle when he shouted, *"Dale!"* Go!

Energy passed through me like a strike of lightning to the heart. I turned, took three strokes, and free fell through the air with the thick lip cascading behind me. The board skipped down the vertical face of water. Engaging the fins at the bottom of the wave, I had only one option: pull in. With immense energy rushing overhead, I held my line and focused on the light at the end of the dark sand tunnel. The exit widened and gave way to bluest and brightest sky. It let me out! I looked down at my trembling hands. My body was jumping out of its skin, by far my best wave at Puerto.

I paddled back out. My heart and arms were moving a million miles an hour. I took a calming breath. Paddling over to the Mexican boogie boarder, I wanted to give him a big bear hug and a kiss, in a macho kind of way. With adrenaline coursing through my veins I said, "Thanks for the wave!"

"*Era tuya,*" he said.

I had to admit; the wave did come right to me. For him, a local, maybe it was nothing, but to me it was everything. I thanked him another five times. Eventually, we got to talking story, and I told him about the journey and the good fortune I'd had spearfishing around the nearby points. His eyes lit with interest. His name was Buho, which in Spanish means "owl." Maybe his nickname was for his wisdom or those big brown orbs he was staring at me with? I don't know. All I knew was he gave me the nod on my best Puerto wave. I would forever be indebted. I told him I could hook him up with some dive gear, including a single-band gun and some old dive fins. He was thrilled. He then invited me out, "*Vamos a salir esta noche!*"

I knew there was a street *fiesta* that night in town. Riding that oceanic high, of course I was in.

"*Claro que sí!*"

We met that night at a cantina where we drank *caguamas* (32 oz beer) watching waves of energy sweep down the street. Florescent carnival lights flashed to a distant pulse of salsa. People embraced *la noche*. Later on, Buho introduced me to his friend Oliver from Salina Cruz. Before me sat a young man bearing a broad grin and confident gaze. Over the growing noise, I found out he was a surf guide. He had my attention. People used to claim that Salina Cruz was a secret spot, maybe twenty years ago, but now it most certainly was not. Big surf travel agencies market it, and all the traveling pros surf there. I mean, hell, they had a WCT competition just down the road[42]. Oliver introduced me to his beautiful girlfriend, Leydi. They had come up for the festivities and the surf competition, which Buho was a judge in.

Fascinated by Salina Cruz and the concept of mandatory surf guides,

---

[42] Professional surf competition comprised of the top thirty-four in the world. Hundreds of photographers and groupies travel with them. It is a big scene, a circus.

I began questioning Oliver. "So if I don't have a guide and want to surf in Salina Cruz, what happens?"

"The locals will kick you out. They won't let you surf without a guide."

"What if someone goes to a break and no one is out? Could he or she just get a few?"

"It's not a good idea." He shot me a look that I took as a strong warning.

"OK, then how much is it for a day with a surf guide?" The words just sounded wrong coming out of my mouth.

"We usually have package tours."

"*Toma.*"

Oliver passed me some *grillo*s (grasshoppers flavored with chili salt and lime) to munch on while I mulled over his words.

The night was energized with Dancing and Mezcal[43]. Lights blurred overhead. Oliver put his arm around me and said, "Hey, I like you, man. You should come to Salina Cruz. I will take care of you. *Eres mi camara.*"

I had my first Salina Cruz *amigo*. A series of coincidences had brought us together. I was excited to see how the next chapter would unfold, the waves in particular. I told them, "I'm leaving to Salina Cruz *mañana*. You guys can ride with me. I won't even charge you."

He caught my sarcasm, and we both laughed like we were the best of friends. The alcohol helped.

Oliver and Leydi thought it was a great idea. Salina Cruz and perfect rights, here we come!

We later ran into Buho and Oliver asked him, "*Estás pedo?*"

Buho looked over at him with sloshed eyes and said, "*Tienes pedo?*"

I was confused. "*Pedo*" to me always meant fart. I asked, "*Pedo?*" I held my nose to suggest a smelly fart.

Leydi giggled. "*Que pedo!*"

I was then taught the four Mexican *pedos:*

In Oliver's case, it meant "drunk." For Buho, it meant "problem." My use was "fart" and Leydi's was "how funny." If you go to Mexico, be sure to know your *pedos*.

That night we were all *pedos*.

---

[43] Similar to the processing of tequila, just a different plant. I think it has a smoother and more versatile-mixable taste.

In the *mañana,* I woke to pounding temples. The Oaxacan sun punished me further for my night of excess. I wanted to hide, but remembered I was taking Oliver and Leydi back to Salina Cruz. When I showed up at their hotel room, I got a series of grunts and hand waves. My presence was bringing harsh light into their cave.

Oliver yelled, *"Estamos crudos."*

He didn't have to tell me, I could see it. They were hungover. I had heard *crudo* used to describe meat, it translates to "raw." Interesting they would use it to describe a hangover. That morning, I, too, felt *crudo*, like raw, rancid meat. They wanted to sleep and catch the late-afternoon bus. I envied them but knew it was time to go.

Back on the road, I looked down at the cup holder. The unpredictable nature of Puerto was not the place for Mike's tube. I learned that early on when it administered my first flogging.

Southward.

People assured that the drive to Salina Cruz was actually three hours, not like the "three hours" from Oaxaca to Puerto. I tried my best to caffeinate and power my way through the *crudo,* despite the fact that my head and heart were slamming me in unison. I pressed on past some of the famous point breaks along the way. No stopping, checking, and debating if it was good or not. I had a target. I envisioned tacos, point breaks, and cold beer waiting for me at the finish line. My fantasy was disrupted by repetitive clanking. Was it the muffler again? No, I had two side pipes coming out of the passenger side door, Mexican ingenuity at its finest. Had I hit something? Was it one of those wild and deranged *perros* that chase and try to intimidate cars? I was forced to pull over on a hill.

Upon inspection, a flat tire. *Que chingada!* My head spun. I felt the sudden urge to vomit in the thick tropical heat. Digging for the car jack, sweat poured off my brow. The search was disrupted by a deep rumbling in the distance. What was that? I pressed on. By the time the jack was out, it had begun to pour. This was not a morning cup of coffee pour, it was the dumping, blinding buckets pour. I looked to the heavens above and opened my mouth. *Agua dulce?* Not quite sweet, but salty.

Out of the squall, two men came running over from a nearby cantina.

"Necesitas ayuda?" they asked with eager eyes.

"I am fine, thanks."

They disregarded my words and proceeded to assist as the rain hammered down on us. The car jack struggled to stretch with the corrosion and sand gnawing at its joints. The incline didn't help either. With the tire replaced, I sponsored a round of drinks. They told me I should look into getting a new *gato*. I agreed. Based on the context, I figured they meant my rusty sand-filled hunk of metal, jack, not a cat.

It boggled my mind how determined these men were to help a stranger. In the States, how often do people stop for a person in need? Is it that we're too busy, don't care, or afraid? Whatever it is, I see room for growth.

The short trip taught me three valuable lessons:

1. Never travel hungover
2. Help a stranger, regardless of the weather
3. In Latin America, *gato* means "car jack"

The next day, I headed to the *llantería*. While waiting for my tire to be patched, a black '80s Volkswagen Beetle sped by kicking up dust clouds. Our eyes connected as he passed. This triggered a *shaka*[44] and a "Hey, mi fren!"

The driver made a quick U–turn. Being a white dude who has spent many years traveling around the Americas, I've heard my share of "Hey, mi fren." These three words generally lead to an offering of drugs, some unneeded, overpriced service, or trinkets. I wanted no part of it. The word "NO" hung from the tip of my tongue.

He parked and swaggered his way down the street. A small man with a spiky Afro wore a tattered Rusty surf shirt, dusty board shorts, a pair of disintegrating sandals, and a paper-thin mustache that clung to his upper lip[45]. He extended his right hand.

I shook his callused hand and waited for his offering.

"Mi fren surfer."

I kept guarded. "Hey man, what's up?"

---

[44] The "hang loose" sign used in the surf culture. This is done by extending your pinky and thumb while closing the middle three fingers. Please keep in mind that throwing a *shaka* doesn't make you cool.

[45] For surfers, picture a Mexican Brad Gerlach.

"*Qué hongos*[46]*? Soy Ramón.*"

"They call me Cory."

"*Te llevo a la playa, mi chingón*[47]*.*"

OK, so that was his angle. He wanted to take me to the beach. I figured he would do this for a special price because we were *frens*.

"No, thanks. I'm waiting on my tire to be patched."

"*Cuál es?*"

I pointed to the Pathfinder.

"*Ah, buena camioneta.*" He nodded rapidly, showing respect and approval. From that point on, the Pathfinder became known as the *Camioneta*, the truck.

"*Qué pasó?*"

He was concerned about what had happened to the *Camioneta*, so I showed him the eight-inch piece of rebar that was extracted from the tire.

He casually looked at it and said, "*Es normal,*" and continued his rapid head nodding. Again, I figured he wanted to be my surf guide for a price. I changed my excuse.

"I am waiting on my friend Oliver, my surf guide[48]."

He was as incessant as an airport taxi driver. "No" meant "try harder." He pointed to his black Beetle caked in Mexican dust and said, "*Vamos en el bocho.*"

"How much?"

"*Gratis, te llevo gratis, mi chingón.*"

He gave me a pat on the shoulder. I've never met someone so excited to take an unknown guy to the beach, for free. The mechanic told me it would be another forty minutes. I asked if he knew Ramon. He shook his head and humbly returned to his work.

What did I have to lose?

"OK, let's go."

---

[46] Originated from *Qué onda?* What's up? If you literally translate *Qué hongos*, it means what mushrooms. Could this imply a deeper connection with the Mexican people and the *Aztecas*, who referred to *teonanácatl* (psychedelic mushrooms) as the flesh of the gods?

[47] Meaning my cool, acceptable, or friend. "Chingón" is commonly used throughout Mexico, especially in the south.

[48] Contact Oliver at Oaxaca Soul Surfer. He'll take care of you, and if you're lucky, he will tell you a few stories.

His entire body buzzed with excitement as he said, *"A la playa, mi chingón!"* followed by another series of head nodding.

We headed toward his *bocho*. I left all my belongings in the *Camioneta* at the *llantería*. I will continue to place faith in the working class and *campesinos* (farmers) of Latin America.

As I got in the *bocho*, a spring knifed into my back. My stomach jumped as the seat collapsed backward. My feet came flying up to counteract the fall. I then sprang forward. I gave Ramon a concerned look. He responded with a *shaka*. I guess that was "normal."

His face beamed as he turned the key. The *bocho* roared to life, bellowing out a cloud of milky smoke. He checked all the gauges, adjusted the mirror, and threw another *shaka*.

I threw him a *shaka* back and told him his car was *chido*. Cool.

"Claro." He gave me a look like I had just informed him that Mexicans eat tacos.

"Te gusta música?"

"Of course!"

Based on what I'd seen so far, I figured he would put on some old school punk music or maybe some Mexican "Banda." Not Ramon, he looked over with the same overzealous eyes and cranked the volume. Loud static flooded the speakers. He held his right hand up as if cuing the music. He paused. Boom. Techno. Fast high-pitched techno beats rattled the *bocho*.

"I'm a Barbie girl in a Barbie world. Life in plastic, it's fantastic…You can brush my hair and dress me everywhere…Imagination that is your creation."

Ramon started dancing and shaking as if he were having a rhythmic seizure. And with that, we took off toward the beach in a dusty Barbie world. He saluted everyone in our path with a raised hand, a head nod, and a *"chingón."* Then he looked over and sang in a deep voice, "Let's go, Barbie. Let's go party. I'm a Barbie girl in a Barbie world!"

I was speechless. I thought that Mike Brant would be the only heterosexual with the audacity to rock this kind of music while in the presence of a complete stranger, particularly another male.

Nope.

Clearly, Ramon wasn't afraid to be himself, which is why his nickname throughout the area is *Chingón*. It's also because most things that he does and describes are *chingón,* cool.

After "chingón," his second favorite word is *"perfecto."* Everything in Chingón's life is *perfecto* as long as it involves the ocean. We took the exit outside of town where the earth flattens to meet the sea.

"What's that over there, salt flats?"

"Simón!" (Of course.)

I guess that's why it's called Salina Cruz. The smell of burning trash wafted in the offshore breeze. The *bocho* parked on an empty dirt lot in front of a rock jetty. On the inside, the sand bottom contoured perfectly to a crescent moon-shaped cove. Chingón said *perfecto* several more times while I looked at the ocean. It lay still. Maybe a lull? Nope. Flat as a Mexican halibut. But for Chingón, it was still *perfecto*. Why? Because it afforded him time to drop some surf stories.

"Esta ola es bien peligrosa."

He pointed to the cross where a twenty-year-old *chamaco (kid)* named Abisael drowned rescuing two of his friends, a local legend, a hero.

On the rocks and mixed in the sand were small black globs.

"What's this?"

"Petróleo de la refinería." He pointed over to the Pemex refinery. I could see the smokestacks and flames from afar. I felt a twist of guilt in my gut for having contributed to the contamination all the way down the coast.

Chingón rubbed his thumb on his index and middle finger, *dinero*.

"El surf cuesta."

"Rompí una tabla aquí y casi ahogué también."

He spun tales of breaking boards and getting slammed so hard that he temporarily lost hearing and almost drowned. Another time he sliced his foot and had to borrow money to go the doctor for stitches. Chingón found surfing later in life, early thirties, just five years ago, and has been paying his dues. He used to be a marathon runner, but one day while running along this very beach, he saw a guy, Noque, surfing solo putting on a tube-riding clinic. Chingón stood on the beach mesmerized and has been caught in her sea-spell ever since. He is the epitome of what it means to be a soul surfer. He lives, eats, and breathes surfing. His life consists of working at the naval base constructing commercial ships, but his heart revolves around the ocean. Any pulse of energy, he's out there. Even on a flat day, like today, he was on it.

Chingón spoke of the origins of surfing in Salina Cruz and of a guy named Patrick from San Francisco, the godfather of Salina Cruz surfing. He came down in the early nineties and taught most of the locals how to surf. A gift they hopefully never forget. He was known as the guy who *"camina mucho,"* walking to all of these remote spots solo in the sweltering heat lugging a giant long board. Talk about commitment. He also surfed with a dive knife strapped to his leg after a close run-in with a tiger shark. According to Chingón, he was the only gringo who could surf these spots without a surf guide. Unfortunately, Patrick had some "issues" in California that would keep him away from his beloved Salina Cruz for several years.

Chingón's parents, his father, known as the *Rana* (frog) and his mother, Nena, are building a house atop one of the many hills in town, and Chingón is their watchdog. Every afternoon he climbs the hill, past the colorful laundry drying in the oppressive heat. Over the vast valley, he sees oil drums and the industrialized port along with the sizzling silhouettes of Christ's cross reigning over the colored-cement homes. *Que calor*[49]*!* Chingón sleeps at the construction site. His presence ensures that no one takes anything. Because they would. Anything that is not welded or locked down becomes *"desaparecido."* Disappears.

---

[49] The two most common phrases you hear around town: *que calor* and *gracias a dios*. Heat and God dominate the land.

Leydi's Cumple Años

"Drive to know, discover, and be bewildered."
–Don Juan Matus

When Oliver (the surf guide I met in Puerto Escondido) returned to Salina Cruz, we became the four *camaradas, amigos*: Oliver, Chingón, Cinco, and myself. You are probably saying, Cinco? He got his name from his large scar going down the middle of his chest. When he was born, the doctors needed to rearrange his organs, mainly his heart. The legend has it that he didn't have a heart, hence the nickname 'Cinco': *SIN COrazón*, meaning without a heart. Despite the nickname, Cinco has a lot of heart. Although he might not be the guy busting 360 airs surfing (nor am I), he is not afraid to go for it. Pointing to himself and then me after a session, he said, "*Somos guerroros Aztecas con el espirítu de jaguar.*"

I had never been called an Aztec warrior with the spirit animal of a jaguar. Based on the fact that the jaguar is one of the most feared and respected animals in the jungle, I took it as a tremendous compliment. Cinco, with his baby face, looked to be in his early teens. I would later find out that he was in his twenties, a father, and works at the fish market. But he still made time for our surf trips[50].

Days evaporated in the Mexican desert sun. We had the privilege of surfing various point breaks by ourselves. I reminded myself that I wouldn't be surfing these breaks if it wasn't for Buho and the wave he gave me at Puerto. Funny how acts of kindness and sharing waves work.

It was the off-season, which also meant minimal swell. It didn't matter. With the right attitude, any day by the sea is a gift; all I

---

[50] Years later, like so many surfers in Salina Cruz, he became a surf guide.

had to do was look at Chingón and his unwavering enthusiasm. On one of these days, we found a tight rocky cove just east of town. It was like nothing I had ever seen, three different waves colliding into each other. The swells would rebound and ricochet off the rocks to meet the incoming wave. We bodysurfed the two-to-four-foot shore break. On a solid swell, I imagined that the place would be suicidal.

About 500 meters beyond the shore break, a crop of rocks rose out of the sea. I told the boys I was going for an exploratory dive. Cinco's face brightened as he saw me grab the speargun.

"*La comida!*" He liked to refer to my speargun as food.

"Let's see. No expectations."

Even in the small conditions, the visibility was poor: cloudy and churned with sand. There was a vertical rock wall that extended down into abysmal depths. Smooth, sand-colored rocks covered in barnacles lined the edges of the cove. The conditions didn't feel right. Even small rockfish looked at me with menacing eyes. Doubt began to cloud my mind. Time to go in. Just one more dive.

On the ascent, three beaconing silhouettes entered my periphery. They were too far away to identify. I took a deep breath and descended again. "Uninterested" was the look I was going for. At a depth of around twenty feet, three large jacks approached from my left; two of them took a wide turn while one aggressively charged in for a closer look. I squeezed the trigger. A silver flash shot downward. The wire connecting the spear to the gun tightened and then pulled me down. Without a float line, I couldn't let go of the gun. I swam over to slow the fish down. I got alongside of him and grabbed him by the gills and then secured his tail-the power source. Ascending to the light, I tried to remain calm. On the surface, the fish struggled and thrashed to break free. Out of the chaotic water, I hoisted the head of the powerful jack and screamed, "*Comida!*"

The boys went wild in celebration jumping and hooting. With the jumbled-up currents and pounding shore break, the exit looked questionable. I called for help, thinking that they would be set spotters and help guide me in. Seconds later, I saw Oliver scrambling around like an anxious dog searching for a place to poop. He was looking for something. He picked what looked to be broken net and sprinted along the cliff. I watched in disbelief as he leapt from the rocks into the ocean. It was his girlfriend, Leydi's, birthday, and he really wanted to bring this fish to the party! *Amor.* Love. Together we secured the fish and got him "safely" to shore.

Dinner and celebrations followed. I told them I would make a gringo special: scalloped potatoes and grilled fish using a teriyaki marinade. Her mother watched over me with extremely alert eyes as I operated in her domain. She cooked rice and beans. After dinner, they asked for my *historia.* They seemed genuinely interested, so I described my San Diego life. A life of teaching, surfing, and adventures with *Mañana.* I spared them the love lost part. The story ended with Panama and Mike. I told them of the Brant family entrusting me with some of his remains and that this was his final send-off, searching for his last ride.

Leydi's mom shot me a concerned look. *"Dónde está Mike?"* she asked.

I pointed outside to the street. "He's in the *Camioneta.*"

Her worried face became serious. *"No puede dejarlo en la Camioneta. Alguien lo puede robar."*

My face read, someone might steal him?

She pointed to the car. *"Ándale."*

Walking out to the Pathfinder, I wondered who the hell would steal someone's ashes. Nonetheless, I grabbed Mike. Their faces brightened when I returned. La Señora enlightened me that I was on a spiritual journey, and that I needed to take great care of Mike. They wanted to hear more about Mike. Uncorking a few Mike Brant stories filled the room with endless laughter. One of Leydi's friends, a good-looking señorita in her twenties, asked to see some photos. I showed her a picture of Mike with his shirt off, hair parted down the middle, standing with perfect posture.

Her eyes flared, *"Que guapo!"*

"Yeah, he was a pretty good-looking guy."

She held my phone, staring deeply at his photo. In honor of Mike, I decided to mix it up. The conversation seemed too normal, too safe.

"Mike also loved dudes," I said.

"Era maricón?" Her brown eyes swelled with terrorized shock.

"No, he wasn't gay. He just loved hanging out with males."

They were perplexed by the enigma of Mike. Mike's eccentricities continued deep into the night. Tail holes, nakedness, wet stories, and beyond. Knowing there were surfers at the party, I circled back to Mike's hair flips.

In surfing, people scrap and fight to take ownership of waves. At the conclusion of the wave, the rider might feel compelled to release some adrenalin. Emphatic body posturing is what we call a "claim." There are subtle claims and barbaric, chest-beating claims. Mike was the former. "Kicking out at the end of the ride with his chest held high, he would flip his blonde hair out of his eyes. The bigger and better the wave, the more dramatic the flip. There was a positive correlation between wave heights and hair-flip ferocity," I told them.

Try to explain all that in Spanish. What defied translation, I animated. I did my best to flip the scant amount of hair on my head.

Telling his stories made it feel like Mike was sitting next to me the entire night, laughing.

Matters of self-preservation had me thinking about the protests that were now sprouting up all over Mexico. When I asked, I got several discouraging stares. I had violated the three conversational rules of Latin America: never talk about politics, religion, and *fútbol* (soccer). People kill over such matters. With an errant flick of the tongue, the blood of a Latino can go from room temperature to scalding hot. I proceeded with caution. They told me Mexican politics were complicated, and that they didn't want to get involved. To me, this meant, "We don't want to talk about it with you, gringo." I could understand their reservations. Latin American history teaches us how political activism is often met with swift and ruthless brutality. What they all agreed on was that turmoil was brewing, especially down south in Chiapas.

And once again, I found myself driving straight into the heart of the storm.

La Política Complicada

"Consciousness is compelled to grow, and the only way it can grow is through strife, through life or death confrontations."
–Don Juan Matus

"Nieto is taking our jobs!"

I had heard this before.

"While he puts in his thugs and people he can manipulate, 3,000 state workers have lost jobs, and there is more to come."

A merchant stood behind the glass counter display, his hands waived wildly as he spoke. Four men stood around a copy machine taking in his lecture.

"We need change." His commanding presence continued, "We have only three parties, and they are all corrupt."

I had heard this one too.

"The killing in La Paz was a guise, a cover-up. What he's doing is killing the opposition.

"Nieto is bad for the people."

His pupils nodded in agreement. It was clear that the men were not here to purchase anything. For me, I just needed to make a copy for my *transmite* "import" papers. I paid the man fifteen pesos for the copies, and told him that I hoped things improved. He sat back down on his stool. He looked up from his glasses and said, "It will only get worse, you'll see."

The conversation had taken place a month earlier, at the border at Otay Mesa, his words weighed on my mind. What the old man had predicted had come to fruition.

On September 26 and 27, forty-three college students at Raul Isidro Burgos (a college in Ayotzinapa, Guerrero, located just outside Mexico

City) had "disappeared." Unfortunately, the word *"desaparecido"* is a word that is deeply embedded in Latin American history. Opposition to those in power suddenly vanish without a trace. Thousands of people have been murdered. Rarely are such crimes investigated or prosecuted. Victims simply join an ever-growing list of *desaparecidos*.

These forty-three university students ("*Normalistas*," as they were referred to) disappeared for their political activism. They spoke out against the interweaving of politics and the drug cartels. Reports surfaced that the state police and members of organized crime had attacked a university bus. The students were removed, put into police cars, and never seen again. The people were outraged. The government denied any involvement. The mayor of Iguala and the chief of police went into hiding. A tape was later discovered of an official of the (PGR) Procuraduría General de La Republica, Attorney General directly under Nieto, saying all the forty-three students were in fact dead. Despite all the evidence, no charges were pressed[51]. The streets around Distrito Federal and Guerrero ignited with vengeance.

Stores were looted and giant statues of the president were burned to the ground. Malatov cocktails were sent crashing into Oxxos, government-funded convenience stores. Many toll booths along La Cuota were destroyed. People were unsure what direction Mexico was heading.

On November 20, roads were blocked for the *desfile* (parade) celebrating the anniversary of the Mexican Revolution. Kids marched in colorful costumes. "Banda" music vibrated the windows, and large sticks of dynamite exploded, shaking the ground. The atmosphere was light and festive. It seemed like the dust had settled from the last retaliation against the government. But as the Buddhists say, perception leads to deception.

Charged with the bloodshed of their ancestors, the people looked to avenge the forty-three *desaparecidos*. Reports came of riots and vandalism sweeping across Mexico. Unsure of where to go or hide, I held my mountain-ward course, San Cristobal de las Casas, Chiapas.

Glass shards covered the road in front of *caseta de cuota* (toll booth). The regular, uniformed government employees were gone. My heart skipped with the sight of masked men occupying the booth. My nerves tightened

---

[51] Information cited from "Latin American Disappeared and Repeating History in Mexico"(Jeff Abbott, Truth Out website).

with the sound of debris crunching under my tires. A man with a V for Vendetta mask and a green, long-sleeve shirt stood over the *Camioneta.* Two other men flanked to his left and peered out from behind youthful eyes, their identities concealed by red bandanas. I took a deep breath and stopped.

Now what?

As I rolled down the window, the cold mountain air poured in. My breath clouded. At over 7,000 feet above sea level, I was a long way from the tropical beaches of Oaxaca. Instead of looking like a scared gringo, I pointed to the sign looking for guidance: it read, "cuota 60 pesos."

One of the men spoke, "*Trienta pesos está bien para la causa.*"

Thirty pesos for the cause was better than paying sixty. The masked man handed me an announcement.

I uttered a *gracias* as I stepped on the gas. I took a look at the paper, which read, "*La opinión pública,*" described the events, and listed their demands. They wanted to see the forty-three students alive or have the president and his officials resign. If not, the violence, protests, and demonstrations would not only to continue, but intensify. It concluded with these words: "In the end, we shall overcome. Our fight is no longer isolated."

Driving through another *pueblito,* I was funneled down a narrow alleyway. Vast tangles of live power lines drooped over the clogged streets. People marched with banners, screaming for justice and retribution. Drums beat. Horns blared. Passion flared. The revolution lived on the city walls. The names, silhouettes, and slogans of forty-three students were graffitied everywhere.

> "*Mateo, el campo te espera* (Mathew, the country waits for you)."
> "*Gustavo, la pelota te dejó* (Gustavo, the town left you a soccer ball)."

Emiliano Zapata's eyes pierced deeply into the people's hearts as he looked on from a multitude of murals. His ubiquitous spirit was fortified by his unflinching gaze and hefty moustache. His revolutionary legacy, along with Pancho Villa's, still carry weight in modern Mexico.

In 1994, a group known as Ejercito Zapatista de Liberacion Nacional (EZLN) declared war against the Mexican state, which it still wages to this day. The group was formed in response to the creation of the North American Free Trade Agreement (NAFTA); the EZLN felt this was just another attempt to further polarize the wealth and resources in Mexico while offering little to the poor, particularly Chiapas. The economic impacts on the corn industry were profound. From 1994 to 2002, corn exports to Mexico doubled. The 6 million metric tons were provided at below cost. This in turn plummeted the price of Mexican corn by 70%. There were no subsidies provided or regulations put in place to safeguard the local interests. This short-sided profit scheme drove many farmers out of business, driving them to support guerilla movements, move to overcrowded cities, or join drug cartels. People in desperate positions do desperate things. The benefits for the few cast violence and political turmoil upon millions of Mexicans[52].

The support and involvement in Zapista villages, primarily in rural outposts of Chiapas, has increased. The group functions autonomously, completely detached from government rules and regulation. Their slogan: When the government oversteps its boundaries, we will be there to defend the people. In the response to Nieto and the forty-three *desaparecidos,* more people have joined the Zapatista movement. How far was this going to escalate?

The uncertainty and civil unrest seemed to galvanize the populace. The political fervor stormed in their eyes and lived in their mouths. The "never talk politics in Latin America" rule disappeared in Chiapas. A restaurant owner believed that the government was not going to send troops, but instead infiltrate the movement and create an internal divide. He also spoke of more vandalism of toll booths in Tuxtla, a Zapatista outpost. One old man complained about the price of eggs going up with Nieto. Others made comparisons to the '94 *revolución.* Some believed that corrupt police were playing both sides by supporting the movement and then trying to discredit them. What I heard the most was "We have to end this corrupt system."

But the question remained, how?

---

[52] Information is cited from "Truth and consequence of Corn Dumping," (publisher: Organic Consumers Association).

On a cold, clear night in San Cristobal de Las Casa, two charred doors of a store leaned against the wall with their hinges completely blown off. Half of the shelves inside were broken; all of them stripped of their goods before the fire. An acrid stench of burnt plastic and coffee drifted down the cobblestone streets in the brisk mountain air. To the right of the door, in giant black letters were the words: *"Puto Peña"* (*"Peña,* the president, is a bitch").

Alongside of this were silhouettes of empty faces of the forty-three *desaparecidos.*

A whirlpool of nervous energy spun around the colonial streets. Two policemen dressed in riot gear guarded the front of the decimated store. One policeman turned and snapped a photo of the carnage. I did the same. None of my friends had heard anything about the events. *How could something of this magnitude not be newsworthy?* I wanted to share to the electronic world what was happening. I felt for the families of the forty-three and the ones in La Paz.

My post produced thirteen likes.

On the way back to my hostel, several people joked, *"Vamos al Oxxo."* Most laughed, knowing that the stores in town had been burned.

That night a third Oxxo and Soriana (the Mexican version of Home Depot affiliated and subsidized by the government) outside of town were reduced to charred cement. The toxic debris still smoldered through the city. Just as the flier had warned, it seemed like the violence and vandalism were escalating.

The words of the announcement lingered: "If Nieto does not step down, the violence will not only continue, but escalate." Most people didn't believe that Nieto would step down[53]. Further conflict seemed inevitable. Days after the toll booths were destroyed in San Cristobal, the police and National Guard came in, reasserted their authority, and reclaimed the toll booths. Members of the opposition were arrested. The state had struck back. I later learned that there were another forty-one *desaparecidos* in Chiapas, too. That brought the total to more than 120

---

[53] Five years later, in 2019, Nieto was accused of taking a 100 million bribe from drug kingpin El Chapo. This was brought to life in his trail, which was exactly what the students were protesting against.

reported *desaparecidos* in the last year. How high would that number climb? Was there a solution?

Entering the *Camioneta*, I was reminded of what I was doing. I was not here to start a revolution. The stacks of surfboards and Mike's remains screamed two words: "SURF TRIP!" The wheels again pointed southward to Guatemala, the gateway of Central America and land of the Maya.

My worrisome mind circled around my expired tags. Would they let me in? I let the unwanted anxiety pass. *If they don't let me in, so what?* I had come this far.

My thoughts then jumped to the next concern.

Guatemala was no safety net; my mind ran through the bloody history and brutal clashes between the government and the Maya. I recall learning in high school history class about the Aztecs, Incans, and Maya. (Mayan is used as an adjective to describe dialect/culture not the group of people.) Little was taught about the existence of modern-day Maya and their everyday struggle to survive.

Es Normal

"Nothing of value, nothing that is real, is ever lost."
–Eckhardt Tolle

Asking directions in Latin America will give you a lesson in inexactness, heavy gesturing, and unwavering confidence. People spoke of a ferry just outside the sleepy beach town of Monterrico (where I had caught a few waves but not enough to satisfy my growing surf appetite) running along the Canal de Chiquimuilla. The dirt road looped its way from the beach and into a thick mass of wild vegetation. With no ferry in sight, I headed over to a small straw-thatched *bodega*. The shade provided a much-needed escape from the flesh-searing sun. A dark-skinned man with jet black hair leaned against the shaded wooden counter. He was barefoot and smiled. After the standard *"Qué tal?"* and *"Cómo estás?"* inquiries, I asked, "When does the ferry come?"

"Aquí está. Ya mismo sale."

He gestured to the water's edge. Logs and planks floated on the shoreline moving ever so slightly in the passing gentle current.

"I'm looking for a ferry for the *Camioneta*." I nodded toward the Pathfinder.

He smiled matter-of-factly, pointing back to the floating planks.

"Thanks."

I was taken aback by his white tank top, which featured a giant rooster-Gallo, the local *Chapín* (Guatemalan) beer.

"That tank top is pretty incredible! Congratulations."

His eyes swelled with excitement as he took action. He now stood shirtless before me.

"Toma," he said, holding the tank top in his hand.

83

A smile beamed from his round face. He shook the shirt like he would be offended if I didn't take it. Finally, I did. His name was Hector. It mattered little that the tank top was stretched and polkadotted by blue and gray paint stains. When a shoeless stranger gives you the shirt off his back, it touches depths in your heart you never knew existed. Now Hector stood before me practically naked. I ran to the car and grabbed a shirt. Thanks to a Guatemalan laundry service in Lake Atitlan, the shirt was now a shade of smurf blue mixed with gray camo, atrocious. It reminded me of Mike's ugly-ass Orion surfboard.

With no ferry in sight, I asked Hector about the current state of Guatemala. I know I'd broken the "no politics" rule, again.

He shook his head with sorrow. "*Está muy mal ahora. Están protestando en la ciudad.*"

I nodded. "Yes, I've read about the conflict."

The people, primarily Maya, had taken to the streets of Guatemala City in protest. They were speaking out against the hydro—electric plant that would contaminate and jeopardize their water supply. Many people had been arrested.

The brackish water flowed passively below. I had trouble digesting what these corporations and government were doing to the Maya.

Hector gestured to a small man standing atop the floating planks. "*Ya llegó el capitán.*"

Was I really supposed to put the *Camioneta* on that waterlogged, barely buoyant piece of driftwood? I paced around the Pathfinder, dripping in sweat. Surely, if Jon "Dealyo" were here, he would be calling me "abundance of caution."

Was there another option? Drive north up through Guatemala City. Did I really want to drive through another war zone? No. What did I have to lose besides materials?

Ah, fuck it. *Dale*[54].

With passion flaring in his dark eyes, the captain waved me on. I stopped. Did they know my car was over 4,000 pounds? He assured me the "ferry" could handle it.

---

[54] As they say, "*Arriesgar un huevo para tener un pollo.*" (Risk an egg to have a chicken.) Don't overthink this quote. It is not supposed to start a debate over which came first, the chicken or the egg.

"*No hay problema.*" He continued waving *Latinoly, "Es normal."*

I put the car back in drive and began dropping down the dirt bank. SLOWLY. He continued the wild waving. *La Camioneta* inched forward... Forward... Forward. Hector looked on. His camo-smurf shirt glowed from the shadows of the *bodega*. At the top of the ramp, some unsupported planks cracked under the weight of the *Camioneta*. How did I let this crazy *Chapín* talk me into th—

Boom!

I looked on in horror as the boat plunged into the water. Loose planks of abused wood jumped in the air. Like a five-year-olds tooth, the planks hung to one another by a meager thread. The gunwale went from two feet above water to less than a foot. With even the slightest swell or boat wake, we'd be taking on water. On the positive side, we hadn't sunk. All seemed dry on deck along the forty-foot driftwood tender.

How was our captain going to move three kilometers down the waterway to Avellana? Raised slightly above the transom was a thirty-horsepower outboard motor. Again, he continued his animated wave to pull forward. The stern of the boat sank, and the bow rose. Twenty-five feet stretched behind the *Camioneta*. Why the sudden movement? He waved to an approaching *combi* (large van).

No way. "*No es normal.*" I screamed, "No!"

The captain motioned him forward. The *combi* inched closer. The driver looked down on us with his tires hanging on the edge. The boat floated just above water. This was insane. He looked at his watch and slammed the *combi* into park. Reason prevailed. Phew.

The skipper shrugged and walked to the stern. The engine fired up, belching out a few puffs of white smoke. I had a flashback to the *Mañana* and her white plumes. Was there a kelp-wrap or something clogging the heat exchanger?

As if feeling my growing concern, the captain issued the words, "*Es normal.*"

We puttered out in the calm, brown water. As we accelerated, the boat fought, with little success, to plane. With a slight jolt, water came rushing in from the stern. Sitting casually on the gunwale, the captain's look conveyed "*Es normal.*" He held the throttle with one hand while the other hand used a three-liter plastic Coke bottle as our manual bilge. We ran closely along lush mangroves. At least if we sank, I knew I could easily make it to shore. Men in wooden canoes slid through the tight mangroves.

The captain continued to throw water overboard. I grabbed another bucket and added to our manual bilge pump. We soon found our bailing rhythm: one of us leaned to one side while the other scooped and tossed. We passed a ferry heading west. A few passengers watched with their jaws dropped as we heaved water from the boat.

I waved and yelled, *"Es normal!"*

The added boat wake sent water over the port side. The waves came crashing in. Our feet disappeared in the murky water. The bailing continued. I had to ask the question, "Have you ever sunk a boat?"

"Oof, hace tiempo." He threw his arm up to the past behind him.

"How long ago?" My nervous mind needed to know.

"Hace tiempo."

"How long?" I refused to accept inexactness.

"Hace algunos años. No hay problema," he assured me.

"OK." A few years ago.

We continued upstream.

True to his word, we made it to Avellana. Time flies when you are throwing buckets. I thanked the captain *Latinoly* (in the suspense of it all I never learned his name) with an excessively firm handshake.

Before me stood a number of sun-bleached cantinas and commerce. Vendors awoke with the sight of California plates. A quick wave to the people, and we were gone. Both the *Camioneta* and I appreciated being back on solid ground. She tore into the asphalt. Signs marked the road leading to the town of Hachadura, the next border.

My thoughts eddied around the Maya locked in battle for existence. Once again, I was amazed at just how little we hear about such events in the United States. I came to Guatemala scared about the violence, gangs, and guerrillas. In actuality, I was more fearful of the state-institutionalized terror, and the horrifically long, growing list of *desaparecidos*. The sign at the border made this situation quite clear: "The state has the right to kill criminals."

Despite the beautiful landscape and good-hearted people, I was ready to move on. The worrier in me resurfaced. *What about the tags? Will I get stuck in Guatemala and eventually be labeled a terrorist?*

Endless brake lights broiled above the road ahead.

Witch's Rock por la Chica Mala

*"I'm open to the guidance of synchronicity, and do
not let expectations hinder my path."*
–Dalai Lama

At the border, hordes of pale tourists hiding under enlarged brims stood outside an air-conditioned bus. White globs of sunscreen dripped from their faces. Sweat whisked off their eco-gear. Their guide, a well-paid bilingual professional, ensured that they wouldn't be inconvenienced by Spanish. He would take care of everything. Where were the ravenous border caddies? I was left in peace to handle my own affairs (the paperwork).

Bam. Bam.

"Bienvenidos a Costa Rica."

Costa Rica (the rich coast) presented a new frontier full of adventure and undiscovered dreams. The plan was to head to Tamarindo for the upcoming north swell. The Northern Hemi swell train was in full swing. Another large storm packing forty-to-fifty-foot seas slammed the Hawaiian Islands. Was it going even half that size in Costa? Doubtful. The energy would surely decay after traveling over 3,000 miles, but by no means would it disappear.

As I left the *frontera* (border), a vehicle ahead of me sped past a sulking woman on the side of the road. The following car slowed, the driver gazed upon her, and then took off. Clouds of smog sank this poor woman further into the ground. Her head sagged under the weight of the Costa Rican sun. She vented to the dirt below. *"Todos son malos. Almas oscuros!"*

I decided to show her that not everyone was *malo* (bad with dark souls). The *Camioneta* and I were going to make her day. Her black, curly hair rested upon a revealing pink top. Rolls of loose flesh bulged out into the tropical sunlight. Despite the fact that it was 2.2 million degrees out, she had a beige jacket draped around her shoulders. Her sullen eyes told a tale of hardship, disdain, and despair.

I rolled down the window and asked, "Buenos dias, where are you headed?"

"Me llevas a Liberia?"

"Sure, I can take you there."

Liberia, an hour south of the border, was indeed on the way to Tamarindo. I pulled over. I'm sorry, Mom; I know I promised not to pick up hitchhikers, but this poor, battered soul was in desperate need of some *ayuda*[55].

"Come on. Let's go." I motioned her over. Her scowl changed to a grimacing smile. She grabbed her large black handbag and came aboard.

"How long have you been waiting?"

"Cuatro horas."

"Four hours at the border? Really. Why?"

"Porque todos son malos."

"Are you hungry?" I offered her some stale Nicaraguan bread. She ripped the clear bag from my hand.

"Qué tienes para tomar?"

I handed her a bottle of water. She GUZZLED it.

"Tienes cigarillos?"

"No." I didn't have any cigarettes.

"Paremos en una pulpería."

We stop at an octopus factory? I shot her a bewildered look from over the blue surfboard between us.

"Una tienda."

With no store in sight, I pointed to the overgrown jungle surrounding us. Awkward silence followed. What hitchhiker consumes bread, water, and then demands cigarettes? Pinback's song "Syracuse" broke the silence, pulsing positive, mellow beats. "Step down in sand…" My mind floated to empty tropical beaches. The palms swayed.

---

[55] Actually, I had picked up loads of hitchhikers from Baja to Oaxaca to Nica. If given the opportunity to help, why not? Latin America is filled with kind-hearted souls. I was inspired to return the favor.

"*Yo quiero reggaeton[56].*"

"I don't have any reggaeton."

"*Esta música es mala, una mierda!*"

Pinback is shit? I shuffled over to some Bob Marley, always a crowd pleaser.

"Don't worrrry/about a thing/Cuz every little thing is going to be alright."

I embraced Bob and the positive island vibrations, mon, singing to her from across our divider, the blue bomber. Sure, she might not understand the lyrics, but soulful music transcends translation. Right?

"*Apágala!*"

Ignoring her request to turn the music off, I turned the volume up and kept singing.

"Rise up this morning/Smile with the risin' sun. Three little birds/ Pitch by my doorstep."

"*Apágala!*" This time she screamed.

Not wanting to fight, I turned off the music. If it wasn't *reggaeton,* she wasn't having it. Here I was, giving her a ride, food, water with good vibes, and attitude is what? *Dios mío.* Maybe she had something troubling her? Maybe it was time to hear her "*historia*"? She had mentioned that she had left her kids in Nicaragua in order to work in Costa.

"What do you do for work?"

"*Soy una prostituta.*"

A traveling prostitute. Endless questions spun through my mind.

"How long have you been in the industry?"

"*Estúpida.*"

"How did you get into the field?"

"*Estúpida. No quiero hablar de esa.*"

My questions were *estúpidas,* and she didn't want to talk about it. She hated my music and the only thing to talk about was her "work," now deemed off limits. Santa Rosa, Playa Naranjo beaconed from the street sign above. Bingo. Witch's Rock would be my escape from the *chica mala.* Like Wes Brant said, "We were living the Endless Summer." In *The Endless Summer II* surf film, one of Wingnut and Pat O'Connell's most iconic

---

[56] Spanish rap with a lot of bass, cuss words, and voluptuous *chicas* in their videos. Prime example: Daddy Yankee.

stops was Witch's Rock. The video showed perfect blue cylinders spiraling off in some hidden tropical jungle. Costa Rican magic! My simple mind now knew of only two things: Witch's Rock, and get this *chica mala* out of the *Camioneta*.

Another forty-five minutes of uncomfortable silence or hostile conversation was unacceptable; the plans had to change.

"I'm not going to Liberia. I'm going to head to Playa Naranjo."

"Me vas a llevar a Liberia!"

"Sorry, but plans change."

She screamed, *"Tienes que llevarme a Liberia!"*

I didn't have to take her anywhere. She said it again. With clenched fists, she struck the dashboard. Now what? Then she pounded her thighs, sending shockwaves of reverberating flesh. Her breath shortened to an uncontrolled pant. *Que cagada* (How shitty)!

I should have listened to my mother.

What the hell do I do now?

The *policía* inspection ahead answered the call.

Slowing down, I looked over to her. "If you don't get out of the *Camioneta*, I'm going to tell the *policía* about your career. You are no longer welcome aboard the *Camioneta*."

She went ballistic, hitting me with a series of *puta madres, pendejos,* and *mala persona*. She threw the open plastic water bottle against the windshield. Water sprayed across the dashboard.

I stopped.

"Ya basta." (Enough!) I pointed out.

She slammed the door shut while bombing me with profanities. This marked the end of "our story," punctuated by bitching. The *policía* looked on from the roadblock 300 meters in the distance. I left her standing on the corner and sped ahead. Two young friendly faced policemen came to the window.

"Qué pasó con la guila? La chica?"

"She is *muy loca*." I twirled my finger and rolled my eyes. We all watched as she sat down and brooded on the side of the road.

"I tried to give her a ride, but she was way too negative. I guess you can't help them all."

"No te precupes. Buen viaje."

I followed their orders and wasn't going to worry about it. I returned to Bob.

"Singin sweet songs/

Of melodies pure and true/

This is my message to you-ou-ou-ou."

A green sign with white letters hung from the post above: "Punta Naranjo Santa Rosa Park 12 km." I followed a utility dump truck down a paved road into the park. *Paved roads? Maybe this wasn't going to be so bad after all. Maybe it was all just a marketing scheme, making surfers think that taking an expensive boat ride to Witch's Rock was the only option?* I thought of my old English student Perrazo from Galapagos and his favorite word, *"Facilito." Super easy.*

Turns out I spoke too soon.

The ranger charged me an $18 park entrance fee. A small sign to Playa Naranjo, the world's largest dry rain forest, pointed left. How do you have a dry rain forest? It rains just enough to classify as a rain forest. The enormity of the densely populated trees eclipsed the sun, the perfect canopy. The shadowed road gave way to loose gravel and finally morphed into some sort of rock-hopping-crater-crawling-challenge. I clung to Bob's words of wisdom, "Cuz every little thing/ is gonna be alright." *Bang.* The slaloming of Mexico and Honduras had given way to some sort of extreme mogul course. I tried my best to mitigate the beating on the *Camioneta*, but it was inevitable. *Bang.* The *Camioneta* bucked. I cringed with the sound of crunching fiberglass. Didn't clear that gap. Oh shit, there's another mogul- *BANG.* In Spanish, they have a word for this: *una paliza* (a beat-down). How much more of this could the *Camioneta* take?

After an hour, I had only gone three kilometers. Turn around? It was too late; Witch's Rock was already firmly lodged in my brain, so turning around was not an option. Besides, I bet Wingnut wouldn't turn around. The question of, is this massive ravine passable, became, what's the best line to mitigate the damage? The road worsened. The boulders dispersed into a creek bed, smaller rocks bouldering out of deep mud pits. Time to use "abundance of caution." I was in doubt and definitely going to walk it out. In the world's largest dry rain forest, I felt extremely alone and at the mercy of the wild. Macaws shrieked in the distance. Underneath that atrocious call, deep growling ripped through the jungle. The canopy shook.

The *Camioneta* stopped. Eventually, little furry black tails revealed their identity: howler monkeys. Most certainly, not as intimidating as their sound. Onward.

The *Camioneta* was paying the price for my jungle fantasy. She crawled forward in agony over jagged rocks and unforgiving terrain. She started sagging on the driver side. The pitted floor would have made for a nearly impossible tire change even with the new-used Mexican *gato*. Oceanward.

Three hours later, with the *Camioneta* crying out for mercy, we arrived. Five fully equipped Tico, Costa Rican, trucks with roll bars, winches, and large mud tires rested under indigenous trees[57]. The Pathfinder proudly donned her California tags. She had earned another much-deserved rest. We found a nice soft landing on a somewhat level, shaded patch of grass. Upon inspection, the rear driver side tire was completely flat. I would deal with it later. Surf now; fix later. Move over, Wingnut, here I come.

An enthusiastic ranger greeted me. *"Bienvenidos al Parque Santa Rosa."*

"Tiene recibo?" I showed him my park receipt.

He opened his palms to the oaks, locust, and the Guanacaste trees (a giant mushrooming tree resembling the Tree of Life). The distant beach was bordered with tall palms rocketing out from the rich foliage.

He switched over to perfect English. "Here you can see tapirs. Sloths[58]. Also we have a few jaguars in the park."

"Jaguars???"

"Yeah. They usually stay far away from this camp. This park extends out 495 kilometers, and this coastline is one of the most important turtle sanctuaries in Costa Rica."

"That's amazing." The surfer within me finally asked the question that was burning inside.

"And the waves?"

"Hay tubos hoy!"

"Tubes, really?"

---

[57] I wouldn't recommend going with one vehicle. Most rental cars would get destroyed on this trail. I would highly recommend asking around, as the road at times is flooded, unpassable, and/or closed.

[58] In Spanish, they are called *perezoso*, which means "lazy." This was one of my nicknames in college, which turned into a verb. We got slothed and watched surf videos all afternoon.

"*Sí, las olas están muy muy buenas. Nosotros decimos tuanis (*cool)!"

Good tubing waves in the jungle! Maybe this was The Endless Summer after all?

After the border crossing, the *chicha mala,* and the tire-bursting mogul run, my excitement level for surf was comparable to a kid skinning-dipping for the first time.

The conversation finished with a few lively *shakas.* (Good vibes!)

A thirty-minute hike through the jungle lay between me and the dream. In my spontaneous detour to Naranjo, I saw zero *pulperías (tiendas)* to buy supplies. My provisions consisted of five gallons of water, four slices of stale bread (thanks to the *chica mala* taking two), and peanut butter. Food was an afterthought. Everything would figure itself out. It always did.

The imagination can really go wild with visions of barrels mixed with the jungle sensations and *The Endless Summer* surf fantasy. Like a jaguar, I sprinted under light streaming through towering bamboo shoots. Giant oaks and locust trees twisted overhead in the ocean breeze. The crashing waves roared through the forest. Was I really about to witness the iconic Witch's Rock? Barreling? "Wingnut" must have left my lips 1,000 times. Maybe the ride had rattled a few screws loose, or were they always loose?

The shaded path slithered like a snake through the jungle, eventually coiling seaward. The canopy opened to an endless black-sand beach. Paradise. A few surfers took refuge from the fierce afternoon *sol* in a small, driftwood shack. Foam ringed a mushroom-shaped rock that rose up from impossibly blue waters. Witch's Rock, a living dream, has the classic setup, with perfectly groomed lines that funnel along a gentle and forgiving sandbar. The north swell offered more peaks than the peeling rights featured in *The Endless Summer II.* Today, it was take your pick. Left or right cover-ups opening to a soft shoulder allowing for maneuvers. I mind-surfed a few empty waves down the beach. I mentally ripped them to pieces.

Three boats bobbed beyond the break. The takeoff zone of about 150 yards was lined with feisty paddlers. Were there pasty dudes with fiery eyes masked in zinc determined to get their money's worth? Yes. Were there drop-ins? Yes. Were there a few stink eyes despite the paradisiacal surroundings? Yes. Would I let that pull me off of my cloud in the sky? Shit no, the soothing tropical water cooled my nerves.

I bet Wingnut would be mellow out here. *Dónde está Wingnut? Hoy Wingnut pasó por acá? Viva el Wingnut!* I think the journey made me a bit looney. Looney for Wingnut! Despite my delirium and the crowd, I managed to find a few waves that made it all worth it.

The boats fled just before the darkness cloaked our world. I was left with the sounds of the wild jungle and surf. I floated along the beach guided by the starlight. My salty eyelids felt heavy. Out of the blackness, a sliver of light flickered from behind the brush. Like a tired sloth, I waddled my way tentward. Stale bread and peanut butter had never tasted so good. That night I dreamt of the perfect day. Tomorrow, I was going to beat the crowd.

Like a burglar in the middle of the night, I slipped passed the sleeping Ticos. I took to the beach not wanting to risk being devoured by the savage jungle. A pair of red macaws screeched through the emerging sky. How could such a beautiful bird give birth to such a heinous sound? Up ahead, movement, flailing motions in the sand. *Una tortuga* making her way back to the sea. Had she just laid her eggs? I steered clear, taking the high line along the woods' edge.

The silhouette of the rock outlined the fading black wall. Well overhead, A-frames, right and left, came out of the night and accentuated the day. I imagined splitting the peak with Mike. I saw him going left on his quad-finned Spectrum getting in his classic pigdog stance looking up toward the falling lip. I took the right. We both got piped. As I kicked out, I looked over to see his chest puffed up followed by a massive hair flip. We raced each other out again for wave priority. I beat him[59]. The image vanished like an oceanic mirage as I continued walking down the beach. Alone.

Untamed jungle stretched for miles north and south along the empty coastline, not a human in sight. There were no drop-ins, no stink eyes,

---

[59] Talk about racing: after getting in a fight over a girl many years ago, we decided to resolve it by a race around the loop at Wrightsville Beach, slightly over two miles. Classic Mike, a nonrunner, sprinted in skate shoes the first several hundred yards. I let him go. After a quarter mile he slowed to a walk. I passed him with a shove in the back and then said, "Suck it, Sauce!" Mike returned to the Henderson Street house, and all we could do was laugh. It was impossible to hold a grudge against Mike.

no *me voys,* no *oyes,* and with eighty-degree tropical water, the setup was as wet as a dream could get. The moment said, "Surf!" The waves weren't big enough for Mike's pipe, so I left him with backpack-guarding duty.

I couldn't paddle out fast enough. The water felt like warm honey. A glassy line popped up and I dropped in to the wave bowling up on the sand bar; no barrel, just a carve section. I raced back out to the take-off zone. The cat-and-mouse game between the lip and I continued for almost an hour before figures emerged from the jungle. It was a Friday, which meant weekend crowds. In just a few hours the crowd approached thirty. Decreasing swell and provisions as well as the arrival of overanxious weekend surfers meant it was time to hit the road[60].

---

[60] And no, I didn't see Wingnut.

Bocas Del Toro and the Swell From Hell

"The great ones of the past have not died, they
have merely changed their name."
–Carl Jung

"Check your brakes, and don't surf Silverbacks."

He removed his sunglasses, revealing his piercing blue eyes. "The road to Almirante is really *loco y peligroso*. Many cars break down. Others just fly off the cliff. So be sure to check your brakes. From there, you can take a ferry to Bocas."

His name was David, owner of Oasis Hostel and a Panamanian surfer.

Sure, I had heard the word *peligroso* (dangerous) a ton of times, but coming from a surfer, I gave the warning more attention.

"You are going to have a great time. I love Bocas. There are plenty of waves to surf, just not Silverbacks."

"Why not?" I was both intrigued and terrified.

"Unless you are a crazy professional surfer, stay away from it! The wave snapped my friend's back like a twig and nearly killed him. It has taken many fishermen's lives too. There is a huge swell heading there next week. Be very careful. It's no joke."

I gave him a meek smile, a *gracias*, and then mounted the *Camioneta*.

From there, we traversed across a river then banked back to the Pan American Highway.

Each time I checked the surf forecast, it grew. It went from four to six feet with clean conditions to ten to twelve feet. Now a surfer knows that this could translate to six-to-twenty-foot faces depending on the angle, period, and bathymetry(topography of the ocean floor). The stomach butterflies fluttered faster.

Am I ready?
Only one way to find out.

Back on the *Panamericana*, the horizon opened to large paved roadways, hotels, and billboards. Five-star hotels advertised surfing and luxurious getaways. In the hills, vibrant-colored cement homes clumped together under dancing palms. TV satellite dishes sat upon the tin roofs, bringing Hollywood and *telenovelas* to the poor. Many have prioritized entertainment over upgrading their dirt floors.

Chinese grocery stores lined the Highway 1, heading toward Chiriquí Grande. Chinese *mercado* domination would be the theme throughout Panama. Was Panama a precursor to what was in store for the rest of the Americas? What did the people think about the Chinese? Most were happy with *"Los Chinos."* They said that before, the merchandise was always missing and overpriced. Now, however, the merchandise is cheap and well-stocked. As the markets faded away, the bottles of Coke, Clorox bleach, and Gatorade remained. The beautiful, rolling green vistas were marred by short-term gains and short-sighted consumption. Across fields, black and blue plastic bags flapped in the breeze. Open stretches of blurring landscape mixed with billowing clouds of burning trash. When will we learn that trashing our planet is trashing our children's future?

On the long drive, I had time to think about the discovery of one of the most coveted waterways on the planet. Over three million years ago, a narrow strip of land lay buried beneath two oceans. With time, an isthmus formed a fragile neck between two great bodies of land. The stretch of jungle and streams served as a barrier between the vast empires of the Maya-Aztecs and the Incas to the south.

Vasco Nunez de Balbao looked to change that. He was the first conquistador to step foot on what is now Panama. He watched a torrid river known by the natives as *Tuira* in the Darien gap (unruly jungle that connects with Colombia) following a course to a distant, unknown sea. Balbao and the rest of the conquistadores had developed a blood-thirsty obsession for gold. They began fighting over the small amount of gold given to them by the natives. The chief's son, Panquiasco, was perplexed about why they threatened to kill one another over these shiny stones. Nevertheless, he told them, "If you follow this path, after a quarter moon, you will find an immense expanse of salt water, whose currents will carry you to a great land with an even greater chief, where you will find such stones lying about."

He was referring to the great Inca Empire of South America.

Balbao pressed onward with his depleted troops through vast jungles with unforgiving terrain full of malaria, punishing heat, and torrential downpours. The desire for gold and the conquest of new lands had consumed his existence. In 1513, his cravings led him atop the hill of Guayabito, where he and his men gazed upon the magnificence of the placid sea below, improperly named Pacific[61]. He had discovered the slender passageway between two great oceans.

Panama and its inhabitants would never be the same[62].

From 1824 to 1903, the region became part of Gran Colombia, what is now Panama, Venezuela, Colombia, Ecuador, Peru, and Bolivia-led and unified by the revolutionary Simón Bolívar against the Spanish. On November 2, 1903, under the creed of "Manifest Destiny," the Americans, led by Theodore Roosevelt, sent troops to Colon, a port city on the Caribbean side. The United States had decided to liberate Panama from Colombia, unbeknownst to either party. It was fitting that the Treaty of Panama wasn't signed by a Panamanian but by Phillipe Bunau-Varilla, a Frenchman, and William Nelson Cromell, an American lobbyist. Together, they worked on establishing a canal, which would be backed by the Panamanian oligarchy. Armador Guerrero was named the first president of Panama and the Hay-Brunea-Varilla Treaty was signed. It legalized U.S. military intervention of the isthmus[63]. The United States "invaded" or "occupied" (depending on whom you are speaking with) the country fourteen times during the following 100 years.

Passing the town of David, the true place of Mike's demise, sent a deep chill though my body. I did not look for the hospital where he stayed. There was serious swell coming, and I needed to focus on the road. Cows

---

[61] Anyone who has spent time surfing or navigating the Pacific knows that it is far from passive.

[62] His efforts were rewarded, and his name is now attached to domestic beer and a metal currency. The people also refer to the coin as Martinelli, the ex-Panamanian president who authorized the minting of the Balbao coins, equivalent to one US dollar. He was later incarcerated for corruption.

[63] Reference from *"America's Prisoner: The Memoirs of Manuel Noriega."*

grazed on the pastures of the palmy plateaus. The road disappeared as it spiraled its way up a looming tropical mountain, shrouded by malicious clouds. The music shuffled to Offspring, "Smash": "When I go driving I stay in my lane/ Gonna wreck this motherfucker's ride/ Cuz I got bad headache." My mind raced back to my early high school days, speeding on the Garden State Parkway down to the Jersey shore with Mike Krantz and Greg Bayvel. The gas pedal dropped. Passing cars on double yellows along the rolling hills, images of round green barrels spun in my head.

Bocas, here I come!

The plateaus quickly gave way to the vertical terrain and the great mountains of Chiriquí. The mufflerless *Camioneta* growled. I kept a nervous eye on the temperature gauge. I laid off the gas and dropped her into low gear. The temperature crept insidiously higher and higher. The humid tropical air thickened.

With the needle on red, I looked for the nearest stop-off. The *Camioneta* began coughing up white steam. The radiator hissed. *Que cagada!* With toxic fluids spewing everywhere, I made an emergency turn-off at a place called El Refugio De La Brisa Del Diablo (the refuge to the devil's wind). The wooden gate blew open along a stone wall to reveal a man resembling the character "Vigo the Carpathian" from *Ghostbusters,* my hero. His long, tightly cropped hair swirled in the devil's breeze. The man before me, a Canadian-Quebecua, stood with his hands at his waist watching the *Camioneta* smoke and vomit anti-freeze. He returned with a bucket to catch the *Camioneta's* hazardous bile. He invited me into his bed and breakfast. The kitchen and dining area offered a spectacular view of the valley below. The Pacific Ocean and the sky fused together in oscillating shades of blue. The peace and serenity of the mountainous view calmed my soul.

Meanwhile, the Caribbean was threatening to eat herself and those foolish enough to challenge her.

Stephane, and his Cuban wife, Olga, had found solitude in these mountains. He led me to the back, where lush gardens surrounded a small pool edging the verdant valley. The blustery wind violently yanked at the trees.

"Let me guess, you are heading to Bocas."

I dipped my head.

"My wife and I lived there for fifteen years, owning and running restaurants. It has changed a lot since we first moved there. It has lost its charm. It's too crowded and commercialized now."

I'd heard that story before.

"How was the trip down here? California, wow!"

I gave him a few of the highlights and finished with Mike's story. He looked over the vivid green foliage. He corralled his long wisps of hair and secured them behind his ear.

"I've seen it happen many times in Bocas. People come to Bocas to escape their problems, yet their problems still remain. Add drugs and alcohol, in "Paradise" where there is a party every night, and you have a deadly combination. People get LOST there all the time."

Bocas seemed haunted. I had read that this was the farthest western waypoint that Columbus had voyaged to. After taking a good look at the waterlogged archipelago, the explorer decided to turn around. Later, it was converted into a depressed banana port.

Today, the surfing industry markets the place as a surfer's paradise.

I lunched at Refugio. The food was phenomenal! After adding some extra anti-freeze and water into the Pathfinder's radiator, I noticed that the grill had become a collage of colorful insects, dating back to our time in Mexico. Enough to impact the air flow. After hosing them off and painting his gravel with their iridescent remains, I thanked Stephane for his hospitality and sage advice. Then *adiosed* him.

The ascent resumed. Up and up. The road jackknifed along hairpin turns above a cloud forest. The road was slick in the misty mountain air. The gauge was uncomfortably high but not in the red. At the summit, I didn't have long to admire the passing beauty of the *Forestral de Fortuna* (Fortunate Forest Reserve) before the see-saw took a downward plunge. The tires desperately clung to the dank, narrow road ribboning along a sheer cliff with guardrails that ranged from untrustworthy to nonexistent.

Multiple crucifixes stood before an abysmal drop. David wasn't joking: "*Loco y peligroso.*"

The white, fluffy clouds of the Pacific had given way to gnarled rumblings overhead. The dark aquamarine horizon stretched beyond the spec below, Almirante. Shane who had lived in the area with Mike, told me, "Almirante is a dangerous shithole and quite possibly the worst place on Earth."

Well, if hell was on the road to Bocas, so be it. The highlands eventually flattened to soggy marshlands. Rolling into the mouth of hell, I was struck with the stench of rotten trash. Overstuffed, waterlogged black plastic bags lay scattered across the streets. Commerce was a mixture of hardware, grocery, and beaten-down motels. Anxious street urchins with roaming eyes wandered around without focus. Mangy dogs, patches of fur and exposed bones, hobbled about. Broken, abused, Chinese-made plastic sandals clogged the sewers.

Shane had recommended stocking up on provisions to avoid island inflation. A myriad of Chinese *mercados* lined the polluted streets. While buying supplies, I kept a close watch on the *Camioneta*. My gut told me to get my ass on the ferry as soon as possible. But there were no ferries until the following morning. A long line of delivery and pickup trucks, loaded to the brim with cheap Chinese goods, stretched from the water. Though we had left the jungle, the dense humidity and clouds of bugs remained. My ears buzzzed with *zancudos*. I accepted that my shirt was going to be permanently stuck to my back.

One of the truck drivers said he was going to pay a guy, *guardia*, to watch his truck and save his spot in line while he got a few hours of shut-eye at a motel. He chuckled, *"Muchas cucarachas."*

Decision time. Spend a night suffering in an overpacked, steamy *zancudo*-infested *Camioneta*, or have faith in this *guardia*, like the rest of the drivers, and head to the cockroach inn. I chose the latter and was guided to my musky little love cave by a small, tight-lipped Chinaman. Yes, I probed his Spanish. A curt amount of Chinish (Chinese and Spanish) followed. How bizarre!

I awoke to the distant beats of a *rumbera* (party). Reggaeton rattled the walls. Time to get the hell out of hell. A few lanky shadows shot down an alley. I walked briskly with my head down, my hands dug deep in my pockets like I was concealing something. I eyed no one, clinging to the misconception that my lowered skullcap concealed my *gringoness*. Whatever. If they robbed me, all they'd get was $50 and a few about-to-be-canceled credit cards.

Imagine feeling this way every day. Imagine living in hell.

Voices and commotion sounded in the distance. A horn blew, announcing the ferry's impending departure. I sprinted back to the *Camioneta*. It was civilized chaos, "normal," battling with the trucks to get on the ramp. Climbing the ramp, I felt much more confident of this vessel's seaworthiness compared to that beaten-up leaky piece of driftwood in Guatemala. *Was she still afloat?*

The *Camioneta* fought her way to claim a crammed spot on the ferry sandwiched between cargo trucks.

Scaling up to the top deck, the sunken archipelago emerged below the black, boiling thunderheads. Anger and rage charged the atmosphere, ready to unleash its fury. The gallant cargo ship beat against the stormy swell. Through the cracks in the sky, shards of light struck down upon the menacing sea.

Was this heaven or hell?

I captured this powerful moment and shared it online. Forty-three people showed their electronic support. Wes Brant commented, "Mike has to be pissed about something."

Graham Greene's description of Bocas, thirty years prior, in his book, *Getting To Know The General,* was a mirror image of what lie before me: "When the clouds whirled apart, we caught a glimpse of the mountain tops and then of the sea boiling below. We landed in a deluge of rain on a small island which seemed to be sinking back into the sea under the weight of the storm. This was the Bocas I had been so determined to visit."

Several months earlier, Shane, Mike, and I had talked about meeting up in this paradisiacal surf destination. Now, I found myself heading to some sinking island chain, chasing after this swell from hell with Mike stuffed in a tiny bottle.

It was beyond baffling.

Shane had told me that Mike's favorite wave was called Sausages, somewhere between Carenero and Big Rock. I wondered if this would be the place for Mike's final send-off. What demons lurked on the approaching shore? Did I really want to know? As we off-loaded in the pounding rain, my blood swirled with sadness, uncertainty, fear, and excitement.

Amid the pelting rain, cab drivers hollered at the passing traffic from a storm shelter. The water seemed to pile high upon the non-existent drainage system. Greene was right, it felt like the island was sinking into the Caribbean. On the ride out to the hostel, I saw soggy, slanted structures lining the shore. Maybe the storm surge would end their structural suffering?

Shane recommended that I stay at the Mondo Taitu, which he said was "Very bro friendly." *Sure, why not?* The swell forecast had me jittery. I could care less where I stayed. The plan was simple: check in and get the fuck out there. Mondo Taitu was conveniently a mere block from the water. I entered a dimly lit, dank hostel devoid of life. It was around noon. Puddles of water welled under cracked wooden stairs. A few browned surfboards lay against the corner wall.

"Hola, hello?"

Nada.

I rang the bell several times. The living room reeked of cigarettes and cheap liquor. Several bangs were followed by a thud. I envisioned someone falling out of bed. A scraggly shadow-dweller emerged; I figured him to be an employee. His head swayed, guided by bloodshot eyes.

"You a surfa?"

"I try."

"Did ya hear Kelly Slater is in town? Greg Long just came too. He got in last night for the swell of the decade."

I hadn't heard.

But word travels fast in the modern world. The hype was on.

He signaled me to follow. He leaned against the fridge to keep his balance. At the kitchen, I was hit with the stench of wet onions mixed with sweaty latex.

"This is a shared space, so do your best to clean up after yourself," the clerk told me.

We continued to the room, occupied by four snoring sausages. Heaven.

"What do ya think?"

I looked out over the balcony. The storm had broken and the sun was bursting from the clouds. There was a huge swell on tap.

Fuck it, this place would do. "Sure. Put me down for one night."

"Did I give you the key?"

"No, you didn't."

He returned to the desk. He spun in circles, fumbling through coins and keys. He shook his head as he closed the drawer. "Welcome. I'll find ya key lata." Then he retreated to his cave.

My stomach churned with anxiety mixed with *café con desayuno* (coffee and breakfast). My gut squeezed. *Baño!* Every toilet in the place was clogged. I scrambled across the street to the local pizzeria. The look on my face read, "I will buy something afterward."

Bowel-evacuation complete, a more comfortable human returned to the hostel.

Scanning the empty hostel, I thought about Casa de Toro, the hostel Shane and Mike ran for several months. I saw flashes of Mike checking in his guests. I imagined them being impressed with his extensive surf lingo and animated personality. I wondered how many times he used the word "mon."

"The waves have been great, mon."

"Let me take your bags, mon." "How was the flight, mon? Meet any girlies? Any land barrels, mon?"

How many times was he apologetic even though he had done nothing wrong?

"Sorry, am I in your way, mon?"

"We had an epic party here last night at Casa Del Toro-Kahuna's Camp of Kooks, you are gonna love it here, mon."

"Place is loaded with dime pieces, mon."

"Let's do the damn thing, mon!"

"Let me know if you need anything, mon."

I was sure my time would come to meet Mike's people and hear some Mike Brant Bocas stories.

Now, however, survival was my first priority.

I was told I needed to take a water-taxi to get to Isla Carenero, a long left, reef point break with several barrel sections. I walked out onto the street with my board shorts, stretched T-shirt, and surfboard in hand. I approached a pack of Panamanians, a peanut gallery of wise men, standing in front of a *bodega* gawking, talking, and drinking while the world blew by. Loaded with adrenaline, I engaged the pack.

"I want to go to *carnicería.*"

They broke into laughter. Finally, when the laughter subsided, one man said, *"Qué quieres comer?"*

More laughter ensued.

What do I want to eat? I replayed the conversation, and it hit me that I had just asked to go to a meat factory. What I wanted to say was "*carenero.*" Oops.

"DISCULPA. I want to surf la PUNTA Carenero."

"*Por allá.*"

They threw their hands over their heads, *Latinoly,* at a point across a small park.

Walking up to the docks, I was greeted by aquatic chaos[64]. Boats were hurled against the pilings in the unconquerable sea. The dock lines moaned in agony. The operators of a few water-taxis shook their heads.

"*No, muy bravo el mar. Muy picado. NO.*"

Basically, no way am I risking my *panga,* my livelihood, for some crazy gringo. At the end of the docks, a boat rocked with surfers.

Bingo. The perfect time to be solo.

"*Cuántas?*" the driver asked.

I let him know I was alone.

He snapped his head back and gave me a "*Sube.*"

I hopped aboard the bucking boat.

The other surfers were from Long Island, New York and were determined to take a look at Silverbacks. If it wasn't manageable, then they would surf Carenero. An elongated channel of only a few kilometers separated the two islands Carenero-Bastimiento.

The captain motioned for me to untie the bow line.

"*Vámonos.*"

Huge lumps of water reared up from the bowels of the ocean as we headed to the tip of Bastimentos. The channel was a churned cauldron of converging currents. With the bow of his boat aimed at a point of overgrown jungle, the captain hit the throttle. We skipped off the top of a large crest, taking flight. The prop snarled as it came out of the water. With great force, we slammed down into the devilish green sea. The warm spray came flying over the bow. My heart almost jumped overboard. I looked back to the *panguero* (captain) and saw that his eyes were wide and dripping with fright. I questioned my decision-making.

---

[64] I once lived with a dude who tattooed the word "chaos" across his under lip. He referred to me as "old guard." I was thirty.

Another *panga* rose and disappeared below the surging sea monsters. Who would be crazy enough to surf the most dangerous wave in the area on the biggest swell of decade? Could it be Slater and the boys? What a sight that would be to watch the best surfers in the world doing their thing on the swell of the millennium. Yes, it had already been upgraded in size, like a fish story.

The best surfers in the world sat on the little water-taxi to our port. They weren't surfing. The heroes of our sport were spectating the swell of the millennium.

A set approached. Time stood still.

My eyes grew. My mouth opened. My scrotum tightened. The ocean drew off the reef. I gave the captain a look that said, "We don't want to be anywhere near that fucker when it breaks." He took notice and headed deeper into the channel. The first wave gathered volume. It lurched up and out, detonating in a square green anvil with a thunderous boom. I had a good, clear look into its evil eye. The following wave was even bigger, approaching more than twenty feet on the face, and several feet thick. Freight trucks could have driven through those tubes with room to spare. Two more followed close behind. Each wave threw a gaping barrel and then turned itself inside out with a huge spit of seething salt water. With a short period of twelve seconds, you could easily get held underwater for three waves. Each wave approached at a different angle. The sea lacked rhythm. Death seemed like a very realistic outcome.

For a moment, the sea quieted.

We pulled up closer to the *panga* with Kelly Slater, Sunny Garcia, and Greg Long looking out into the gladiator pit. Had they been out?

"How was the go?" I fired over.

Silence.

Two motors continued gurgling.

Sunny gave me a searing stare. He didn't need to say anything. His narrowed eyes read, "What do you fucking think?"

I looked over at Kelly, who just laughed at my stupidity.

Excuse me for asking. That's OK; I guess we looked like kooks (Hawaiian lingo for poop) pulling up with tiny boards knowing we were not going to ride Silverbacks that day. Later, via social media, photos of them surfing the break appeared.

All I know is, that at the peak of the swell, no one surfed Silverbacks.

We circled back to the point and joined a swarm of sea-men. There had to be close to two hundred guys out. I saw guys I had met in both Nicaragua and Costa Rica. Everyone had come to Bocas for the SWELL EVENT. The waves were going off, offering well-overhead barrels. The current ripped down the point. It was out of control with guys dropping in on each other, throwing boards, breaking boards, and a few leash tangles for good measure.

I did my best to stay out of the way.

In the surfing world, we call this a zoo, packed with wild and domesticated animals. I got a few waves and then sat down at the end of the point. One wave shut down on me. I stepped off, thinking it would wash over without incident. Wrong! It steamrolled me, tightly pinning me to the bottom, and ripping my shirt over my head. I wrestled my shirt off underwater and stroked for the surface. *Time to go in?*

The swell was forecasted to pump for the entire week. I thought back to all the good luck Mike and I had had on our surf trips. This was no exception.

Back on land, I toasted one up to my boy in the sky.

After one night of dealing with drunk dudes sloshing around the dorms till the small hours, I changed hostels. I moved to Hostal Luego. There a dude, Frank, an NJ-California transplant, talked of his Silverbacks flogging. He had gone the day before the swell peaked. He was not shy about displaying his battle wounds, telling us what it was like to be backhanded by a sea monster. It looked like a Siberian tiger had dragged its claws against his back. The wounds garnered instant credibility.

They were the only DUDES out. He said he was with traveling pro surfers and even they had trouble, but managed to get a few serious tubes. The only way to make the wave is to backdoor the backless beast. Frank's first wave apexed, leaving him with one option: abandoning ship. He went down hard with the lip. Getting lip-launched on a wave like that is life-threatening. He was slammed on the bottom and grated along the reef. After the intense burst of energy, it took him five full stokes to make it to the surface, meaning it was a solid twenty-plus feet deep.

What kind of power drives someone to that depth?

He said he had been surfing Bocas for over ten years and had never seen any swell that big.

Would I ever get a window where it was more approachable? Just the thought was terrifying.

I reminded myself that I wasn't in the surf industry; I wasn't cool, and most importantly, I had nothing to prove. That being said, I didn't come all this way to just listen to stories. Bocas had loads of options from reef slabs, right and left point breaks to barreling beach breaks. With the swell forecast, retracing Mike's path would have to wait.

I gave Silverbacks one more look, taking my 8'4. On the boat ride out, I was a gnarled ball of nerves. The swell had dropped slightly with sets still approaching twenty feet. Even mind surfing the wave was impossible. Entering the water looked suicidal. No one was out. Not a good omen. *No gracias.* I knew it wasn't meant to be. I felt relieved. A *pinta (*beer*)* was instantly cracked. I headed over to Paunch instead.

I would have to disagree with some of my friends who labeled Paunch a fat mush burger of a wave. On this swell, it was anything but soft. The bottom of the wave dropped out with visible reef close below. If you stuck the drop, you were getting barreled, without a doubt. After another great session at Paunch, high on endorphins, I headed back to town. Yes, people were perplexed to see a gringo driving down there. Under a saggy palm, a dreaded surfer walked along the sandy road. I decided to acknowledge his presence with a "SURF."

His response was shocking. He turned around.

I couldn't believe my eyes.

It wasn't just any dready dude strolling down some sandy tide-dependent, marginal-non-existent Caribbean road, it was Terry Dorman. Before me was a kid who used to live on my block in Long Beach Island, Brant Beach[65]. He and his brothers Bryan and Ken-Kennums, along with Whitewater Wesley, Billy-Dizer, and Mike-Busta Bust started skim boarding and boogie boarding as groms. Dr. Daniels-Birdman and occasionally Shelly-Shell Bellz showed us the beauty of surfing and the glide[66]. That initial taste of the oceanic life has never left me. Now, Terry stood getting unintentionally fucked with by me. He told me he was

---

[65] Yes, I think it's another strange Brant "synchronicity."

[66] Despite being in great physical shape, Dr. Daniels died in his forties from a heart attack while in the mountains snowboarding in Colorado. Some say it was the change in altitude. It was shocking. His stoke and passion for life will never be forgotten.

staying in town for the next few months learning Spanish. Being the last "kids" of our families, we both took on the role of the black sheep-traveling surfer. To the conventional Northeast family, we were space cadets, lost on this planet. But we were space cadets with giant, shit-eating grins from Paunch's aquatic elixir.

One thing that Bocas doesn't lack besides waves is dudes. Despite a handful of female chargers, most are males. From Paunch to Bluff, the lineups were packed with pros and hungry surfers. Kelly Slater later said that Point Carenero was one of the most crowded breaks he had ever seen, up there with Snapper Rocks on the Gold Coast of Australia. I translated that: "It's one of the most crowded spots in the world." Maybe it was from all the hype on this swell?

But like anywhere, every place and every swell has windows of uncrowded waves.

On one particular session at Paunch, I found myself flanked by my old neighbor, Terry, as the waves approached double-overhead with just a few other guys. Thick emerald walls of water heaved onto the reef, leaving us to hoot each other over the ledge. The waves grinded down the line, ending in a blast of briny air. I witnessed the same smile I saw almost thirty years ago as he took off on a knee-high shore break in Brant Beach. We traded off waves, howling in a sea of disbelief. We had a little over an hour of memorable waves and poundings.

The arrival of two boats filled with fiery Latin surfers closed that window. I took a small inside wave and headed to shore. Riding the whitewater in, I couldn't help but think of what a small and beautiful world we live in.

With declining swell, it was time to address the real reason I was there: Mike Brant and his Bocas legacy.

First stop, Mariposa. In Spanish it means "butterfly" or "gay;" Mike would have embraced both definitions. Locals, like Kahuna, referred to it by its former name, the Lemon Grass. Wes and Shane both told me to find a girl there named Suki. Shane hadn't returned to Bocas yet, but I felt compelled to forge ahead. Bringing a Canadian from Hostal Luego seemed prudent. I can't remember his name. Let's just call him Phil.

So "Phil" and I had no idea what we were getting ourselves into. Maybe Mike had pissed on her bar, had some leftover debts, broke something, and then banged someone's girlfriend? Maybe she was going to kick my ass for even speaking his name? Maybe Phil could serve as a shield? Maybe Mike had taught her to surf, and she had fallen in love with him? Maybe she would dump glitter on us?

That was Mike. You never knew what to expect, even in the afterlife.

The place was packed. Live, jazzy Caribbean-flavored tunes electrified the tropical night. Three open walls faced the black sea. It reminded me of Dockside in Wrightsville Beach. I envisioned Mike running around trying to please people: "Is everything alright, mon?" "Are you having a good time?" "Can I get you anything, mon?"

An energetic, tan woman approached from behind the bar, her black, curly hair merrily bouncing upon her shoulders. We were warmly greeted by brown, attentive eyes and a hospitable smile.

"What can I do fo youz?"

A heavy British accent was the last thing I had expected to come out of her mouth. Would I get loaded first and then broach the subject of Mike, or just get right to it? She peered deeper into my eyes. I saw confident feistiness there. Maybe she would kick my ass after all? I fished for words.

Where do I start?

"Wes Brant and Shane told me to find you. I drove some of Mike's remains down from North Carolina."

She froze. Her mouth opened in shock, looking at us like we were ghosts. Tears began to pool in her eyes. She left the bar and came running around the corner and gave me a huge hug.

"How the hell are you, mate?!"

"Drinks on me tonight."

"Any friend of Mikey is a friend of mine."

With that, she slapped me on the shoulder. Phil, too, was stunned. When she left to make our *piñas,* he looked at me and said, "Mike must have been one hell of a guy to make that kind of impression."

I proudly nodded. "Yep, that's my boy Mike. Everyone loved him."

"How long did he live here?"

"Four months?"

"*Four months!* That's it? I would have figured they were lifelong friends."

"That was Mike for you."

It didn't take long for people to identify with Mike and his eccentricities. They were drawn to him—or repulsed. The fact that Suki rolled with Mike and Shane meant that we could skip the formalities. I imagined the outrageous boundary-pushing experiences they had shared.

That night, Suki treated Phil and me like we were family. She shut the place down, and we traded Brant stories deep into the night. The laughter bellowed out onto the street. Phil did his best to follow along. She talked of the Mariposa being a second home for Mike. He worked for food, which was excellent, and helped out with their other place, the Jungle Lounge.

Suki's eyes sparkled with love. "We were 'Bruki': Brant plus Suki."

After hearing her stories, it was apparent that Suki embraced Mike for being Mike. Heterosexual boundaries were dashed with glitter, pink bikes, and Disney princess songs until the morning sun.

Meeting some of Mike's friends and feeling his impact in that area filled me with gratitude. I felt fortunate to have experienced his brilliance and am honored to call him a friend. Balmy hours dissolved into days and days into weeks. Like so many visitors before me, I found myself caught in the Bocas time warp.

Did I find Mike's wave?

No.

The moment never felt right with the Caribbean's frantic, short-period energy amid a maelstrom of ravenous surfers. But the explosion of swell activity in the North Pacific told me that it was time to move.

Now or never.

Boarding the ferry to the mainland, I couldn't help but think back to one of the last things Mike wrote me, a quote from the movie *Point Break,* which he often quoted and made fun of: "Some guys sniff for it, others jab a vein, all you gotta do is jump, Johnny. I can't live my life in a cage, Johnny[67]."

Mike drew a line through life like no other. He wasn't just a pioneer; he was an artist.

---

[67] I imagine of all the characters in that movie, Mike would have been Bunker Weiss, aka Lupton Pittman. Others said Mike was Bodhi. Before growing his hideous dreads, he definitely resembled him, young Patrick Swayze.

The ferry roared to life, rattling the *Camioneta*. Exiting into the tropical breeze, I set my sights beyond Almirante, beyond the Darien Gap, to Colombia[68], the gateway to South America.

The search wasn't over.

Mike in his ELEMENT.

---

[68] At the time, Ferry Express (known as *Ferry Estress*) ran from Colón, Panamá, across the Caribbean (slightly over 300 miles and around a twenty-hour trip) to Cartagena, Colombia. They no longer take cars. Now, if you want to drive to South America, you have to put your vehicle on a container ship, which costs around $1,000, and could take several weeks. *Suerte!*

MB's surfboard bench on the South End of Wrightsville
Beach offers a great place to sit and remember the
good times shared with Mike. Thanks to Vic for
making this happen. "Keep Ya Head UP" is a song
from Tupac Shakur, one of Mike's favorite rappers.

Taking a painful look within.

Broken board compliments of a South end drain pipe.
MB loved to snap my surfboards. What a SAUCE!

Byram, building his own "personal legend."

McBrant going OSS(Open Shirt Sausage).

Mike looking for shade around C Street. Classic
pigdog on a solid three (out of five) logo day. Photo
compliments of Tony Butler and Wblivesurf.

Pache. Pachucho. Lion heart.

This was the large sheepshead that birthed the story
Farting Back to Life. Beware of harvesting larger reef fish
that may contain high concentrations of bacteria.

Silverbacks, in all her glory, untouchable.

Los Chingones with Mike on *Leydi's Cumple Años.*

Author dropping in on a memorial day in northern Peru.

Celebrating the end of a historic day (from left to right) with: Corocho, Tarantini, Grecia, Camilo, Author, Lucho, Gustavo, Pache, Daril.

Fin del Mundo (End of the World) with Mike overhead.

Tarantini (Gustavo's dad) adding some MB
flare, camo+flames, to the *Camioneta*.

Part III

Into the Unknown

"Synchronicity is an ever-present reality for those who have eyes to see."
−Carl Jung

In the rising sun, the turquoise morning sea awoke. Frigate birds spiraled above, looking for *desayuno* (breakfast). Colombia's coastline grew under the waning harbor lights. The boat shuddered, as it had all night, under the ceaseless pounding of the Caribbean. A Spanish fortress loomed above the colorful colonial hills.

Pirates beware.

Hundreds of years ago, Spanish galleons loaded full of gold, silver, and bad karma had set sail across these waters. The Incan stones were going to make them wealthy and famous beyond comprehension.

But menacing ships appeared on the horizon. Their voyage would be cut short as English pirates headed down from Belize to intercept them[69]. On the high seas, there was no judge or jury. Might made right. And the volatile waters below flowed with indifference to the nefarious battles of men. The tropical shades of blue endlessly swept shoreward toward Cartagena de Indias.

Outside the port, Colombia's new rulers resided in sky scrapers, oil tankers, and cruise ships.

---

[69] Belize was an English pirate's dream: barrier reefs for protection and an abundance of timber. This is also one of the reasons why the main language in Belize today is English.

Deserted

The balmy air inside the *Camioneta* thickened with fear. I drew a long, deep breath. I channeled my burning nerves to the task at hand: we needed to get out of there, fast. *How the fuck did things go south so quickly?* Only an hour ago we were flying high upon the clouds of the Caribbean Sea. I really, really regretted smoking that big fat *porro*. My eyes bled, and my soul quivered. As the key penetrated the ignition, I knew there was no turning back. I looked over to my *guapa co-pilota*, and reminded myself that if I died, it would be with a smile on my face from this Colombian beauty.

I had met her four days earlier in Taganga, a little tourist town on the Caribbean. Before getting to Colombia, all I kept hearing about was how amazingly attractive and *caliente* the women are. I was super single and in a new country. Panama was astern and *Carnaval* season lay ahead. The stars were aligning with the pendulum of life surging forward, so when I saw a group of *Colombianas* day-drinking at the hostel Divanga bar, I went for it. The bartender sat talking to a girl in wide-brimmed straw hat, short frayed jean shorts, and a snug white T-shirt. I grabbed the wooden barstool beside her. I was struck by her passionate, coffee-colored eyes; they beamed with unbridled energy. She was twenty-one. Her name was Veronica, and she wanted to dance with me. I was intimidated. I gave her the classic gringo joke I once heard in Ecuador. "When us gringos dance, it's like we are killing ants[70]."

She laughed, showing her perfect teeth against her well-rounded red lips. A few drinks loosened the lips, hips, and it was time to dance salsa. I pulled her tight. I could feel passion pounding out of her chest. After a few whirls, we were dripping in sweat. Our wet bodies clung together. I could feel the moisture of her warm breath. My hairs on my neck stood up, and goosebumps erupted all over my body. Her luscious lips connected with my earlobe. My heart galloped. Her sensual voice issued the words, *"Bailas como si estuvieras haciendo el amor."*

A common saying in Spanish is *comida hecho con amor*, food made with love. But I've never heard what Veronica had just told me, "Dance as if you were making love." I felt rhythm pulsing through me like never before. I was in love.

The music switched over to reggaeton. Yes, I knew this song, Daddy Yankee! *"Cómo te voy olvidar? Cómo te voy olvidar?"* (How am I going to forget you?) Daddy Yankee was speaking the truth. There was no way I was going to forget Veronica. Our flow improved. She "seemed" impressed. I sucked less at dancing reggaeton than salsa. What followed next dropped my jaw to the dusty dance floor. It was where the word *"caliente"* and "Colombia" forged an eternal union. The dance is called *El Choque.*

It felt like I was being struck by lightning during an earthquake. I swung my head around to find Colombian girls on both sides of me. Another male charged the dance floor and had a girl's leg over his shoulder before I could even say, *"Dios mío."* He dropped her floorward with his pelvis gyrating to the beat. The dance floor became a whirlpool of flying limbs and sweaty bodies. The repeated collisions of bodies, I imagine it is where the dance gets its name, *El Choque* (collision-car crash).

Songs pumped down the dusty streets. Sure enough, the *tiburones* (land-sharks) heard the call and began to tighten their radius. The pulsating orb of wet, caramel-colored bodies grew larger and larger in that tiny bar. I took a time out. Waiting for drinks, I looked up at a music video, "Latinoamérica" by Calle 13. It began with the beating heart

---

[70] *Cuando un gringo baila si estuviera matando hormigas.* If you are a gringo o gringa that dances well, my apologies for the generalization, but the comment never fails to make them laugh.

of *Pachamama* (Mother Earth). Flashes of the countryside and poverty-stricken faces seized my breath. An old woman with far-reaching eyes sang up to the sky from some distant farmland,

"Tú no puedes comprar la lluvia. Tú no puedes comprar el sol."

"You can't buy the rain. You can't buy the sun."

Her earth-colored eyes knifed into me like the Mayan's sorrowful eyes of Guatemala. The intensity of the images, lyrics, and beat shook me to the core. The message was clear: despite all the exploitation of Latin America, the people will always have nature and their soul, which is not for sale.

When the song ended, reality became loud and argumentative. It was time to leave. Despite the fact that there were a bunch of shots thrown back, friendships made, and good times had, emotions still flared. No one wanted to pay the tab. The bartender took action. She snatched a guy's Android and said, *"Cuando pagues la cuenta, aquí está tu celular."*

"When you pay the tab, the phone is yours."

The guy was livid. *"Puta madre!"* He threw his hands up and his friends tried to calm him down. His body stiffened with his malicious gaze. Did he want to get physical with a female bartender?

Veronica gave me the look that said, *"Vámonos."*

At the next bar, the *salsa choque* continued. I found myself in another love sandwich, grinding til we hit the floor. Once again, after several songs, I had to let Veronica go; she was in a league of her own. Everyone took notice, watching her in a dance trance. She was not thinking about her cell phone being stolen for the third time, power outages, the oven-like heat of a concrete home, or corruption. She was possessed by the beat. Her body shook, ebbed and flowed with grace punctuated by seismic movements. A number of on-looking males drew closer, and then flailed backward.

When the song ended, she returned.

"What happened?"

She leaned over with the sweat beading off her thick black brow. She pulled her moist, curly black hair from her face.

"Los mandé al carajo."

She told them to fuck off. What a woman. For the remainder of the night, she was the undisputed queen of the dance floor. I felt fortunate to witness her in her freest form.

The clock read 4am; *so much for spearfishing tomorrow at first light.*

Veronica told me she was ready to go to her *casa*. My adventurous mind spun into overdrive. My eyes darted across a Colombian map on the wall, trying to connect two words: VERONICA and ADVENTURE. Where to? Jungle? No, stick with what you know, stick to the coast. I followed the map to the tip of South America.

"How about coming to Cabo de las Velas with me?"

"*Mañana me voy a Carnaval.*"

"Me too. How about in a few days?"

"*Sería muy chévere.*"

After several days of the outrageous street parties of Carnaval, I went to Santa Marta[71]. Veronica bubbled with excitement. I tried my best to suppress my raging hormones. The tropical landscape heading north gave way to a cactus-studded desert. Driving through towns like Camarones and Riocacha, it felt like Baja all over again. The world at large is bombarded with images of Colombia: dense jungles, coffee plantations, drug cartels, cocaine, and violent kidnappings. The desert and "safe" tourist towns of the Caribbean had already dispelled a few of these myths for me. I wondered how many other unknown treasures Colombia held. Once again, the open road filled with mysticism and discovery.

We drove over a painted star.

"What do those stars mean?"

Veronica ran her thumb across her neck and stretched out her tongue. "*Muertos.*"

They were all over the road. Once again the *Camioneta* was passing across an elongated graveyard.

Colombian gas is expensive, about $5 a gallon. Bordering Venezuela, a country with cheap gas, La FARC(Las Fuerzas Armadas Revolucionarias de Colombia, Colombian guerrilla group) and others have found smuggling *gasolina* to be extremely lucrative. How does one smuggle *gasolina*? In a pickup packed to the gills with barrels of gas. There's no concealing it. If-when discovered, a high-speed chase follows. How do you think a high-speed chase through the desert is going to end with a pickup packed with gasoline?

Long stretches of asphalt cut through lands where cactus outnumber people. Fruit stands of guayabas, fresas, cocos sporadically populated the

---

[71] The final resting place of the "Great Liberator," Simón Bolívar.

road. Gas signs, probably selling illicit Venezuelan petrol, seemed to be the best seller. With my gas gauge on E, our options totaled zero. We pulled over.

An ancient man whose body resembled a weathered piece of driftwood crouched on his battered knees, put his mouth around a dirty hose, and pulled hard. Within seconds, he scrambled over to the *Camioneta* to begin filling. With the hose inserted in the truck, he leaned over and spat out a mouthful of gas. I cringed at the thought of what of his internals looked like. With the tank filling, I walked over.

"How does it taste?"

"Nada, para mí es costumbre. Así es la vaina[72]."

I know some people love the smell of gas (like my friend Munz), but to get accustomed to the taste of gasoline? I could do nothing to improve his situation, just fork over the 100,000 pesos and swap a few road stories.

His señora sat expressionless, rocking behind a cement wall and breastfeeding another *hijo*. After a slight lift of the head, she returned her eyes to her dust-filled horizon. I thanked the man, and we returned to our desert adventure.

What to do on such a flat, endless desert road? Would we sit back pondering the enigmatic questions of life? No. With the wicked heat and this stunning woman beside me, a pelagic thirst surfaced that only a *chela* could cure. We stopped at *una tienda*.

After drinking a few beers, Veronica lost her *verguenza* (embarrassment) and began speaking English. The *Camioneta* became our mobile language school. I told her of how I was working on a Latin American slang list. Her eyes animated as she said, "Well, out here in the desert, some say, '*Oye mamaburro.*'"

She lost herself to laughter. I had trouble imagining walking up to someone and saying, "How's it going, donkey fucker?"

She slapped her thigh, shaking her head. "Sometime *es* true."

Even my inquisitive mind didn't want to pursue the conversation further.

With the linguistic exchange in full force, the amusement was unending. We cruised blissfully through the day until night covered the parched earth. In the absence of light, in a foreign country, everything

---

[72] I would later interpret *así es la vaina* to "*es normal,*" or "that's how it goes."

becomes more menacing. My eyes strained to interpret the conflicting shadows. Swaying brush now looked like soldiers doing stretches with their AKs. Oil rigs resembled vampiric praying mantis sucking the Earth's blood. Do those machines ever sleep?

We weaved our way through the oil fields toward a faint pool of light. Small dirt roads with puddles of loose sand offered a plethora of pathways. I looked at my phone and a blue circle pulsed from a map. Here we were approaching the end of the world, and this creepy little "intelligent" phone was still tracking us.

The layered lights grew from the black desert. On the outskirts of town, there were carports and *palapas* running along the beach. The soft oceanic melodies told us that we had arrived. Motorless *pangas* and driftwood lined the shores of this tranquil fishing town. We popped a tent and sat along the water's edge.

What to do?

"Prende un porro?"

My eyes got redder and more intimate things became comical. I haven't laughed so much in my life. Yes, she was only twenty-one, but her wing-it, badass, shit-talking attitude made us a perfect fit. I think we annoyed our neighbors swinging wildly in hammocks, laughing the night away. We bathed under the scintillating stars. Veronica shook her head in disbelief.

"Brightest stars I seen in my life."

They were spectacular, but the dreamer within wanted to push it further. What would the starlit skyline be like without the town lights? A beaconing flash briefly illuminated the empty point. I sharpened my eyes. It was *el faro* (lighthouse), and it was calling.

En la mañana, while breakfasting, we watched the *pangas* buzzing out over the glistening tropical waters.

"Let's go take a look at the point by the lighthouse."

"Por Qué no?"

Colombian tourists swam among the celestial water while their tour bus sat idle above. Our eyes opened wide with the anticipation of a Caribbean embrace. Maybe a meal lay beneath that radiant blue sheet of tranquility? Veronica removed her clothes, revealing a black one-piece. She strolled along the soft sands toward the sea. I grabbed my dive gear. The aquarium below offered mind-numbing colors and coral caves. Small wrasse with florescent yellow tales cautiously eyed me from their abode while a lizard fish passed along a sandy patch of ocean floor. I abandoned my hunting duties and followed him. He fanned out his brilliant purple wings. Beyond the beauty, I got the message: "Don't mess with me."

I saluted him and surfaced for air. Looking around the desert cliffs and expansive blue, I was alone in my private underwater world.

I relaxed. The dives deepened. I spotted a small ledge around thirty-five feet giving way to a drop-off. I emptied my mind, and plunged below. Leveling off at the bottom, something felt wrong. A distant noise grew. The disturbing vibration grew stronger and louder. My lungs began to warm. And then they began to scream for oxygen. Ascending was a diver's worst nightmare: an incoming *panga* at full throttle. Quite the predicament. Knowing that the only way to appease my burning lungs could lead to decapitation. I kicked toward the surface with my spear directly above me.

Bursting from the surface, my lungs ballooned with air. My eyes widened. The *panga* was headed straight at me, only a few hundred yards away. I dug my fins into the water to raise high above the surface waving my gun from side to side. *I'm here! Don't hit me!*

They held their heading, me. Closer and closer they came. One hundred meters-eighty meters-sixty meters. At that moment, I contemplated diving down. The *panga* mowed ahead. I packed oxygen into my lungs, getting ready. Just as I was about to dive under, they turned, throwing water and wake over me. I choked on the mixture of air and water. Their laughter rang over the sound of the outboard engine.

As Veronica would say, *CARAJOS.*

Were they aware of my presence? Abso-freaking-lutely. Did they say anything to me? No. But their intentions were clear, scare the shit out of me. Maybe they were being territorial of their fishing grounds? If you have a problem with someone fishing in your waters, even though the ocean belongs to no one, at least say something. The reckless *pangueros* could have made a sad ending to the desert romance.

Heading back, I looked at my goodie bag. It held a red snapper and a small mackerel. A successful harvest meant fish tacos for *la gente*. We spent the rest of the day hanging in the shade with the local fishermen and indigenous merchants. The Caribbean Sea dazzled us with her ever-changing shades of infinity. Long, deep breaths of satisfaction filled my lungs.

At sunset, people packed up and headed back to town. We hiked to the bluff at the top of the point with our wings soaring in the cooling ocean breeze. The sun cast a golden shade of orange on the last clouds of dust from the departing cars. Alone at last. Veronica's beautiful face shined upon the vast seascape. It all felt like a lucid dream.

Off in the distance, a fading squawk of a seagull dissolved into the ocean's whisper. This was it. The world, and all of its problems, vanished in that moment.

We claimed our camp; ten kilometers of winding labyrinth-like, sandy dirt roads separated us from town. We were at the tip of South America, making our own rules.

"*Toma*."

She handed me a *porro*. I knew as a *caballero,* I had to at least light it. Well I did just that and then some. A huge plume of smoke came billowing out of my mouth. I coughed and then laughed. Then I coughed some more and mustered up a "Buenas noches".

She heeled over, giggling. My face hurt from my permanent grin. This is how life was supposed to be, fun! Watching the last rays of light disappear into the darkening blue, we glided down the rocky terrain back to our secluded campground. The tent was set up, and I started to cook some rice *con pescado*.

If coming out here needed any more vindication, I looked up at the Colombian night sky. Strobing stars overwhelmed our ceiling. They were greater than any human could comprehend. The star-laced night was ours.

"*Marvillosas*."

Veronica's almond eyes gleamed in the starlight.

"Did you hear that?"

"*Qué?*" she looked confused.

"That."

"*No escucho nada.*"

She looked at me like I was crazy. Maybe she thought I was just stoned and paranoid?

I heard it again, a muffled sound coming from the water. My eyes squinted into the pitch-black wall. *Nada*.

Out of the blackness, a piercing light sliced through the night like a sharpened blade. It was directly in front of us, maybe a hundred yards offshore. After a few minutes of circling, it ceased. The motor fell silent. We heard nothing and said nothing. My nerves knotted. Until we figured out what was going on, we tried to minimize our existence. No phones. No stove. No light. Maybe they were fishermen?

But what kind of fisherman rides with no running lights and then sporadically turns them on? Lobster fishermen fish by night, but they leave lobster traps and have lit buoys-traps. Having just dove the cove and point, I knew there were no buoys or traps.

We remained quiet, hoping they would just leave.

They didn't.

Reality was frightening. We were at the end of the world, on the border of Venezuela and Colombia in a remote desert area. Surely, this would be a strategic point for drug traffickers.

The enigma continued. The light and motor would turn on for a few minutes and then off. They were either searching for something or dropping off something. I tried to keep my cool. *Think. Maybe we should just go chill out in the tent?*

No way. There was nothing chill about the situation. We were in the middle of nowhere, miles from help. If they rolled up on us nestled in the tent, we would be fucked. Great time to be stoned out of my gourd.

Suddenly, the boat fired up its engine and approached the shoreline then stopped. The bow light shot off into the desert just barely missing the *Camioneta*. Being Mr. Cool went flying the fuck out the window. Time to leave. If they found us, there was no way we could say we hadn't seen anything; they were right in front us. After packing up the gear, we crept over to the *Camioneta*. I kept a cautious eye on the ink-black sea. Once I started the engine, there was no turning back. Veronica's brown eyes were wide with terror.

"Ready?"

"*Lista.*"

I breathed deep and ignited the *Camioneta*. My nerves lit on fire as the mufflerless Pathfinder roared to life, announcing our presence. I floored the gas pedal. As we flew in and out of unmarked craters, the surfboards became fiberglass projectiles. The paths stretched out like a demented labyrinth.

"Which way?" I screamed. "Right or left?"

Before Veronica opened her mouth, I had already chosen, left.

The *Camioneta* was filled with gas and adrenaline, no brakes.

The next fork approached.

"*Derecha!*" she screamed.

She was learning fast. My mind and imagination were my worst enemy. Thoughts of the movies *Casino* and *Seven* fused together. Heads in boxes and being buried in the desert mangled my mind. If they found us, they had options: bury us in the desert, or feed us to the sharks. Would they call ahead to one of their *compañeros* to cut us off? A blinding light shot through the back window.

"*Mierda!*"

They were coming after us. My heart was trying desperately to hammer out of my chest. I became religious. *Please, Lord, just let me get through this. I won't squeal. I didn't see anything. Why the hell did I smoke? Things can go south fast around these parts. Mike, if you're up there, pal, I could use a little help.*

The light spun and then disappeared, and then reappeared. Then it hit me. I laughed. Through our twists and turns, we had emerged alongside of *el faro* (the lighthouse). Wow, that was some good Colombian *hierba*.

Records were eclipsed in the adrenaline-filled escape. Still flying high as we approached town, with zero bullets in us, I wondered what the traffickers thought when they heard the *Camioneta?* I wondered if they thought about the absence of the muffler and how bad the Mexican Libre and its *topes* were.

That night it never felt so good to be alive, safe, and around other people. Being in the presence of a Colombian goddess didn't hurt either. My heart continued to pump in overdrive as we walked along the serendipitous shores. The street lights of town mattered not. The stars had never looked so brilliant!

The next day, I had to ask the question, "Were we just paranoid, or was there a real threat?"

I needed to know. Heading to breakfast, I asked an old, salty *pescador,* "Is there any night fishing out at *el faro?*"

He cocked his head; his pale eyes swelled with suspicion.

"Absolutely not, no one fishes out there until around 4am. Why do you ask?"

My gut stirred. As many people have told me, the best way to survive in Latin America is to be deaf and mute.

"Just wondering. Thanks."

His look said it all. Last night's scare was real. I thanked him for his time and felt life once again racing through me.

The following day, we went down to a beautiful beach in Santa Marta. We reveled in safety. Who knew what perils lay down the road? I wished Veronica could have continued on as my *co-pilota,* but she was heading to Europe to visit her sister. I told her of my plans to head south to Medellin-land of the *Paisas.* She said she heard it was *peligroso* and laughed. I had heard my fair share of kidnapping stories, but had also heard great things from my friends Adam and Catalina, *una Paisa,* from Medellin.

Which face of Colombia would I encounter?

The Best Trip Untaken

"It is in your moments of decision that your destiny is shaped."
–Tony Robbins

After three weeks of overcrowded city life, stressful ferries, run-ins with traffickers, and *Carnaval* in Barranquilla, it was time to get back to the main pursuit of this trip, riding waves and chasing rainbows. I looked to Colombia's Pacific coastline to chase a giant storm that had spawned off the coast of Japan and mutated into a mega-tempest sending XXL fetch southward to Hawaii and the Americas.

Before leaving Medellin, I had my brake pads changed. I told the mechanics I was planning on traversing through the jungle to a remote beach. The mammoth-sized Colombian stopped his work and rose up from his knees. His frame shadowed my existence. His dark eyes cut into me.

"My uncle was kidnapped in that area for over a month. The narcos figured him to be rich. He told them he was just a poor teacher. Then they suspected he was a spy. They wanted to know who he was working for. They tortured him by pulling his teeth out to get answers."

He looked at me, wrench in hand, grease smudged across his black face. "And you, gringo with your California plates, what are they going to do to you?"

It was an answer I didn't want to know.

"I will tell you. It will be one of two things: either they will think you are rich and your torture will be worse than my uncle, or if they don't think you are rich, they will think you are working for the CIA and the outcome will be even worse.

"Don't go there. If you do, you will regret it."

His advice shot a crippling fear down my spine, imagining the hellacious tortures. It felt like I had cheated death[73].

The waypoint was reset to Buenaventura, Colombia's only "official" Pacific port.

---

[73] I would later read the book *Two Wheels of Terror*, where a California guy was kidnapped on his *moto* and held for more than a month by EPL (Ejercito Popular de Liberacion, Popular Army of Liberation).Around the year 2000, the number of kidnappings in Colombia rose to over 3,000 kidnappings annually. In 2015, the number has dropped to around 300 for the entire nation.

La Camioneta del Dios

*"Real adventure is defined best as a journey from which you may
not come back alive, and certainly not as the same person."*
–Yvon Chouinard

With Medellin in my rear view, the road opened to rolling blooms of
yellows and greens. Crisp country air blended with a brilliant Colombian
sun. *Parilladas* scented the hills with barbequed animals. I was officially
in the Colombian "Coffee Route." I embraced the freedom of the open
countryside.

From what I've gathered from this trip called life, coincidences are
neither random nor isolated. They are part of a greater story. A series of
synchronicities had led me halfway down the American continent. When
and where would the voyage end? My drying finances and deepening credit
card debt told me only a few more months. Wes Brant continued to make
the case for keeping the "Endless Summer" alive. He suggested that I "get
Mike barreled at the end of the world." He posted a link showing some
Spaniard finding empty waves at the southern tip of America. It seemed
too remote to fathom. All I knew was I was on a trip of a lifetime, and I
needed to get back to the Pacific.

The hospitality of the *familia Latina* was one of the driving forces
to the trip. I will never forget the unconditional generosity, kindness,
and love they have shown a foreigner. So when Daisy, Colombian, and
Lots, German, had told me months earlier in Panama to look them up in
Palmira (just outside Cali) if I was ever in Colombia, I took it as a sincere
invitation. And after my encounter in Medellin, I figured it was time to
reconnect with people I knew.

Daisy's mouth dropped on her doorstep when I showed up one night with a pair of bloodshot eyes and in great need of a place to crash. The thirteen hours of driving from Medellin, through the *café* route, showed me beauty that defies description.

The first thing Daisy asked me: "Are you hungry?"

"Yes, por fa."

"My friend has a restaurant just down the street."

"*Chévere.* Awesome!"

She dropped everything to take me there.

It was fitting that her friend would have a New York-inspired *restaurante. El local* was filled with the décor of Frank Sinatra, the city skyline, and sports paraphernalia. It felt like I was in a Devo video filmed at an '80s sports bar. Sinatra's world-famous song came on. "Start spreadin' the news..."

I grabbed a seat below photos of the Yankee baseball legends Darryl Strawberry and Don Mattingly.

Frank continued, "I want to be a part of it/ New York, New York."

The mother, la señora, of the owner greeted me with extreme attention. She quickly determined that I was a good match for her daughter Marcela. She said, "I have a daughter for you. You need to take her with you to the U.S." Everyone started laughing at her forwardness. Latinos love this joke, take her or him back with you. #The American Dream.

I figured her to be a charity case because her mom was selling her so hard. Ten minutes later, a Selma Hayek look-alike came waltzing down the stairs. She shyly smiled as the señora told "their story" of how she crossed the border with her two girls. They staved off scandalous border coyotes, human traffickers, and dehydration to make their way to Arizona. From there, they headed to New York City, where they lived for seven years. She said the family loved New York. Her eyes beamed, listening to her *hijita* speaking English. Marcela was a part-time English teacher and a full-time beauty queen. You could tell she was drawn to me and the prestigious gringoness oozing out of my skin. If she wanted to practice her English with me, *no hay problema.*

Fate would have it that we were both heading in the same direction, the Pacific Ocean. The family had been trying for years, unsuccessfully, to visit their dad, a well-connected naval cook based out of Buenaventura.

The señora told me "Papi" could help me navigate the coast for waves. It seemed too good to be true.

Daisy painted a different picture. "My family and I love the beach, but we don't go to Buenaventura. It's too dangerous. That's why we go to Panamá." She continued, "You thought Colón was bad. Buenaventura is a scarier, more intense version of Colón. The people are more desperate."

I wish I had listened to Daisy.

The señora, however, assured me that it would be fine and that her husband would take care of us. After my time spent in steamy concrete jungles, I was ready to believe.

The señora told me that God had sent me and my vehicle to the family. I was a blessing. "*La Camioneta del Dios*" had a nice ring to it. Who would have thought, *the Camioneta*, God's chariot!

One big happy family piled into the *Camioneta*, Marcela riding shotgun, Isabel (a teenage beauty queen from the barrio), Maribel (Marcela's eight-year-old daughter), and the Señora. They said it was a three-hour drive. My experience would not allow me to be fooled. We quickly lost an hour looping around Cali's chaotic, traffic-choked streets as my *co-pilota,* Marcela, caught up on sleep.

Leaving Cali, we passed through iridescent *barrios* with neon-colored clothing drying in the *sol*. As we passed the burning colors on an uphill turn, the *policía* waited for us. My heartbeat skipped with the word, "*Documentos.*"

While he was inspecting my documents, I rolled down the window to show him that I was indeed driving a grandma, daughters, and granddaughter. I painted the heroic picture of a gringo delivering the family to their father at the naval base in Buenaventura. He bobbed his head in approval. His intensity lightened. *La Camioneta del Dios* was set free in less than two minutes.

Driving through the mountains, I told the girls about the vehicle's great metamorphosis. She went from being an ordinary 2002 Pathfinder used for an office commute to Easton, Pennsylvania, to a teacher's metal coffin slugging it out on Highway 5 in San Diego, to the *Camioneta* battling *topes* in Mexico, to God's blessed chariot in Colombia. Things were looking up!

Just on the outskirts of Buenaventura, we passed a small cluster of swamp dwellings. La señora pointed to marshland of rotten stilts and straw roofs.

"*Es bien peligroso allá.*"

"Why?"

"*Allí los narcos alimentan los muertos a la tierra.*"

Translation: "That's where los narcos chop people up and feed them to the earth." The señora's words were not what I wanted to hear heading into the unknown. Like in Mexico, I reminded myself I was wasn't involved in the drug trade. I was taking these *Colombianas* to see their Papi in God's chariot. We would get an easy pass, right?

Wrong!

Imagine pulling into a Colombian "danger zone" with a family, all women, with a bloated surfboard bag strapped to the roof and white Californian tags flashing in the sun like a lure. Then add being lost. What happened to the "We know the city. Don't worry. We will guide you. You will be taken care of."?

We were like an injured gazelle being circled by a pride of hungry lions. I didn't have time to be upset. Two teens with enraged eyes leapt to their feet and sprinted after us. Their hands waved frantically as they shouted. The *Camioneta* and my pulse accelerated. The next corner saw more bulging orbs of desperation. More followed. Two guys pulled alongside on *motos*, banging on my window and telling me to follow them. I once again cursed my surf appetite for getting us into this situation. At every turn, malnourished humans burst into motion. I wished "Papi" would have appeared out of the ghetto heavily armed to clear the way for us. He didn't. I floored it over to a non-threatening elderly man to ask for directions to the ferry.

Pulling up to the docks, a supposed safe-haven, we saw more wild animation. We were told the ferry would be leaving in fifteen minutes. My mind was a blender of angst, find secure parking for the *Camioneta*, unload the women and gear, get food, and get on the ferry. I was being pulled in every direction.

"*Boletos!*" Señora screamed.

Don't forget the tickets.

She had asked me before if I had money. I didn't know that meant, can you pay for the entire family's ferry tickets? She said they had no money.

How can you travel without money? There was no time to argue, only time to act. I swiped my credit card for the tickets, unloaded the gear, left the señora and the girls at the boat, and floored it out to a parking garage. We would find food later; we were getting the hell out of Buenaventura. I said a prayer for *La Camioneta* and left her in a paid parking garage.

As Marcela and I headed back out on to the streets, predatory eyes followed us. Our walk became a trot. They tightened their pursuit. I looked at Marcela, and we began running. I stopped when I heard a thud, something crashing behind me. I turned around.

It was Mike lying on the ground. Our predators paused. I crouched down and picked up Mike's vial. I lifted him over my head, showing him to the crowd. A beaming smile overwhelmed my face.

"I present to you, my friend Mike."

Everyone froze in dead silence.

I couldn't believe the bottle was still intact after flying out of my backpack. I slipped Mike back in his camo-cozie and stuffed him securely into my backpack. Mike's ashes weren't meant for this Colombian ghetto.

Our followers remained paralyzed. Maybe they thought I was some sort of *brujo* (witch doctor)? I didn't stop to ask. Whatever it was, we were left alone.

We pressed on.

We arrived to the docks to the sound of twin 250hp engines growling. With the boat fully loaded, the señora flagged us over. The thirty-two foot ferry had a narrow beam, built for speed. We moved our way to the only remaining seats, on the bow. I glanced up to the sky as we pushed off the docks. We were extremely fortunate to have escaped unscathed. I strongly felt Mike's presence.

The headwind freshened over the emerald water. Accelerating, we were hammered by the ocean's punishing beat. The boat bucked over the short-period wind swell and plowed into angry cross waves, sending spray over the bow. Everyone was soaked. After spending most of my childhood on boats, I learned that there's a way to take waves head on while easing off the throttle to soften the impact[74]. Not this captain, he was full throttle. In the jungle heat, my balls plunged to new depths. The problem being, they were cushioning my impact. *Bang, bang*, ouch. After readjustment,

---

[74] My father's second boat was called *Wave Whacker*.

my spine crunched. An old man behind me winced in agony. I stood up to brace myself and tried to offset our anguish with jokes, telling the other passengers, "I don't want my *huevos* (eggs) to be scrambled."

No one laughed.

The captain kept the throttle pinned. Mutinous eyes shot back at him. The elderly man behind us began insulting the captain with "*carajo*" and "*puta madre-pendejo.*"

The captain eased off the throttle. The bow sank, and the ocean swallowed the bow. The captain couldn't find the balance between stationary and full throttle. He returned to the latter. Then Marcela's daughter began crying. Did this deter the captain? *Negativo.* The old man behind me had had enough. He lunged at the captain. The other passengers held him back. I shook my head in disbelief.

After an extended period of spine-jarring slams, we arrived to more frenzied commotion. Being the only white guy around mandated extreme attention. Offloading the bags, I noticed the señora sagging motionless upon the gunwale. Her head hung over the water. She said her back was hurt, and she couldn't walk. She grit her teeth as we carried her and her belongings to the cab. I circled back to the boat to see if there was anything left behind. Butted up against the transom was the señora's human-sized-bag of provisions, now reduced to a rancid puree of smashed eggs, fruit, lettuce, and potatoes. Not only was everything pureed, but it also reeked of gasoline. *Had we been leaking gas?*

We took a cab to our "free" accommodations. Thanks, Papi! We traveled down a narrow, muddy trail surrounded by vivid green vegetation. Rounding the coast past an airstrip, we came upon our bungalows on a flat stretch of manicured lawn. Papi wasn't there.

Everyone was hungry. Was I going to let the family starve?

"*Vámonos.* Let's go eat."

We walked under the fury of an afternoon squall. The deluge and roadside puddles reminded me of Bocas. After we ate, Papi arrived. His plaid fedora shook side to side as he fought back the tears. It had been seven years since they had last come to visit. Seeing the look on his face made all the hardship worthwhile.

Though he was in his fifties, he had the exuberance of a child when he spoke of the wonders of his jungle outpost. The señora's condition improved, *gracias a dios*, and she got back to her religious ways. The following morning, while breakfasting, she reached for my hand. I was startled. She held it, wanting me to recite biblical verses with her.

I reclaimed my hand and told her, "Thanks, but no thanks."

She continued pushing to a point where it got confrontational. Here I was eating, in peace, and she felt the need to impose her religion on me. She claimed that my soul needed saving.

My rebuttal, "Look, señora, I try to be a good person. Did I not transport your family here? Did I not pay for your ferry tickets to get here? Did I not feed the entire family while we were waiting for Papi? I respect your religion, but please don't insist on saving me."

One night we awoke to the blood-curdling wail of the señora. We found her slouched over in her bed writhing in agony with back spasms. Her screams to the heavens tore through the heavy jungle air. She leaned over her disheveled sheets and vomited. I felt guilty for bringing her on that back-breaking ferry ride. I had tried to do the right thing by uniting the family. Now look at them, super *triste* and discombobulated. What to do? We contemplated airlifting her to Buenaventura.

With time, the señora's condition improved, but the message was clear: time to go. She vowed never to return on that ferry; Papi would have to come visit them in Palmira.

Surf?

On the first day, I paddled out to a small beach break. Tall hills of wild green entanglement overlooked a tight sand-rock bottom cove. The waves were waist to chest high. Kids watched me from the cliff. Three small, unsupervised black stick figures hiked down. Once on the sand, they fearlessly charged the water. In a spectacular projection of water, backwash met an oncoming wave, burying the kids in the emerald-green sea. Their heads surfaced, squirming to keep afloat. I paddled over.

"*Tabla! Tabla! Tabla!*" Their gurgling little voices pleaded.

Their extra weight sank the board. I got off and pulled us toward shore.

"Bueno, who wants to go first?"

One of the kids shot out of the water like a cannon. I had my answer. I pushed the boy into a smaller wave, figuring he would just ride it on his belly. To my amazement, he transitioned from his knees to his feet. He was up! For a second, he crouched over the short board. Then a back-wave sent him and the board flying high into the air. Did he just bust an air on his very first wave? Yes. His name was Byram. He was twelve years old and a fearless natural talent, a growing legend. We spent the next hour swapping waves. The other two kids were content with belly riding. They couldn't get enough of it. Later, I was joined by one of the local surfers. He paddled over. He looked toward Byram with enamored eyes. He told me he was a special kid, who climbs fifty feet for coconuts, and how a tourist once tipped Byram for his help. He went straight home and gave the money to his mama. He also donned a nice mohwawk. Super grom!

He pointed south.

"Conoces la punta?"

I shook my head. I hadn't surfed the point.

"Quizás mañana?"

The ferry was leaving tomorrow at 11, plenty of time.

"Sounds good. See you tomorrow."

The right point break broke off a rock and ran out toward a river mouth. The indigo-green jungle extended over the teal-green sea. The waves, long crumbly rights, stretched out like a liquid dance floor. Dodging driftwood, we traded waves. The other guy slid down waves on a hand-carved wooden finless board-alias. At the bottom of the wave, his board spun out of control. Throughout the session, he spun all over the place with his mouth stretching to his ears. We hooted each other into waves, and I was reminded of why I love surfing. He was a stranger, but felt like a brother, connected by the pure joy of the wild ocean. As the good times were flowing, the family emerged on the shore calling me in. The ferry was leaving.

I was relieved when Papi said he was returning with us. Having a male presence in the *Camioneta* who knew the area changed the dynamic completely. On the way back to Palmira, Papi signaled me to pull over at an empanada stand. He took us around back to a sparkling clear mountain river. The rushing water gleamed as it flowed along the lush green banks. Papi motioned for me to jump in. I felt a rush of exhilaration plunging into the cool freshness of Colombia. Others joined, including Papi. Floating in a river surrounded by exuberant faces, I felt the true brilliance of Colombia. I knew the rest of the trip was going to be just fine.

I dropped the family off that night in Palmira and went out with Daisy and her friends for a night at the *discoteca*. Celebration was in order since things could have gone horribly wrong in Buenaventura. The following day, after a good deal of *adiosing*, I left for Ecuador. Images of snowcapped volcanoes, the Amazon, and the enchanted islands had me super-charged with excitement and wonder.

Las Islas Encantadas

"He has asked to search for wisdom on all waves of the sea."
–Kalui Nalamele

We fastened our seatbelts. Speeding down the runway, my imagination took flight. Iguanas, giant turtles, crystalline water, and barrels rifled in my brain. The wheels left the ground. My stomach tingled. I did my best to keep my expectations at bay, for expectations can be a surfer's greatest enemy. Many come to the islands with preconceived notions of "tropical paradise," and many leave disappointed. The arid climate, blustery winds, demoralizing heat, uncooperative waves, and wildlife can be a major letdown. Then there's the sun radiating off the lava rocks, scorching most gringos to a crisp. On top of it all, you have an expensive flight, park fees, and regulations about where you can go and what you can do. That being said, the people and the legends of the islands are what keep me coming back.

Years ago, I taught English at a university on San Cristobal. It was there that I first met Javier Agama, who was taking my class to pass the TOEFL test as part of his master's program, even though it has nothing to do with his competency in the field. I was happy to have him in my class. His eyes were always filled with life as he "practiced his English." He also told me magical tales of enormous whale-sized fish and forgotten islands.

For Javier and most other Latinos, hospitality is second nature. He took me fishing. We picked fresh fruit from his luscious gardens in the highlands, alongside a large husky named *Oso,* who fattened himself on passion fruit and guanábana. Javier educated me about his *finca* (farm) and the soil of unequaled fertility. He spoke about the Agama family's impact

144

on the preservation of the giant land tortoise. For hundreds of years, pirates and the local population had almost dined them to extinction.

"*Muy rica.*"

Elders' eyes twinkled with nostalgia when speaking of the ancient turtle soup. Not any more, the Agama family set up one of the first sanctuaries that looked to protect these ancient animals. In time, the rest of the islands and their inhabitants made a much greater effort on behalf of wildlife conservation and protection.

Several years after meeting Javier, he asked me to be the godfather to his son Ivan. In his family, he is known as Negrito, which translates to "Blacky." Yes, he has a nice tan. Does he take offense to his nickname? No, why should he? He is who he is and the nickname contains no malice. When I come to the islands, I stay with them at Casa de Nelly.

The *hostal* is named after Javier's wife, Nelly. He calls her *la jefa*, the boss, because she is. She also might possibly be the nicest woman on the planet. Her smile is welcoming, and she loves to take care of her *pasajeros* (guests). Please ring the doorbell. Luna, their silky terrier, will be there to greet you[75]. Nelly will help you with anything you need; just don't ask Nelly to speak English. When this happens, she smiles and yells to her children Roberto, Andres, Ivan, or Analia to come to her rescue. They do, and life rolls on.

Life rolled in the form of jarring plane turbulence. It made me think about how I came to the islands in the first place: Mark (aka Bruce Lotion). We taught English together in Peru, and he pointed me in the right direction of finding employment and diversifying the dream.

When hearing that I taught English in Galapagos, the most common response is, people live there? Yes, the total population across all the islands is somewhere around 30,000 and increasing. Despite the laws enacted in 1997 banning Ecuadorians from moving 677 miles from their continent to the enchanted islands, people continue to find a way. How? Some marry locals or others just come by boat and live illegally. There are more employment opportunities on the islands, which have seen economic growth of around six percent, comparable to China. But the population growth and spike in tourism have put the ecosystem and the habitat in

---

[75] Rest in peace, *Lunita*. I'm sure there are endless *motos* for you to bark at in heaven.

jeopardy. This imbalance could destroy the very reason people come to the islands in the first place: the wildlife.

Some believe that the islands are cursed. An entire book, *La Maldición de la Tortuga (The Curse of the Turtle)*, was written about the "Mystic islands that erupted out of fog." The book tells of marooned pirates dying of thirst while other unfortunate souls-political prisoners and criminals-baked to death. Many slaves lost their lives, like the ones in Isabela building the "Wall of Tears." Some of the earlier settlers suffered horrific deaths laced with betrayal and misfortune.

Then came the woman of divine beauty to the island of Floreana with her two lovers. She declared herself the empress of the island. Lore has it she would seduce men and conquer their souls. Then one day she disappeared. Was she murdered? Mysterious deaths and poisonings of her adversaries occurred afterward. Some say she still haunts the island at night as a bat. They call her the *Baronesa,* and she waits for you.

On the island San Cristobal, fables of Sr. Manuel Cobos dance in the mouths of the locals. Cobos created his own world and currency. He was the self-proclaimed owner, king, and god of the island. He farmed sugar cane and coffee and treated his slaves with extreme brutality. Mutiny was his karmic payment. His servants stormed his house and killed him. They say that on a still, quiet night, he can be heard riding his horse through the highlands, looking for revenge. If you find yourself in Progreso late at night and hear the *click clack* of hooves, run!

In the months that I lived on the islands, I witnessed two surfers fall victim to the curse of the turtle, Paki and Lolo. Paki was a hard-charging legend in the bloom of his surfing life. He was always the guy to talk to, always on one of the biggest waves of the day, at the best parties, and always had a beautiful girl under his arm. When he was found hanging in his bathroom, most were shocked about the reported suicide. I believed the report to be bogus. I had seen him earlier that night at the *discoteca, La Isla*. He was doing his usual dancing with girls and high-fiving his friends. His smile and personality were as big as ever. I believe someone from the mainland whom he had pissed off or owed money to killed him and tried to cover it up.

The next tragedy was Lolo. He was a soft-spoken, humble human with a streak of wild. When a big wave at Loberia popped up, he wasn't afraid to turn around and go. I can still see him with a giant grin on his face bouncing down the line. He was an experienced and respected dive instructor. On one of his dives to León Dormido, his equipment failed, and he was found floating, dead. Both of these watermen were under the age of thirty-five.

Volcanic peaks broke through the clouds. I wondered which of the legendary locals would be on the island: Umberto, Rosita, Billabong, the Lobos brothers, Wilson, Bolívar, Giovani, Gordo, Mateo, Toto, or Eddie.

The plane arched over the island engulfed by indigo-blue water as ribboning Southern swell lines wrapped along the coast. I closed my eyes, diving deeper into the dream. My mind spiraled out of control before the brilliant blue tube, Mike's tube. My neighbor watched as I bounced with adrenaline in my seat. The huge south swell was the remnant of tropical cyclone Pam that had hit the Australian coastline several weeks earlier. Its energy reconsolidated along the roaring forties into a monstrous maelstrom almost the size of Australia. The bulk of the energy would be arriving the following day. How big would it be?

Javier and Ivan were there to greet me at the baggage claim. It is rare to see them without a smile, only two times that I know of. Once when Javier had a kidney stone, and the second time was when Ivan got smashed on the reef, compliments of Punta Carola. Negrito laughed at me as I barreled my amoebic blob of a surf bag past the gate, knocking over the bags in my path.

I jumped in the back of their white pickup and breathed in the island's enchanted air. The sun's fury made my skin feel like it was melting off my bones. We passed a school wall decorated with beautiful murals of wild sea creatures. The message read: "We conserve and protect our natural habitat." Was that what was really going on with the proposed five-star hotel at Punta Carola? What would happen to the marine iguana and sea turtle sanctuary? And what about the world-class wave? I grabbed a hold of the back hatch of the truck as we launched over another speed bump. Passing the bakeries, the sweet smell of chocolate donuts and *pan* overwhelmed my senses. I waved to the kids, hanging out on their bikes on the well-maintained sidewalk. You could feel their joy. I wondered what the island they inherit will look like. *Will there be anything left to protect?* Only time will tell.

Arriving to Casa De Nelly, my little paradise, I marveled at the wooden sea lion benches, hammocks, and the turtle-frigate bird chair. Relaxation. I waited under a shaded palm for them to show me a room. I had mentioned to them that I had made the journey with my friend Mike. Unbeknownst to me, Nelly heard this and became frantic. She said to Javier, "No one told me that Cory had a friend with him. I had Cory in for a single room."

Nelly returned with her usual happy face and led me to a room with two single beds. I thanked her and dropped on the bed drenched in sweat. *Que calor!* She later asked to meet Mike. I told her he was in the room. We entered.

"Dónde está?"

I pointed to the night stand were Mike's container was propped up against a light. She jumped back and covered her mouth in horror. Pointing with a trembling finger, she asked, *"Qué pasó??"*

I spun Mike's story. I assured her that he was a harmless and gentle soul. She normalized a bit, and told me that in Ecuador they have a custom of spreading the ashes of their loved ones around the edges of the property to protect the family. For Mike, a surfer, the ocean seemed like a fitting place.

That night I awoke to the arrival of Pam's energy. The roar of the ocean was broken up by the relentless barking of the macho sea lions patrolling the waters. In the *madrugada* (dawn), I ambled down the hill toward the pier. The pier and its docks danced in a sea-drunk *salsa*. The boardwalk was already under water. Carnivorous waves cresting over the pier pried my sleepy eyes wide open. The water-taxis that once filled the bay were gone. Spray in excess of twenty feet soared through the sky. Pier lights shattered with the ocean's power. What would that energy do to a human? How big would that be at Loberia? My stomach knotted like old, salty fishing line.

As the day broke, the giant south swell ignited the bay from *Cañon* to *Playa Man* and *Suicidios*. Hmm, a break called "Suicides," I wonder why. Could it be because the wave heaves onto exposed razor-sharp lava rock?

The coterie of hot-shot groms were all doing their thing at Playa Man, putting on a show for their bronzed *hembras (chicas)*. This was the most user-friendly and visible surf spot in town. It also happens to be directly in front of a university filled with female biologists. Suicidios drew the macho men, the guys with something to prove. I cringed watching consecutive guys get pulverized. Not a single wave was made. The reward was bar banter at Iguana Rock or Barquerro later that night. They would waddle in, chest puffed out (*pechón*), head held high as they asked, *"Dónde surfeaste?"*

"Yo surfé Suicidos."

"You did?"

What I watched were dangerous-looking beat-downs. No thank you. Please keep in mind that every spot has its day. And today was not the day for Suicidios. Among the aquatic carnage, I managed to get a few at a break around the corner. My session ended in a snapped board. Walking back, under the brutality of middle Earth's sun, felt like being burned alive. I fought my way back to Casa De Nelly for a *bolón* (a green plantain dumpling), a cold *maracuyá* (passion fruit) drink, and a much-needed siesta.

Que calor!

Sensory Overload

"The obligation to endure gives us a right to know."
—Jean Rostand

My thoughts refused to abandon the Carola hotel project; it sickened my soul. Was everything good in this world, here to be exploited, stolen, developed, consumed, and underappreciated? What could I do? Surf. Purge my malice-filled mind. As I pedaled my way up the hill, board in hand, against the torching sun, I could hear the steady banging of *El Cerro*. This once beautifully vegetated mountain peak was now reduced to giant hideous crater of scarred earth. Did my $100 park fee go toward the decimation of this mountainside? Could I get a refund? How deep would the destructive pit go? What happened to *conservamos lo nuestro?* The island conservation propaganda now seemed misleading.

Reaching the top of the hill, boiling in anger, my seething negativity evaporated in the glassy blue horizon. It demanded my complete attention. Golden sparkling gems glinted off the flattened sheet of water. The wind didn't dare breathe on the ocean's divine work of art. Undeniable gaiety pulsed through me.

The sun-glazed liquid rose to a pronounced pyramid, then unfolded beauty in both directions, not a drop of water out of place. Zero people out. *Could this be happening?* I "YEWED!" myself down the hill. Picking up speed, the wind caught my board and threatened to pull me off the road. Not today.

I locked up my brakeless bike and headed down the path. A few Galapageños, waiting for a taxi, saluted me with *"Buenas olas."*

I gave the guys, a *"Chévere"* with a thumbs-up and sprinted down the beach.

As I approached the water, five surfers headed out. So much for my solo session. They looked familiar. Three young bronzed Guayacas, Ecuadorianas, and their cool, bearded dad, escorted by my old Galapageñan friend, Gordo. Everyone knew what the ocean was offering. There were "smiles for miles" with the anticipation of the reward. Surfing, and the thought of surfing, lets the mind run wild with endless possibilities. Most fantasize about tubes!

"Tubaso!" Gordo yelled.

Paddling over the translucent bay, my skin bubbled with energy. Competitive paddling seemed out of place. I breathed deep and slowed down. I took a moment, for the moment. Sea creatures ebbed and flowed over the craggy reef below. Why can't life just be that easy? To my port, disturbed water molested the surface. A French snorkeler surfaced. She pulled her tangled, seaweed-like hair from the mask while the snorkel dangled in front of her mouth. She pointed below, gargling a single word in her heavy accent: "Wraya."

I slipped off my board and plunged into the blue magnificence. An eagle ray soared through the water like an eagle gliding through air. Its aquatic line was the epitome of effortless efficiency. Out of the corner of my eye I saw bubbles rise from the ocean floor. A marine turtle rested in deep meditation. Can anyone think of a greater way to begin a surf session? My inner wave-glutton made a suggestion: how about a wave?

Leaving the bay, the lineup beheld five-to-seven-foot waves pounding the reef. Another dark-haired Galapageño emerged from nowhere to my inside, Wilson. What a way to see someone after a five-year sabbatical from the island. His shirt had a photo of Cartman from *South Park*. It read, "Respect My Authoritah!"

Wilson, with the way he air drops into waves, commands respect.

His face lit up. *"A los tiempos hermano. Qué tal?"*

"Everything is good." I held my hands up to the surroundings.

His confident demeanor is reflected in his paddling. The peak was his. It was a full-on reunion when my old student Bolívar joined the party. *"Épico!"*

Wilson wasted little time asserting himself at the middle of the peak. His arms stretched out wide like a swooping albatross as he eyed his landing. He landed, leaning on his toes going left and pumped down the race track. The next wave saw Bolívar fall from the clouds, heading right at me. His expression looked calm in the face of danger. He grabbed his rail as the mouth of the ocean opened wide.

It was on!

Another perfect set approached, to be divided among friends. Tono, the bearded dad, looked over his shoulder, *"Por esos días surfeamos."*

These days are why we surf.

"Definitely!"

This is why I spent my entire adult life making decisions to be in these moments.

A turtle surfaced, keeping a curious eye on the peculiar humans. The face of the waves glowed in the setting sun. In California, we call this "the golden hour," the last hour of daylight. Swirling blues were illuminated in the golden light. In the presence of such enchanted beauty, it is easy to get caught spectating and not surfing.

A chorus of *"Dale!"* brought me back to the present.

"Te toca a ti."

My turn. On the boil, as a natural footer, going left was out of the question. The orange and purple parrot fish below got slurped along the bottom as the wave sucked off the reef. My hands cut through the water like a blazing hot knives through butter. The board and fins engaged as the paw of the ocean rose overhead. Two options were before me: one, rip the face off the lip, or two, look for cover. As an aging dude, I went for the latter. The wave threw open, revealing a vast spectrum of colors. The view melted my mind, short-circuiting in the sensory overload. Coasting to the channel, I closed my eyes. The visual sensation went straight to my soul. It felt like I had just gazed out of the eye of the universe.

"What a day!"

Riding my bike back in the dark, I heard the machines grinding away at *El Cerro*. My oceanic mirage had vanished, but I was still holding her charge. I decided to channel my energy toward the protection of this fragile ecosystem and the wave at Punta Carola[76]. *Maybe others will put more energy into protecting what they love?*

---

[76] I channeled my energy by picking up a pen and writing the following story.

The Punta Carola Experience

*"Our memories of the ocean will linger on after
our footprints in the sand are gone."*
–Unknown Author

Looking at old photos and thinking about the project proposed at Punta Carola made me nauseous. It was like losing a son after not seeing him for a while. No, that would be too generic, too clean. It was more like the movie *Indecent Proposal*, where Robert Redford offered Woody Harrelson $1 million to sleep with his wife, Demi Moore. After some brief discussions, the money prevailed. The relationship was never the same.

Well, the money is on the table.

The *playa* was once known as lover's beach, a romantic place to cuddle up on the sand among the iguanas and turtles to the lee of the lighthouse and well, make love. When I first asked the locals about the wave, most said *"tubaso"* and spoke of man-eating barrels the size of cargo ships. This extremely fickle wave was, is, and will always be embedded in local folklore[77].

That being said, you don't relive the flat days but the glorious ones. I present to you, The Punta Carola Experience, *la vida Galapageña* taken from a journal I kept when I was living on the islands in 2010:

It was 6am. The burning star, *el sol*, was still a force to be reckoned with. Roosters were wide awake, they've been up since 3am. My breakfast was laid out in the university cafeteria. All I had to do was show up. I gazed out into the azure expanse. The outer reefs "El Bajito" told me everything. If *Bajito* was breaking, feathering whitecaps plowing over a red channel

---

[77] I have been to the islands several times without seeing this wave break.

marker, Carola was on. My cold *maracuyá (passion fruit)* juice calmed my warming nerves.

Level 3 English Grammar began in ten minutes. Together we numbered six. On such a day, time slowed to a giant land turtle's gait.

"Did someone reset the clock?"

"No teacher, correct time. We still have thirty minutes."

What to do? The section was on the family. The teacher's notes suggested I play the unit CD. In those early days, I used the notes. I needed all the help I could get. It was a song, entertainment at the very least. I needed a distraction. The pulsing sea was breathing just outside the classroom walls. The song began, and sing we did. James Taylor's, "You've Got a Friend,"

"When you're down and in trouble/ and you need some love and care… You just call out in my name/ and you know wherever I am. I'll come running just to see you again."

I walked around the room, encouraging the students to sing along. The marker was our microphone. The five males in the classroom nailed it.

It was 9am. Class finished. Homework: Write about your family members. Describe them physically. Include what they like to do, their hobbies. Of course, there were many questions.

"Teacher, how describe?"

I modeled. "My sister's name is Suzanne. She is fifty years old, and she has red hair and blue eyes. She likes to drink beer. She always laughs at my father's jokes. Sometimes she enjoys going camping along the river. She doesn't know how to speak German, but she knows how to drink their beer."

After the questions were sorted, small talk followed. Some students can be like Pit Bulls: once they have you locked in conversation, they won't let go. Carola pulled on my vitals. I had to free myself. My heart pulled stronger with every beat.

This particular day, Guillermo kept on talking about how much his wife loves to cook onions for him. Extremely random, but yes, this onion conversation was keeping me out of the water while Carola was going ballistic. "OK, you are a very lucky man. Be sure to include the importance of onions, not just to your family and Galapagos, but all of Ecuador."

Am I a bad teacher? Debatable. But what about those times I stayed late, or all the outside material I brought in to class? Please keep in mind that Carola rarely breaks. Today was her day.

With the class locked up, I headed up to my dorm room. The hallways smelled of bleach and flowers; Ester was at it early this morning. Soon enough, she would be at my room. Upon my return, the room would be filled with those sweet, flower-scented toxins. AHHH.

It was 9:15. Board shorts on. I was already sweating like a pig, no escaping the intensity of the Equatorial *sol*. Shitty Sundown, Ecuadorian sunblock, ran down my face. My eyes burned. With my old faithful, my 6'9 Hennek pintail, under arm, I was *listo*. I mounted my beat-up, brakeless bike from Maximo, the university caretaker/concessions owner/ bike graveyard manager/permanently sunburnt from walking all over the island running errands for the uni guy. Once in motion, the gears began to pop. *Papapapa-Pow.* They finally chose a gear undetermined by me. Tourists gawked at the wild beast biking. I gave them the *"es normal"* look. Once the forward momentum began, a rewarding breeze greeted my skin.

Rounding the infamous loading docks of Predial, my eyes met a sea of smiles and a chorus of *"buenas olas"* from the dockworkers. They were offloading goods for the local supermarkets, perhaps, Galamart?

If only they truly knew what kind of energy was coursing through the ocean.

Rick's quad was there. Rick, a Northern Californian (NorCal) transplant, stalks the island for waves with a T-shirt covering his bald head from the sun's brutality. He was always a mellow and welcoming face, and his parked quad told me it was good.

I scurried along the path, hopping from one lava rock to the next and sprinting the sand patches. *Cuidado,* the geckos were everywhere and always one step away from getting crushed by frothing giants. The longer I did this, the more I reminded myself to slow down. How many toenails did I need to donate to these rocks? The narrow trail of approximately 500 meters wound its way through endemic fauna, primarily cactus and manzanillo trees. The thick vegetation amplified the experience, providing the perfect canopy and acoustics for the powerful surf. The booming crash was like a lightning strike to my nerve-endings. A slight opening in the thorny brush offered a sneak peek of sweeping turquoise avalanches.

I recovered my breath when I reached the beach. An inside wave ploughed past the lighthouse and sped down the point. I waited, watching Bajito, the outside indicator, for a set. Clearing the sunblock from my eyes, I found shelter under tangled bushes. I tried my best to put the brakes on my racing heart.

How big was it? The reports in those days were never accurate. Hawaii sometimes served as an indicator but angles and south swells could erase the swell's energy along the point. Was it going to be fun-sized or death-defying? The end result was like Forrest Gump's box of chocolates, "You never know what you are going to get." That was the thrill of surfing and the great unknown.

9:40am. The sun, ruthless. It singed my body like I was an egg thrown on a sizzling cast-iron skillet. Walking along the sand, I was once again struck by the sheer beauty of the place: the waves, wild vegetation, animals, and Caribbean-colored water. No wonder it's a marine turtles and iguanas nesting sanctuary. In the distraction of wildlife gazing, I realized that I was a kook walking down the beach with my sandals on. The sand of the cove has the coarse feel from years of the land-devouring seas. Rounding the well-defined bay along the lava rocks, beware. Large, unstable chunks of asymmetrical slime-covered lava rocks await. Eagerness has lost many fins, caused dings, and claimed toes. Not today.

The other potential hazards are the resting *lobos marinos* (sea wolves) that wait for you. They let you get close, and then give their best snap-growl -moan-open-their-jaws-wide-to-show-their-decaying-serrated-yell owish-brown-teeth-and-hit-you-with—that-vile-fish-breath. The sound is a cross between a lion's roar and a goat's baaahhh. They love to intimidate tourists. After the victim jumps back, they flop their heads down and resume their *siesta*. I envisioned them comparing notes at the end of the day. Whoever made the frightened human jump highest, won.

The south breeze ripped up the wave at the top of the point. The wind flew up the face, throwing spray as the toothy wave barreled down the point. Control the froth. Don't be hasty. Wait for the set to pass. Gauge the size, and time the paddle out.

Carola's enchanting blue lines built upon the horizon. As I stood atop the rocks, my lungs filled with energized mist. This feeling was best described by John Muir: "Enjoyment enough to kill if it were possible."

Viva Carola[78]!

This recent trip with Mike, Carola didn't break the entire month. Others said they hadn't seen her break in years. That being said, I will never be able to erase the memories and the sensation of flying across her gaping walls. I thought this would be *the place*-the wave where I could get Mike barreled. It would have been nice to end the story in such a way. But as the Arabs say, "It wasn't written."

On the last morning, I walked out with Mike to look at Carola one last time, maybe before she was violated and changed forever[79]. What could I do? I walked with the exuberance and giddiness as if I were about to surf her. All the old emotions pumped through my veins. I walked out behind the lighthouse and took a deep, calming breath. Removing Mike from my bag, I envisioned his eternal stoke stretching out across the sleeping sea. I dumped SOME of Mike along volcanic coastline. A perplexed marine iguana watched from a nearby lava rock. A sudden surge came and returned the ashes of my friend back to the sea. The iguana vanished.

Ashes to ashes. Dust to dust. Sea to sea. Hopefully, when Carola returns to power, Mike will still be there to look after me.

---

[78] One day I hope to have some of my ashes scattered here.

[79] Months later, the local population rallied together in a large-scale protest against the hotel project. Their bravery was rewarded, and the project was canceled. Power to the People!

Hijo de Dentista

"A hero is someone who has given his or her life
to something bigger than oneself."
–Joseph Campbell

Outside of town, waiting for gas at a *grifo*, I asked the man if he knew Pache. His golden-tooth grin stretched wide before he began chuckling.

"Pache, es mas conocido que la ruda."

He's better known than the Peruvian root-found everywhere and used for everything.

Everyone had an opinion about Pache.

"Es locaso," he's really crazy.

"Es bien soñador," he's a real dreamer.

"Es caballero," he's a real gentleman.

"Es una vida cajuda," he has led a foolish life.

"Tubos lo siguen," tubes follow him.

"El vendió su alma," he sold out.

"Pache has only had two loves in his life: The first was the ocean; the second was the ocean."

The common denominator is that when Pache is mentioned, the people energize-Latino.

An entire book should be written about Carlos' "story," and it would be *buenaso[80]*. A day in the life of Pache, sees the inconceivable conceived and the impossible made possible. In his presence, you will repeatedly

---

[80] If you go to Peru, the most common words you will hear are *buenaso* (really good) and *huevón* (friend, fool, or guy). Put the two words together, and you're Peruvian. How are these stories? *Buenaso, huevón! Note: based on phonetics, Peruvians often change the v to b and write: Buenaso, huebón!*

ask yourself, *did that really just happen?* It sure did. When shooting him a perplexed look, your gaze is met by his molarless smile (thanks to his *papá*, Leiter, the dentist). His weathered and caramel-colored skin is topped by a thick, black, resilient, sand-filled mop.

Pache had had an opportunity for a "normal life," but he gave up his father's dreams of being a dentist when he dropped out of dental school. Now, people tell Pache's tales of great heroism, herculean strength, romance, fights, rescues, and tubes. His life is what Don Quixote read about and could only dream of. For Pache, it's just called *la vida*. Surf stars travel the world making an excess of six figures marketing this glamourous, youthful, and rebellious lifestyle. Yet, one day with Pache would have most saying, "Damn that dude's radicality is untouchable." People like *Chingón* and Pache are the true underground surf heroes of the "third world." They have given everything to live this surfing life.

I will do my best to portray just a few of the many faces of this enigmatic chameleon, Pache. Welcome to the stories of the people's champion and the Wild Wild West of Latin America.

Pache the Enigma

Seven years ago, we stood on the edge of a sheer cliff over-looking the infinite brown. The dramatic dunes collapsed into a ravine glinting with broken glass, vials, and syringes. Prescott, who had been teaching English in the area, pointed to the placid Pacific. His eyes were hidden under neon yellow-tinted shades and a sun-bleached mesh hat. He shook his head at wind-driven whitecaps fizzling northward. Scattered rocks covered in seaweed poked up from the surface leading into a sand-filled cove. My neck and back baked under the fury of the Peruvian desert sun. Black plastic bags swirled in the howling offshore winds, carrying the memory of death wrapped in defecation. White-tipped vultures and frigate birds sailed high overhead.

Pres broke the silence. "I swear, this place gets world-class surf."

He flashed a broad *sonrisa* as he relived the glorious waves of the past. I wanted to believe. I turned around to a non-existent trail through a field of trash and asked, "How the hell did you find this place?"

"Pache took me here a while ago. I try to get Joe-another English teacher-to come here, but most of the time I surf the place by myself."

"Pache?"

"You don't know Pache??"

"No."

"He's a local legend! He was the first surfer in this area and pioneered most of these breaks. He has been surfing these points for over thirty years. This is a small town; I'm sure you will meet him soon enough."

I would learn the legend of the wave and of Pache. Both have many moods that I would come to know and love.

Pache the Lion Heart

The stage was set. My arrival to Pache's house saw a massive storm freighting up the coast from the depths of the polar seas. The buoys off the coast of Chile were reading fifty-six feet at twenty-three seconds. Given the southwestern direction, the bulk of its energy was aimed straight at the Peruvian coast.

Viewing surfing as a religious pursuit, we see each surf break as a place of worship; the sun, the moon, and the ocean as our gods; the tube as the Holy Grail, Duke Kahanamoku[81] or Eddie Aikau[82] as our prophets; and the ever-changing swell charts as our holy "book." Surfers check them hourly and live and die with their oscillations. Everyone knows, everyone speculates, everyone talks. Everyone except Pache. He's a surfer from an era that said, "Today, I'm going surfing." Did he know what the size of the swell would be? No. All he knew was that he was going.

I spent the afternoon hanging out with his dad, Leiter, a non-surfing

[81] A Hawaiian Olympic gold medalist in swimming turned surf ambassador and lifesaver. Many claim his surf exhibitions in Southern California in 1912 and Sydney, Australia in 1914 are what birthed surfing in these countries. His heroic surfboard rescues revolutionized lifeguarding and have saved thousands of lives.

[82] Legendary Hawaiian big-wave surfer and lifeguard, who repeatedly risked his life to save others. He volunteered in the Polynesian Voyaging Society with a crew attempting to retrace their ancestor's voyage to the Tahitian Islands(2,500 miles) on a double-hull canoe. They capsized in the open ocean, and Eddie decided to paddle for help. He, and his board, were never seen again. Yet his legacy and spirit lives on in the sea.

dentist in his seventies[83]. His genuine gaze and deep facial lines exude great wisdom and contentment. We talked of love, life, happiness and Latin American adventures into the evening hours.

I looked around and finally asked, "Where the hell is Pache?"

Leiter shrugged. "*Quién sabe?*"

Nobody knew.

Not even Pache's father, his roommate, knew Pache's erratic movements. Leiter's milky blue eyes dropped down to the streets below. Horns blared as we sat on the porch above the main strip in town. I had entered the land of noise making. Forget about an ordinance, from sunrise to sunset and all hours of the night, eardrums in Peru take a severe beating from the ubiquitous barking dogs defending their turf, to the high-pitched sirens of the *combis* overpowering the toy horns of the *motos*, to the triangle banging from a garbage man trumped by an enraged elderly man hobbling and screaming "Heyya!" A newspaper salesman, of course. Whistles, kisses, and cackles came from the pack of young males, "*chibolos*" gawking at a passing female. Emphatic "*oofs*" flew from the beer-slugging-circle of males out front of a *bodega*. Then there was the *soya*. Of all the obnoxious noises, la señora and her *soya* were peerless. Armed with a giant megaphone mounted atop a *moto*, she continuously circled the *barrios*. The señora's recording (selling her juices) looped on FULL VOLUME.

"*Señora llegó LA SOYA, chica morada, jugo de manzana, jugo de maracuyá, avena con fruta. Señora llegó LA SOYA....*" The sounds began at five in the morning and continued deep into the night. I wondered if the señora ever slept. When they passed, I asked Pache's dad, "Does that soya lady bother you? Isn't that repetitive announcement at full volume obnoxious?"

Leiter grimaced like I was pulling out one of his teeth, and said, "*Es insoportable.*" He continued shaking his head.

Like most small towns and our small world, a lot has changed and much has stayed the same.

Over the acoustic assault below, I could hear a formidable rumbling from the growing sea. Was Pache going to turn up for the approaching swell event, the swell of the year, the swell of decade?

Two days after lighting up the famed Chilean point break Punta de

---

[83] His office is just on the other side of his living room.

Lobos, tales and photographs spread of gargantuan surf. Surfers talk surf. SURF. Pico Alto was well over twenty-plus feet and proper Chicama broke. We all knew it was coming, but how big would it be at the spot, I will call *La Caleta?* This spot has been a long-kept secret between myself, Prescott, and Mark. That wave became our secret lover. For years, we became well-acquainted with her endless lines[84].

The break packs a punch. Surfing that wave and her relentless conveyor-belt current takes its toll on the body. At times, we couldn't find anyone who wanted to surf it. In the beginning, the wave seemed taboo, and the local groms stayed at a shadowed cove, a much smaller, softer, and user-friendly wave. So when one of the kids did paddle out at the point, it was *buenaso.*

I was eager to reacquaint myself with our desert flower. The peak of the swell was the following day, which was calling for eleven feet at twenty-two seconds. Walking to the point through the trash fields is a shock to the senses. An array of colored plastic bags fluttered around rocks and shrubs. Warped wooden and rusty shacks lined the path. Plastic bottles, broken sandals, and cardboard littered the landscape. A canine skeleton smiled from the sand below while the breeze sandblasted the fur from his corpse.

At the top of the pass, I was baffled to see that the virgin point break had been deflowered. For the first time, there were two cars parked atop the bluff. Neither of them were Pache's Sazuki. After years of tight-lipped secrecy, the point had finally been exposed. Loose lips sink ships. Now, there were not only cars, but also a small *casita* on the *cerro.*

Concha su madre[85]!

I had to accept that the times had changed. Who was I to say who can and can't surf here? I was just a gringo. Corduroy lines rose from the brackish horizon, which was dotted with oil platforms. The surfers jockeyed their position to intersect the incoming waves. One guy dropped in. The wave had a soft roll-in on the outside. Once the bending band hit the inside sandbar, it threw open. The guy raced in front of the

---

[84] One day with Pache, we named the three sections: Pachucho (Pache), la Preciosa (Prescott), Coreva (Cory).

[85] Commonly used throughout Peru. It means "damn." It originated from the phrase: *Vete a la concha su madre* (Go back to where you came from: your mother's vagina).

barreling locomotive. My nerve-endings were set ablaze. The wave looked as good as ever.

Enough watching, I flew down the powdery sand dune.

The offshore winds ripped at my board. I squinted as the sand daggered my tender skin. Along the slope, thousands of glass vials, syringes, and broken beer bottles twinkled in the sunlight while black plastic bags swirled in the wind like leaves in the autumn air. Some things hadn't changed. My eyes scanned beyond the unidentified ribs protruding from the sand to the slimy rocks for entry points. The rocks and currents hadn't changed either. Dynamic dunes shadowed the curved shoreline.

I remembered our horrendous clothes: we used to bury them to hide them from the local thieves. Yes, our clothes were stolen several times while we were out surfing. A tax paid for surf discovery and exploration. Yes, it was a far cry from tropical tubes, but nonetheless, it has a special residency in my heart.

Another line swelled along the point, and two *chuls* (unknown males) paddled for it.

They both dropped in.

"*Oye!*"

The guy in front, at folly, turned around and kicked off the wave. The other guy raced down the wave, but the whitewater mowed him down. The wall continued to spin off, unmolested.

I ducked under the first round of whitewater, tasting a trace of crude oil. Surfacing, I was whisked down the beach by the infinite sweep of the southern seas. Rounding the end of the point, I punched under the peeling lines. Making it out of the impact zone, I paddled hard as a guy flew off the back of the wave, landing right beside me. Too close to ignore, I engaged.

"Nice wave!"

Most dudes love it when you compliment their waves, an ego boost for the macho man. Instead, I saw an intense disdain. He stopped paddling, not a good sign.

"*De dónde vienes?*"

I instinctively responded with three words: "I know Pache."

Shaking his head, he paddled back to the top of the point. This used to be my get-out-of-jail phrase. Most guys responded with a thumbs-up, *chévere*, or a shaka. It didn't matter where I went; it had a perfect success rate, until now. Not only was there a small crowd, but some dude was vibing me, and I hadn't even caught a wave. Does he know that he just rode the *preciosa*? I bet he has never seen a proper wave link *preciosa* to *coreva* and have it turn itself inside out into a gaping, sand-filled cave. As I paddled to the outside[86], the negative vibes continued from this guy, whom I suspected to be from Lima. Why? Because I saw a nice SUV on the hill. Most locals up north can't afford such luxuries. Most have to scrape together all their *soles*[87], *dinero,* for a *combi*, colectivo, or cheap bus ticket just to get to the ocean.

Attempting to rally the crowd against me, he continued, *"Mira este gringo."*

One of the guys interrupted, *"Tranquilo, es local."* He motioned, like I was a part of the group. It was Camilo, a local body boarder. As they say in Peru, un *corcho* (cork).

Relieved, I paddled over to Camilo. "Where is Pache?"

He threw his hands up, *"Quién sabe?"*

Again, nobody knew.

Among the other surfers sat a Brazilian, with his GoPro, filming the "secret break" and the surrounding area, giving a Portuguese narration. *Are you kidding me?* The Limeño had a problem with me paddling out by myself, and this guy was here documenting everything with impunity? Where was the justice? I imagined he had paid to surf there.

Dropping in on my first wave, all the tension faded away. I was hit with a sense of gratitude. What a privilege to have glided across these powerful walls. With my legs warming and my heart humming, I kicked out. Lit with life, my smile couldn't be unglued. The waves took center stage for the rest of the session. Each set stacked higher upon the magenta pastels of the afternoon sky.

That night I awoke to Peruvian artillery shaking Pache's tin roof. My veins thickened. My breath shortened. I tossed and turned in the sand-filled sheets, thinking about mountainous walls of water.

---

[86] In Spanish, they say *adentro*, which means "within." An interesting oceanic perspective; whereas we "English speakers" view it from land, saying outside or out the back, farther away. I like *adentro*.

[87] Interesting, the name of the currency means "sun," coming from the Incas' relationship with the all-mighty sun god.

The following morning, looking out of Pache's two-story house, I could see lines cresting above the beachfront shacks discharging their heavy artillery. Pulverized vapor hung over the coast. I kept an attentive eye on the sea. Despite my tornadoing gut, I stuck to the morning ritual, *café y avena con fruta* with Renato and Frecesia, great Peruvian cooks also staying at Pache's[88]. During the morning preparations, the door blew open and slammed against the wall. There stood Pache, my hero. His eyes were alive and focused. We both knew where we were going. No more talking, checking, speculating-the day had finally come. Pache looked ready to retake his position at the throne.

Looking down the point, we saw that the ocean had turned into a wild and unruly beast. *Combi*-sized barrels sped down the point, unclaimed. No one was out. A vast sweep of turbulence tore down the beach. Endless, heavy-watered walls of dark chocolate layered the horizon. I tried to envision ducking under the rolling battering rams. *How the fuck were we supposed to make it out?*

Pache held a tight look on his face but smirked with eye contact. The set totaled twelve waves. I knew timing was everything, yet there was no way around not taking waves on the head. In the past, we would have deemed the spot maxed out, unsurfable. Today, we had a number of takers.

Nervous and excited banter ensued as we descended the dunes. I was not listening. The ocean had my complete concentration. But my concentration was derailed by a sharp pain in my right foot. Looking down, I saw a rusty nail extending from my bloody flesh.

I stopped.

As I pulled the nail out, I heard, *"Concha su madre."*

Pache turned around asked with a soft voice, *"Estás bien, mi gringa?"*

His eyes smiled. It was his gentle way of telling me harden the fuck up. I knew why we were here. My foot and tetanus were the least of our problems. Gustavo and Camilo paddled out first and got ripped down the point. The ocean lulled enough for them to make it out.

Perfect timing!

"Vámonos!"

The rest of us, Pache, Lucho (Pache's business partner and *pata*),

---

[88] They now work at a restaurant Mahalo in Punta Hermosa Beach, just south of Lima. The food is *buenasa, huebón!*

along with Darril (a fourteen-year-old local *chibolo* facing his deepest fears) paddled out. The paddle marathon had begun. The first duck dive revealed the power of the twenty-two-second period swell. I struggled to hold onto my 6'9, caught in the fury of the liquid blender. Rising to the surface, I took a giant gulp of air. The torrent sea cared little of our plight and charged at us like an enraged bull. I flipped the survival mode switch, and with all my being, stroked for the horizon. The following wave looked even bigger. Gustavo was in position. He swooped down the face and ducked inside the angry brown cave. My mouth opened as I watched the wave regurgitate itself and him down the line.

Tubaso[89]!

The bar had been set.

The following wave, Camilo's body went vertical with his flippers flailing over his head. The board skipped and bounced off the water like a flat stone on a calm lake. The inside section looked poised to devour him. He accelerated forward and just as the lip was going to annihilate him, he launched out the back. Like a flying frog, his legs split.

There was no time for congratulating. I kept paddling. Reconnecting with my breath, I regained my composure and paddled to the top of the point. I saw Lucho down the beach. He was going to make it out too. I looked for Pache and Darril. Where were they?

This wouldn't be good if Pache didn't make it out. Some had claimed that Pache had sold his soul because he and Lucho were taking people to this spot for profit. They also built the small house on the top of the point and were looking to sell more seaside lots.

A dot, almost half a mile down the coast, rose from the shore pound. Pache wasn't making it out. I felt for Pache. Not only were people calling him a sell-out, but now he just got benched by the very spot that he had put on the map. He returned to shore. Was his head down in defeat? No. He was running back up the point with added determination, ready to give it another go!

My focus returned to the ocean, which was trying to bury me in an aquatic tomb. I heard the chorus of *"Dale!"* from down the line. *Go!* The approaching wave blocked out the platforms. The offshore winds blinded

---

[89] "Aso" added to any noun makes it bigger and stronger, so *"tubaso"* would be a solid tube.

me as I hung atop the sea cliff. Did I really want it? I remembered Gustavo's and Camilo's waves and gave a few more strokes. The bigger board allowed me to roll down the face like a smooth drop on a roller coaster. Getting to the bottom, I looked back at the wave, dwarfing my existence. A long wall stretched out in front of me, and I weaved my way up and down its curvy face. It was brown-water snowboarding at its best! I eyed the exit as the wave built for a beach-thumping closeout. Popping off the back the wave, I had no time to relax. More chocolate avalanches were approaching.

After making it back out, I looked for Pache. He materialized out of the foamy froth way down the beach. He had punched through. His arms looked like waterlogged noodles. He slowly paddled his way up to the take-off zone. I guess this was the changing of the guard. Pache has been surfing here since the early eighties, so many placed him in his fifties. No one knew for sure. Maybe his glory years had passed?

La Caleta was about maxed out with sets in excess of three meters. The rapid current made positioning an endless struggle, but the energy in the water was electric. Everyone was screaming each other into some of the best waves of their lives. Limits were being pushed. There was no hassling for position, the perfect lineup. If you wanted one, it was yours. You could feel that this was not just an epic session but a historic one. This day would be remembered years from now. Finally, Pache got in position, the ocean climbed from the darkest depths of the Humboldt Current, the world's most nutrient rich ocean current. This was his moment. He had to go; the wave had clearly chosen him. The crowd went nuts.

"*Pache! Pachucho! Dale huebón! Yeeww!*"

As the wave bore down on him, it clipped him in the back. He was sent belly-flopping down the face at mach speeds. Just when we thought the whitewater had eaten him, he emerged from the angry white cloud. Pache snarled while holding on to the bucking bronco. His dark eyes bulged with the immense energy of the ocean. Watching him take off, I was reminded just how unique a person and surfer Pache is. There was no doubt that he is a goofy-footed surfer, right foot forward. But then why does he wear his leash on his right foot? He popped up, regular foot looking for the barrel and then changed his stance to goofy, also looking for the barrel. On the beast before us, Pache straightened out and finally switched to goofy. In doing so, it looked like he was going to let the wave reel down the line without him. A catastrophic beating looked inevitable.

What are you doing, Pache?

His eyes dilated. His teeth clenched. Then for a moment, all the tension in his body released, and he flashed his winning smile. He stood tall as the giant swallowed him in her colossal dwelling. Pache disappeared. Then like a sea-sorcerer, he reappeared from her deep bowels with his hand held high.

The crowd went berserk!

"Pache! Tubaso!"

I couldn't believe there was any doubt. He did what he has been doing since the beginning. I looked over to the crew and said, "That's why we call him the tube master."

"El Maestro!"

How could anyone who pulls into a barrel of that size be a sell-out? I understood how some of the locals were against surf tourism and exposing the break; on the other hand, if someone was to gain something from surfing, then why not Pache, *El Maestro*? He was the one who taught most of the locals how to surf in the first place. What has he given to the local surfing community? Everything, he has given everything for moments like the one we just witnessed. I don't know how many times he stood tall in such barrels with no one watching. I would call him the Jeff Clark, Mavericks Pioneer, of northern Peru.

Lion Heart.

Junior-La Historia de Esperanza

*"And, when you want something, all the universe
conspires in helping you achieve it."*
–Paulo Coelho

In 2008, surfing brought me to Talara (northern Peru), to teach English at the LyB Language School. I heard epic tales of the area and its perfect barreling sand-bottom point breaks. I had heard enough. So when Brandon, the flying Canadian, offered me a job, I hopped aboard Transporte Chiclayo. After teaching English at ICPNA Chiclayo (a chain school) for five months, working late nights and weekends while being micromanaged, I embraced the chance for change.

At Brandon's school, we taught a variety of classes throughout the day, from kids' school to Punta Arenas, a private school and community for the *petroleros* (oil workers), to night EFL language classes for teens and professionals. One of my favorite classes was my 6:30 Intermediate Integrated Skills Class. Some students were highly proficient, others knew a little, and some knew *nada*. The idea was to use a grammar book while integrating other skills: listening, reading, writing, and pronunciation. Before me sat a class full of overachievers, a teacher's gem in the desert. This class actually did their homework, asked the right questions (i.e., the ones I knew the answers to), participated, and most importantly, laughed at my jokes.

In this class, I remember a teenager who sat in the front. He came early to class and stayed late. He was always fully engaged and super-focused. His eyes glistened for grammar; he was always wearing a smile, always practicing his English, always hungry to improve himself. He hung on every English word. His jet-black hair was spiked forward, accented by his rock 'n roll and punk shirts. He was cool.

From day one, I noticed there was something different about him. He took copious notes, but had an unorthodox way of holding his pen. I've never seen anything like it. I was intrigued but wanted to be respectful of his space. His name was Junior (*Juniorcito* if you wanted to get cute).

He would later tell me his life's ambitions: he wanted to be an English teacher and learn how to surf. I tried to envision him teaching and surfing, but had difficulty. Based on just linguistic ability, he wasn't the best in the class. His *amiga*, Claudia, was the natural English Language Learner (ELL), but Junior was tenacious.

I was perplexed by his existence. Whether he had an accident or was born with this disability, the result was clear: he couldn't use his fingers. He walked fine, was articulate, and obviously didn't let adversity affect his attitude. He was the class's happiest and most enthusiastic star. What happened? I really wanted to know. In my country, we beat around the bush. We talk around things and try not to offend. In Peru and Latin America, there are no bushes to beat around; everything is direct and to the point.

"Junior, what happened?" I pointed to his hands.

Having heard this question his entire life, Junior took no offense to my query. In fact, he assured me that it was "not a problem." As he unpacked his "story," I didn't notice any remorse or self-pity. He said, "I'm fortunate that I wasn't paralyzed or killed." He was given another chance at life. And indeed he has been making the most of it.

So what the *concha su madre* happened?

First off, have I mentioned that Peru is the Wild Wild West? With no regulations, hazards become part of everyday life. Broken bottles, debris, syringes, reckless *combi* drivers, ravenous dogs, or moto-taxis driving down the road with four feet of impaling rebar protruding out each end.

The incident happened back when Junior was Juniorcito. What happened was a parent's worst nightmare. A five-year-old kid was playing at the neighborhood *parque* when disaster struck. The saying "left high and dry" comes to mind. He had been see-sawing with a girl when she decided she'd had enough. Junior's counterweight was gone. Gravity laid its heavy hand on him, and the next thing he knew he was flat on his back with no feeling in his body. Had he fallen that far? Not likely.

At the hospital, they noticed that a nail had inserted itself directly into his spine. Nails at a children's park? What the *concha su madre* do we do now? The community galvanized around the family; the accident had left him paralyzed. His parents were shocked but extremely responsive. They took him to a number of hospitals, which changed little. They eventually began to consider alternative treatments. Through the use of acupuncture, his mobility returned within a year. But the accident had cost him the command of his hands.

Seven years have passed since Junior told me of his dreams of teaching English and surfing. Roaming the sun-bleached streets of Talara, I wondered, *what of Junior?* I eventually ran into him living at the Waves for Development house in Lobitos. His smile and enthusiastic eyes were as bright as ever. I was taken aback when he opened his mouth. His determination and hard work had paid off. His English fluency was *buenaso*. He joyfully pulled out his cell phone and said, "Look, Cory, I'm surfing now!"

Mouth agape, I looked at photo of him streaking across crystalline water on a perfect little chest-high nugget peeling across the groomed sand bottom shoals of Lobitos. He was crouched just in front of a nice tube.

"What a wave!"

I fought back the tears, thinking about all the adversity Junior overcame to get in that perfect position, SURFING!

Changing the subject, I asked, "What are you doing for work?"

"I'm an English teacher at ICPNA Talara." Junior's eyes beamed.

"Really? Unbelievable!"

We decided that I would observe one of his classes. Like a proud parent, I watched him deliver his lesson with confidence and clarity to a classroom full of excited learners. His activities were varied and engaging. Before I knew it, class was over.

At the end, I let them know that all of his success was because of me. It was a bad joke, but of course, everyone laughed, my cue to exit.

As I drove south to Piura, his story rolled over in my mind. I thought about the strength of his soul and his commitment to his dreams. Many second language learners start off with similar ambitions, but few succeed.

I couldn't determine which I was more impressed with, his surfing or his teaching, probably the former. He mentioned that he drew the line at a meter and a half, a few feet overhead. Waves big enough to scare most landlubbers.

People have taken notice of Junior's growing talents. His friend and colleague Luis-Miguel gushed with admiration when he spoke about Junior. "There is nothing he can't do. In fact, he does things that many can't do!"

Junior continues to reach new plateaus, most recently in the worlds of painting and skating. I would later see some of his breathtakingly beautiful murals around Lobitos and his art gallery behind Cora's restaurant. He had told me that every seven years he was going to do something different. Junior is one of those rare people who excels at everything he puts his heart and mind to. His inspirational story reminded me of the quote from the book *The Alchemist* by Paul Coelho, "When we strive to be better than we are, everything around us becomes better."

He was indeed raising the bar for himself and his *patas* (friends). I'm excited to see what the future holds for Junior and how far he and his friends will soar.

Viva Junior!

Pico Alto, Manya

"The energy that holds up mountains is the energy I bow down to."
–Mirbai

I had already been in Punta Hermosa (beautiful point), a beach south of Lima, for a week, and like always, I looked to the ocean for salvation. I was desperately trying to erase *la perra* incident from my mind. It was a traumatic story involving a pack of feral dogs, a mastiff, and Chino's Pit Bull that I deemed to repulsive to share.

Chino?

Despite the fact that he's Peruvian, he said it's because he looks like a Chinaman. His black jerry curls bobbed under his hat as he laughed. His horizontal slits stretched. God, I love the directness of Latin American nicknames. His bloodshot eyes and his pungent aroma suggested an herbal supplement that added to his Chinoness. Chino isn't a local to the area; he's Cusceño. Coincidentally, he surfs. I asked him, "What is a surfer doing in Cusco?"

"Demasiada fiesta."

He shook his head for a moment then concluded with a self-induced laugh. As an owner of a Cusco *discoteca* on the tourist trail, there was no escaping the *fiesta* for him. Every night was another excuse to party: some Latina, some *gringa* volunteer, someone's last night, a lost job, a new arrival, one of Peru's many holidays and on and on. It sounded like Bocas all over again. It was apparent that the partying had taken its toll on a man deeply entrenched in his forties. His longing gaze past the gated walls to the gray sea told me that the ocean had brought him back.

Punta Rocas lay hidden beneath a sweeping fog bank, which depressingly blankets Lima most of the year. We sat in the car, looking into the milky white haze. Chino looked into the cup holder and picked up Mike.

"*Qué es?*"

"That's my friend Mike that I was telling you about."

Mike's story had Chino's full attention. I watched out of the corner of my eye as Chino stared deeply into the bottle. It was as if he were looking into a mirror, a portal into his own soul. His trepidation filled the *Camioneta*. Chino nervously joked that he too could end up in a bottle if he didn't change his ways.

I looked him square in the eyes and told him he was right.

When the gloomy fog lifted her old gray skirt, we were greeted by long, unbroken Pacific lines. The surf was pumping! Chino had an unorthodox surf style but wasn't afraid to whip it on a solid three-meter wave. We found ourselves in the lineup without a huge crowd, getting glassy-blue perfection. We returned from the water high on life.

Yes, I had surfed some fun waves, challenged myself at medium-sized Punta Rocas, but something was still missing. One box remained unchecked. At the pinnacle of the surrounding surf breaks sits Pico Alto. As the name indicates, it's a tall peak. How tall?

Locals use several words to describe it: *Una ola immensa. Olón.*

On a solid, long-period south swell, the peak can reach over ten meters in height. This wave is extremely heavy and garners respect from big-wave surfers around the world. My curiosity stirred. With my days in Punta Hermosa numbered, it felt like the right time to take a closer look at the notorious peak.

After our session, we headed to the local *cevichería*. They didn't have any fish, so I went for the *pollo tallarín* (spaghetti with chicken). Within an hour, my stomach constricted like a boa around an injured chicken. *Pucha!* As much as I love the food, Peru once again has taken its toll on my innards. Sitting on the toilet, I felt my life force being blown out of me. After a few rounds with the *baño*, I walked out to the bluff. The sleeping goliath had awoken. I couldn't tell how far out it was, maybe a mile? Out of the cold, seamless sea, the wave stood up to the sky, forming a very pronounced peak.

From a distance, it looked doable, not too deadly, just a drop and a mound of whitewater. Not wanting to do this alone, I reached out to

Chinito. I figured his carefree, nonchalant attitude would be perfect for the mission. I paced up and down the hallway, waiting for his door to open.

"Chino, Chino!" I was yelling louder and louder.

Nada.

My nerves started to take hold of my body. My stomach did Asian acrobatics. My mind shot mental daggers. I know how critical I can be of myself, and I still had a long road ahead. There was no escaping me, myself, and I, so I suited up, like a fool, a gringo *Cojudo.*

I tried calming myself by connecting with my breath. My senses returned to the present. The wetsuit felt cold and lifeless. The icy floor vibrated from the distant *cumbia* beat. Walking out to the cliff, I made eye contact with the *vigilante.* He sat is his small hut, guarding the neighborhood. He responded with *"Buenas olas."* He cast a mischievous smirk and raised his eyebrows.

"Yes, really nice!"

I was terrified. Before paddling out, I reminded myself of all the potentially life-threatening events I had survived. **The ocean had brought me here. I had to trust her.**

The large bay surged with agitated orange foam. A river-sized rip quickly slurped me "inside" the sea. I submerged my head. The cold water lit my endorphins. Paddling through a giant foam pit, I picked up a foamy orange beard. Too afraid to stop, I kept paddling. Any idle time could allow my abundance of caution to win the inner argument. At the very least, I could sit on the shoulder and assess the conditions.

Where the hell was the peak? LOST in the wild sea. It took another five duck-dives till I got my first up-close view of the infamous peak. The wave jacked up like an angry volcano. *Dios mío!* My heart fluttered. I paddled as if death itself were chasing me to the channel. Flooded with doubt and fear, I questioned if I could survive the beating. I can't do this. It was foolish to even be here.

Maybe this was just a surf check after all?

The other side of me insisted that I had to find the right one: there's no such thing as paddling out and not catching a wave, right?

After about forty-five minutes of set dodging, scared shitless, my doubts became incapacitating. The shifty peak leapt up and then the bottom abruptly collapsed. The drop didn't even look humanly possible. I kept telling myself, *one, and then you're done. I really shouldn't be out here. I'm not a big-wave surfer, nor do I have the equipment.* A wave swung wide and looked like it had a nice entry point. Wrong. It broke way earlier than anticipated and battered me down its disappearing face. Refusing to be bucked from my board, I eventually got to my feet as the wave fizzled out. Did that foamy shoulder-hop-of-a-wave count? My instincts had already answered that question. I paddled back out.

A human emerged out of the raging foamy currents, paddling over on a massive gun, a surfboard resembling a giant kayak. He was wearing a lifejacket, an inflated pad-not the inflatable vest. He grabbed the water with intensity and precision. His eyes lasered with extreme focus. From a distance, I could feel his piercing gaze. His salty face tightened as he paddled over.

"Qué tal?"

His tone and body language said it all: "What the fuck are you doing out here?"

I had no answer.

He paddled past, saying, *"Vamos. El mar está chico tienes que aprovechar."*

(I had to take advantage of the ocean while it was small?)

What planet was he from? He headed straight for the peak. These were some of the biggest waves I've ever seen in my *perraso*[90] life. He signaled for me to follow him.

I had no choice.

Sí señor, hellman. As we got farther out, massive volcanic peaks overwhelmed the horizon. I heard the word, *"Munyu"* as he too scratched toward the channel. Each wave climbed higher into the sky. The last wave erupted spray past the heavens. We narrowly escaped. I felt a surge of awe and terror in the presence of such open-ocean energy.

As the set subsided, he spoke. *"Sí, está grande."*

It was big. At least he acknowledged that.

"Esta ola tiene mucha poder."

He continued to speak to me as if he were both instructing me and scolding me. His final tip was to never try and duck-dive the wave because of its power. Minutes later, we both found ourselves out of position as

---

[90] An inexperienced surfer in Peru is known as a *perro* "dog." In English, we call this person a "kook." Surfers are a welcoming group, aren't they?

the South Pacific unleashed another round of leviathans. He looked at me, signaling he was going to throw his board. I thought I could make it around. Next thing I knew, I had a giant 10' board coming straight at my head. I followed suit, and left my board. I braced for impact. Buried under salt water, I felt strangely comforted knowing I had someone next to me. Back on the surface, we corralled our boards and quickly bolted for the channel. Luckily, only one wave steamrolled over us. The universe yawned, and we propped up on our boards.

"*Soy Andres. Yo vivo acá.*"

He pointed over to a clump of hillside houses. I had no clue which house was his, but I imagined it was nice. My eyes refused to leave the horizon. Andres grabbed my attention with his booming voice, "People don't paddle out solo here." He then relaxed and explained the lineups. I figured my 8'4 Linden mini-gun and I would just sit inside of him, as he had a 10-foot rhino chasing board with tremendous paddle power. After a few pathetic attempts at catching a wave, my doubts resurfaced. I continued with the excuse, had I had a bigger board, I would have caught it.

As if tired of feeling my conflicting energy, a monstrous wave charged me. There was no hiding. No excuses. The peak swung wide and inside of Andres. I was in the spot. I found myself on top of a canyon staring down into the blue abyss. I popped to my feet with the bottom dropping out. The freefall drop shot my organs up to my throat. I felt the board disconnect from the wave, *manya*. Here we go, the worst beating of my life. My arms spread wide, struggling to hang on. The balls of my feet dug into the board. The fins reconnected with the wave and shot me off the bottom toward the safety of the shoulder. I was going to make it. Adrenaline pumping. "Yew!!"

I emptied my lungs. My chest stretched open. So much for acting like I had been there before. I didn't care. I had caught a proper wave at Pico Alto! By today's standards, big-wave surfers would call the day marginal, but for me, it was monumental. Paddling back out, my body hummed. This was where the surfing addiction comes from. One more (*una más*) became two and three.

With the shades of afternoon darkening, and four waves under my belt, I determined I'd had enough. I felt lucky to get a few and not meet my salty grave, yet.

Remembering his comment about not surfing alone, I waited for

Andres way inside in the channel. He paddled deeper into the sea in search of his last ride. He went for one, contorting his body back and forth, straining every fiber. Nope. My heart dropped into my stomach. The sky blackened with the arrival of hulking sea monsters. It was the biggest set of the day, and there was no escape for Andres. He wore the wave right on his head. I reckoned that his chances of surviving were much better than mine. I scanned the cauldron of whitewater. A piece of his board surfaced, viciously tombstoning back and forth. I cringed, trying to imagine all the tension on his leash and limbs. His head shot up from the boiling whitewater. His arms looked heavy as he grabbed his board and paddled over. With night overcoming the somber sky, he issued the word, "*Vámonos.*"

"What a day!"

I thanked Andres for his local knowledge. Without him, there was no way I would have positioned myself for those waves. *Manya!*

Riding another oceanic high, the wheels once again pointed *sur. Southward.* Deeper into desert of the unknown.

The Path to the Surf House

"Forget the self, and you will fear nothing."
–Don Juan

Chile and its unruly energy has always scared the shit out of me. The country knifes down the Pacific like a dagger straight to the heart of Antarctica. Cutting down the "Roaring Forties," its shore is constantly battered by swells from some of Earth's most violent storms. Now add frigid water, volcanic eruptions, earthquakes, and tsunamis. My knees were quaking before I crossed the border.

Beneath the growing fear, there was hope that Mike's wave lay further down the road. That hope pushed me across the border, under the giant roadside star that read: "Chile."

A man in green fatigues came marching over with confrontational eyes. He spoke a rapid type of pidgeon Spanish. All I understood was

"Bienvenidos a Chile. Cómo estai?" Welcome to Chile.

I responded with a naive smile.

He narrowed his coal-colored eyes as if offended by my stupidity. *"Cachai?"*

"Come again?"

Just when I thought I was getting a handle on Spanish, I got Chiled.

He pointed at the stuff inside the *Camioneta,* then pointed to an X-ray machine inside the customs building. The word that had me concerned was *"TODO."*

I opened the back hatch to verify, "Everything?" I shot him an incredulous look.

"Sí, tiene que bajar todo."

Unpack my entire mobile home? My body language read, "This sucks!"

Sensing my hostility, he responded with more coherent Spanish. *"Esas son las leyes Chilenas. No estamos en Peru."*

His voice sounded of uncompromising authority. What I understood was "These are Chilean laws; this is not Peru." The message: You have to follow the rules here, unlike Peru.

He stepped back and joined the rest of his rigid cronies to enjoy the show. The daunting task of unloading my sandy shit-pile lay before me. Once again, I was an *extranjero* spotlighted in a foreign land, a spectacle. It wasn't just the officials who were eyeballing me but the entire pedestrian borderline. They shared the bewildered look: who is this gringo? I heard a soft *pobrecito* from one of the señoras while I dragged my bloated amoeba-shaped, dusty board bag past them. A man looked at me with empathetic eyes, and said, *"Que cagada!"*

I dipped my head in agreement.

Back and forth. Back and forth. It felt like a public chastising. My will and spite kept my head held high, not allowing them to break me. My personal debris piled high upon the sidewalk. Three hours later, I returned to the official and pointed to the empty *Camioneta* and said, "Anything else?"

"Listo," he said curtly while tightening his black gloves.

"Oye, carabineros." He signaled with a swift overhead motion. A K-9 cop led the charge.

My nerves warmed. *Tranquilo.* My mind sailed to Arica and its heavy waters. The ocean was close; I could taste the salt on my lips.

The dog's bark disrupted my aquatic daydream. The *carabinero's* eyes enlarged like a fat kid looking at a dessert menu. Drugs? I knew I'd never brought anything aboard the *Camioneta*; then I remembered the hitchhikers and other suspicious characters hanging out in and around her. I held my breath. *BREATHE. INHALE. EXHALE.* The well-groomed golden retriever paced around the area where the kitchen supplies once were. The *carabinero's* suspicious eyes read, "You got something to tell us, gringo?"

I shrugged my innocent shoulders. They ordered me to fold down the seat. A honey-coated bottle fell from in between the seats. The dog pounced on the opportunity to lick the shit out of some honey imported from Peru, Piura's finest.

"It looks like the dog is hungry."

"*No, no tiene, hambre,*" he retorted, with a fresh coat of blush upon his pronounced cheekbones. His eyes dropped to the ground as he corralled his lustful companion and issued the magic word: *"Pásale."*

Off to the races! Off to unlock the mysticism that is Chile! The final American frontier! After loading my belongings at a back-breaking pace, I counted four fingers between the sun and the sea. This meant I had about an hour of daylight[91]. The wind-whipped ocean meant onshore wind, not a welcomed sight-except for aerial surfing, not me. Nonetheless, a spot-check was mandatory. I began looking at Google Maps, having done zero prior research. **At least I had been consistently unprepared throughout the trip.** Why change now? I figured just south of the city was the famed *Isla*, and the legendary wave El Gringo. This wave was known for its brute force; dangerous rocks; and steep, hollow take-offs. Like so many other spots around the world, the wave is compared to Pipeline in Hawaii. They call it the Chilean Pipeline, and the city of Arica, the poor man's Hawaii.

Going through the big city, I was struck by the sheer magnitude of the port and number of containers and tankers. Commerce was bustling. I was rerouted from the *Panamericana* to some back road due a military march. The area seemed guarded and ready to stave off any northern aggression. The soldiers marched heavily armed with their killing machines.

Weaving through the congested urban streets, I relied on sight and scent to find the beach. The beach I found was clearly not El Gringo, but I had found water. As I got out to stretch my cramped legs, the cold Chilean wind ripped through my tattered sweatpants and instantly shrank my *huevos.* The cool waters off Peru now seemed tropical. Time to layer up and ask for directions. The ocean, a chaotic unorganized mess of ferocity, hammered gnarled rocks. The cold breeze chilled my aging bones. *Que frío!* Was I really going to try and surf that?

Thus began the routine that accompanied foreign territories and scary waves. The concoction of self-doubt, intimidation, and fear swirled in my blood stream.

I decided to ask a family picnicking at a grassy oceanside park.

---

[91] Special thanks to a woman I once dated named Red who taught me that trick. I also wouldn't bet against her in pool!

The man quickly rose to receive me. His handshake was extremely firm.

"*Hola, cómo estai?*"

At the border, I learned that this was the Chilean version of *cómo esta*.

"Excellent, thanks! I'm looking for the beach known as El Gringo."

The *padre* turned and told the family they were leaving. Was it something I said? The family began packing up. I was confused. Do I just leave or stand there?

Feeling my angst, the man returned. "*Somos Chilenos o Chileneses. Síganos.*"

"Really?"

"*Sí, claro.*"

He creased his lips, displaying his bold chin. I couldn't believe how quickly they were willing to change their plans to accommodate a complete stranger, a gringo, to a wave called El Gringo. I hoped they were not expecting some sort of surf exhibition. My confidence was hovering around zero. I looked in the mirror, saw wavering blue eyes of a dirt bag whose pronounced mustache gave a slightly misleading air of confidence. The bubble vest complemented by some green-stained and deteriorating sweatpants completed the image that read: "I just drove down from California, who gives a shit."

Returning to the task, I tailed the family up the coast. My heart warmed, recalling all the random acts of kindness found across the Americas. These people, who have suffered so much at the hands of our corporations and government, drop everything to help. Maybe I just look like a charity case?

If you answer that question now, I won't hear you.

My guess had gotten me close to the target; I was just two kilometers too far south. As I drove down the narrow bridge to the *Ex Isla del Alacrán* (Scorpion Island, named after the island's scorpion-shaped hook), the south winds ripped across dark water. Powerful, jumbled-up lines wrapped around a small cove. The small waves trickled in to form a left. The predominant south wind was offshore and kept the surface texture smooth. What filtered in was just a fraction of the size of what loomed on the other side of the *Isla*, El Gringo. Around the corner, clouds of whitewater erupted over flesh-eating volcanic rock. I could feel the intensity of the wave. There wasn't a surfer in sight; no way was I paddling out to try my hand at blown-out Chilean Pipeline. I was relieved and worn out from the border dance with the *carabineros.*

The entire family sat in the car with the windows up, sipping *mate*[92] (herbal tea), observing me observing the waves. Even the sun was cold. I walked over.

"Do you know of a good, cheap hostel in the area?"

Once again, the man said, "*Síganos!*"

His wife hopped out of the car and jumped in the *Camioneta*, and we were off. She skillfully guided me around the busy streets of Arica. She had a determined set of eyes that said, "This gringo is going to find his destination." Quick and easy, we arrived at a place called the Surf House.

Before the woman returned to her family, I said, "You must have a lot of faith in strangers, riding around with an unknown man."

She said, "Yes I do. My hope is that you go back to your country and tell your friends about Chile, so more gringos come down."

A handshake did the moment a disservice. **I gave her a hug and felt proud to be a human, which in turn, motivated me to return the good vibes down the line.** I was blown away, and I hadn't even gotten in the water yet. She had completely offset the *carabineros* and the border EVENT. She departed with the words "*Bienvenidos a Chile.*"

I had a newly found optimism for Chile y los Chilenos. It's amazing what a simple act of kindness can do.

A chalkboard in the middle of a small surfboard read: "*Bienvenidos a Surf House.*" As I entered the place, a nice-looking *mina* (girl) greeted me. I dropped my backpack and looked around. I knew I was staying, but just wanted to get a feel of the place. On one side, there was a coffee shop with pastries. It looked comfortable and clean. The surfing photos seized my attention. Waves of unimaginable size, of which man did not have the capacity to paddle in to. They were towing in with jet skis.

The *muchacha* approached, pointing to the photo. "*Es el dueño Kurt.*"

Holy shit, the wave looked to be about fifty feet on the face, and the hostel owner, Kurt, was surfing it.

---

[92] Very commonly drunk in the "Southern Cone": Chile, Argentina, and Uruguay.

"Amazing!"

She let me continue wandering. Taking in all the big-wave shots throughout the place and all these big-wave riders calling the Surf House home sent a terrifying shockwave through me. Of them, one of the most accomplished big-wave riders of all time, Shane Dorian, referred to Kurt and the Wave House as his family. I could only imagine the waves they had charged together. I felt dreadfully out of my league.

Maybe I should have ended the trip in Peru? I quieted the self-doubt and said, "I will stay for about a week."

Her face perked up, and she assigned me to the upstairs dorm.

The energy at the Surf House hostel churned pelagic emotions within. I felt the power and proximity of Earth's bottom, without even entering the water. I had difficulty subduing my fears. The unknowns of the area terrorized my mind. Maybe a few drinks would help extinguish my firing nerves? I was on vacation after all, and I had just driven to Chile (eight months and more than 15,000 miles later).

Bursts of laughter erupted from the downstairs lounge. Minutes later, I had a long line of Chilean craft beers sitting before me. Jorge, the beer pusher, was Chile's great ambassador. Jorge appeared to be in his early twenties with short, black hair accompanied by a baby rattail, pretty standard for a traveling-circus-technician. He was the only *Chileno* staying at the hostel; the rest of us were foreigners. He was the face of Chile and eager to educate us on Chilean slang.

Cachai weón? (Do you understand dude, friend, or fool?)

He was also impossible to say no to. His persuasive and genuine smile encouraged overindulgence. Heavy fermentation flowed deep into the night.

Yes, there was a surfer. His name was Nick, from Vancouver Island, stout beard, built like an ox, anchor tattoo on his chest. He frequents Chile and had posted up in Arica for weeks, or was it months? His brodown of the land and sea was exhilarating and further inflamed the nerves. His hazel eyes rolled back into his head as he uncivilly laughed about the punishing waves. His wild eyes beamed with oceanic energy. His love for surfing was undeniable.

He spoke of a huge, barreling wave in the Atacama Desert. After hearing about Nick's first experience there, a two-wave hold down[93] made me almost wet myself. Imagine this burly Canadian telling you of a wave pulverizing him and filling him with fear. If the wave did that to him, what was it going to do to me? My body filled with fear, then beer-then more fear and more beer. *Ahh, fuck it. Maybe a few piscos to celebrate life?*

And no, this wasn't Peruvian pisco[94]. This was 100% *Hecho en Chile. Viva Chile!*

The Peruvians are quick to counter, *"Quién hizo Pisco primero?"*

For me, it didn't matter who made the liquor drink first; that first night my sheets were luffing in gale-force winds. The plan was to do dawn patrol with Nick, and a German named Lars, who said he wasn't drinking. He was focused on surfing. SMART.

In the morning, I awoke to a thumping cranium. My new best surf mates were gone. First official day in Chile, blowin' it!

I must have made a great impression on them. Last night, I swore the *Camioneta* and I would be ready to charge El Gringo at first light. *Que cagada!*

I collected myself and headed down to the carpark with indifference to the anguish and self-loathing bouncing between my ears. The sea wore a silky-smooth blue gown. The tide seemed too high with waves unloading right on the rocks, not what you want for a barreling wave of consequence. Each violent crunch further enflamed my swollen blood vessels. I figured I would watch the boyz and see how they did. They were the only two rubber men floating in the water. I was impressed with Nick being able to drink all night and be the first one out, the beauty of youth and being a surf maniac.

A Chilean approached. *"Cómo estai?"*

"I'm hanging in there. Thanks."

He cast me a dubious look. *"Weón, huele como un bar. Huele a Pisco."*

Remembering what Jorge had taught me, I responded with *"Mi primera noche en Chile fue la raja."*

My first night in Chile was the ass (awesome-badass).

He responded with unexpected laughter and new-found friendliness. I guess *la raja* was the magic word in his book. He proceeded to educate me on the area. Apparently, among the boogie boarding community, the

---

[93] Buried under salt water for two consecutive waves.
[94] Pisco Chileno is much sweeter than the Peruvian version.

wave is known as Floppos, named after a boogie boarder who pioneered the spot but then passed away in a car wreck. He added that a pro surfer named Seabass (Sebestain Zeitz from Hawaii) loves this wave and comes all the time. The entire time my eyes were fixed on the lineup. Were the boys catching anything? It looked slow, except for the waves blowing up the rocky shore. I didn't see anything positive for me to paddle out. I gave it a pass. Live to fight another day.

Back at the *hostal*, I met the myth, the man, the legend: King Kurt. He probably stood at about five feet. Though he was small in stature, he carried a strong, confident aura. I could tell he knew and had felt things that most mortals never would. Witnessing and feeling the power, glory, and fury of the Roaring Forties and Humbolt Currents had rubbed off on his being. As I've seen with many surfers, the oceanic experiences shape how they conduct themselves on land. Despite my initial intimidation of him and his big-wave resume, he was quite friendly and helpful in describing the surrounding area and the waves. Not all the waves in the area are death-defying, just the ones Kurt seeks. Surfing giant waves is what he lives for.

Death would be the theme of the first few days. Kurt too had recently lost a good friend, a Peruvian big-wave surfer named Aldo. He finished a Pan-American *moto* race in first place and let off the gas as he crossed the finish line. The guy behind him was at full throttle, attempting to overtake him. He caught up to Aldo, resulting in a deadly collision. At those speeds, both were killed instantly. They had a paddle-out for him at Pico Alto. The ocean was as flat as a ceviche cutting board. I imagined a much easier and less blood-curdling paddle-out than the one I'd had. As the ceremony commenced, the crowd began to undulate with swell. The undulation rose higher and higher, until the sleeping giant awoke. Kurt believed it was a result of all the energy in the water, big-wave riders coming together, and Aldo sending them some love. It was the perfect send-off that saw many of the guys get some solid rides.

I thought back to Mike's paddle-out and how special it was. The flatness of Wrightsville Beach left no doubt that none of us bros were getting any rides.

The ride I was looking for still eluded me. I had traversed almost the entire continent looking for this send-off, closure. *Would Mike's barrel ever come?*

Talking more with Kurt further filled me with dread. He too was thinking about heading south to the right. He thought we could maybe tow into a few. He suited Nick up in the inflatable jacket. Nick looked like a deer in headlights as the vest compressed his large lungs. We laughed to ease the tension. Kurt felt our nervous energy and pulled the inflation. Nick quickly ballooned and more laughter followed. I turned around and looked at the photo of Kurt towing into a fifty-foot wave at *El Buey*. It seemed like a twisted joke, thinking about the beating that the wave would inflict. What was I getting myself into? The neurons were ablaze, thinking about towing into a giant cavern and barreling Mike. Was this how it was going to go down?

The second night in Arica was a sleepless one. It wasn't due to surfing El Gringo the next day, which was forecasted to be slightly overhead; it was actually the swell behind it that was getting Kurt excited. In our shared dorm were a few girls all curled up in their cozy beds, deep asleep. Tomorrow, they would take the ten-hour bus ride to San Pedro (the Atacama Desert, the world's driest desert)[95]. The Lonely Planet guide was securely packed in their oversized backpack. Their iPhones were fully charged. They had not a care in the world. I envied them. My thoughts returned to doom, drowning, and an aquatic burial.

---

[95] It rains less than an inch here each year.

Kurt and the Right of Fright

"It is not death that a man should fear, but he should fear never beginning to live."
—Marcus Aurelius

Kurt parked his big, black rig on a hill overlooking a dirt lot. His truck proudly donned a bumper sticker that read, "Go Big, Go like Aldo." He extracted his yellow 8' Bushman semi-gun. It dwarfed my 6' Klimax quad. The sight of his gear left me feeling outmatched and that I was making a terrible mistake paddling out. After taking a quick look at the conditions, Kurt decided the tide was too high. He opted for his nine iron. Yep, he was going to crack a few balls waiting for the tide to drop. He started hacking away, lofting balls over parked cars below. The sun came out, and he took his jacket off and talked surf with his buddies. His black T-shirt read, "Sex after Surfing." After about forty-five minutes of good times and whacks with his *weones* (friends), Kurt decided it was time to paddle out.

I followed Nick to the keyhole, a small break in the lava rock that channeled out into the lineup. I tried to ignore the pieces of rebar sticking up from toothy volcanic rock. Nick looked back and said, "It's an easy paddle-out." He then laughed himself off the rocks into the turbulent gray whirlpool. The surge swept him over the mine field of razor-sharp mussel-urchin-covered rocks. I stood there feeling my pulse in my throat. The surge deposited him on the side of a boulder. He clung to the rock with one hand as the ocean rushed over. The sight had me asking, *what the fuck am I doing here?* Nick pushed off the rocks again to scratch under a thick slab of barreling water. He just managed to sneak under it and was out. Easy?

I needed to get out there and think less. Otherwise I would be the dude who just stood in a wetsuit at the keyhole continuously wetting himself. Kurt had already established himself among the tight pack of surfers. He lined up a wave and took off sideways, sliding down its vertical face. He outran a carnivorous cave and in seconds was paddling back out for another. His hair was still dry.

Jumping off the rocks, the cold water hit me, which electrified my senses. The current was ripping toward the snarling rocks. I didn't look back, I just kept stroking. Making it out, I took a moment to gather myself. I knew if I sat too long, my nerves and joints would freeze up.

After nabbing a small inside wave, I reminded myself that this was surfing. I had done this before. The waves became less menacing, and I had a blast surfing clean overhead barreling waves with ten guys out. On land, we toasted with a round of Heinekens under the warming sun. The moment faded, and then it was time to pick up one of Kurt's kids.

The little five-year-old grom took shotgun and talked little. He didn't surf but liked soccer. One would think that all of Kurt's kids would be hard-charging ocean-goers. But Kurt matter-of-factly pointed out that you have to give the child the space and freedom to become who they are supposed to be. After getting to his house, I saw a few of his kids run up to the truck to greet *papá*. The smallest one swaggered over. His eyes held Kurt's wild intrepidation. The future of Chilean big-wave surfing stood before me. It's interesting to think about how different siblings can be. *How can one be drawn to a dormant grass field and the other to outrunning cold-water avalanches?*

My mind didn't venture too far away from the upcoming south swell. The time had come. The peak of the swell was just two days away. When driving through the Atacama, it's better to leave late in order to avoid overheating. Hey, what about the "no driving at night" rule? I'd like to see you question a man of Kurt's ilk, who might put you into the biggest wave of your life. My lips remained pursed. With a glorified hellman in the car, what could go wrong? No one was going to mess with us.

Then we got stopped at a *carabinero* checkpoint.

Before he opened his mouth, I said, "We're coming from Arica and going to a city south of here."

The man cocked his head sideways and asked, *"Por Qué hablas bien español?"*

Never had I heard that one: "Why do you speak good Spanish?"

"I learned from talking in the streets."

He gave us a nod of admiration and waved us through.

"*Pásale.*"

In the setting desert sun, Kurt pointed to the hieroglyphics carved in the nearby hills. These difficult-to-discern lines reminded me of Nazca. Perhaps the same girl with the etcha-sketch came through the Atacama Desert, or was it extra-terrestrial visitors? I tried my best to focus on interpreting the lines and not on the possibility of drowning. The deep magenta glow upon the cooling desert put my hyperactive mind at ease. I lowered the windows to breathe it in. The stars hovered just above the swells of sand with the Southern Cross illuminating the way.

The *Camioneta* was filled with talks of Pinochet, the seven ruling families who control the majority of Chile's resources, and how Chile has modeled its government and healthcare system after the United States.

I found Kurt's "screw-the-system" approach to be very refreshing. He devoted the majority of his energy toward his passion and his family. He hadn't let the pursuit of excessive wealth infringe upon his liberty and freedom. Some have suggested that he increase the size of his *hostal*. His rebuttal: Sure I will make more money, but with it will come more employees, more problems, more stress, and ultimately less surf time. Why would I need to do that when I am supporting my family just fine?

I swallowed the urge to say Amen.

He continued on about his friend providing medical attention to him and his family without buying into the corrupt healthcare racket. Amen.

Brake lights painted the desert dunes red. Kurt threw his hands up in protest, "*Maldito taco,*" and exited the *Camioneta*. He said nothing more. I was too intimidated to ask him where he was going. He disappeared down the road. With his destination unknown, our destination without him, our guide, was even more unknown. I guess hellmen don't do traffic like the rest of us suckers. After thirty minutes, the crawl of the *Camioneta* quickened to a walking speed. There was still no sign of Kurt. Nick and I joked about him not coming back. Maybe it was some sort of hellman test, leaving us to find our way to the break?

The *Camioneta* was toting serious gear like never before: tow boards, ropes, jackets, and CO2 cartridges. After five kilometers traversed, one hour gone by, Kurt's silhouette nonchalantly ambled through the red sea. *Es normal.* He told us he'd gone for a run. He needed some exercise. He can't stand being stuck in a stationary car. He informed us that there was bad accident ahead; we later heard that it had claimed four lives.

The detour banked a hard left. Traffic looked like it was dropping off the side of a cliff. Kurt looked at me with stern eyes and said, "It's like surfing: when I tell you to go, you go." The line of cars dropped down the face of the hill and funneled onto a bumpy dirt trail. The car in front of us slowed. Kurt gave me the look: "Go!" The adrenaline pulsed through me as the *Camioneta* climbed the bank for the pass. Kurt dropped his head in approval. The next car was on flat ground approaching a curve. Making the pass, the *Camioneta*'s tail blew out before she grabbed hold of solid earth. Driving had never been so fun.

Fully aware of the wisdom beside me, I did my best to absorb and learn as much as possible. When Kurt spoke, I listened. When he said to do something, I did it. Was I a grom again? I didn't care. I had something to learn from someone who has such a unique approach to life and surfing. The experiential wisdom that comes with riding giants makes the rest of life's trials and tribulations matter little.

He mentioned how it was important to stay positive and relaxed in bigger surf. Keeping everything light and being confident settles the nerves and is much more conducive to pushing limits. The life-jacket and jet ski assist add confidence. I kept thinking, *Do we really need to tow in? Is it really going to be that big?*

With an entire civilization erupting from the desert, the *Camioneta* was once again on crowded city streets. Mufflerless with the side pipes roaring, she set off car alarms, announcing our arrival. As I lowered the window, the mist filled the Camioneta with the ocean's electric charge.

When we got there, Kurt's friend described the surf as "*Está pequeña.*"

OK, small. Maybe I can sleep tonight after the long journey through the world's driest desert? Resting my head on a small bunk bed, I listened to the sea. Periodically, out of the stillness of the night, the air shook with the ocean's ominous voice. Small? My veins swelled.

The next day by local standards was small: two meters and building. Firing rights in a big city with no one out, *En serio?* One of the guys at the *hostal* said, "Beware of the gremlins."

"Gremlins?"

"Yes, the body boarders. Once one of them gets wet, they rapidly multiply."

Everyone laughed. After looking at the breaks and the mobs of boogie boarders, I realized that his statement held some validity. The right, maybe due to its power and size, lay unmolested by the gremlins. They say the wave can break as high as the beachfront buildings. I had seen the photos of building-sized waves.

BREATHE.

Checking the surf in shorts and a T-shirt made me feel like I was back in San Diego on a warm, windless winter day. What a difference from the north. Paddling out, we saw the first line raise up on the reef. The deep cobalt blue lightened as it discharged its load. As it peeled down the reef, I was struck by its mass and ferocity. Could I survive that hold down? Nick turned to me, laughed, and proceeded to the take-off. I followed, thinking, *Nick's going to get me killed.* The day finished with some amazing rides. Did we see Kurt? No. We figured the waves were too small for him.

The question the following morning was, what lay behind the blanket of seething mist? It sounded like a war zone. BOMBING! There was tense energy as we suited up. The swell had stepped up another notch, so I opted for the 8'4. Nick was on his trusty 6'8, his biggest board. He of course nabbed the first one on the inside. I watched him drop down a velvety blue mineshaft. My eyes followed the back of the wave unloading down the point. A huge wad of spray flew through the air. I guess he made it. He paddled out with a grizzly grin on his face like he had just stolen some kid's lunch.

My turn.

An immense blue mountain lumbered over the horizon. My body went numb. Paddling into position felt like an out-of-body experience, probably because my body wanted to be somewhere else. I free fell down the sheer face. Making the drop, I squared off the bottom and prayed for the channel. I could feel a huge cavern breathing behind me. As the wave compressed, it shot me out to the shoulder like a cannon.

Flying to the safety, oceanic energy burst out of me like a high-pressured fountain. My leg started uncontrollably shaking. *Was I having a seizure?* No, it was 100 percent pure adrenaline! I sat in the channel to recover my trembling body. Wasn't this what surfing was all about? Getting yourself in difficult positions, and hopefully, surviving. The greater the difficulty, the greater the reward. My reward was still pulsating through me.

Nick paddled for the next wave and missed it. You could see the frustration on his face. I knew he wouldn't miss the wave behind it. He tore into the water, lining up the wave. He breathed fire down the face of the dragon. It piled upon itself, and tossed him through the air. The spray fanned off the peak of a wave so large that it created its own weather pattern. I saw his fins slice through the air. His body hovered over his board. He stuck the drop, engaged his rail, and leaned into a wave easily three times his size. The board knifed through bluing water as he transitioned his weight to turn up the face. The cascading whitewater hammered down just feet from his tail block. The wave let him slide around into the pocket and sent him racing into the channel. His mouth was a giant donut of disbelief. He looked at his hands as they shook with adrenaline. We had experienced a new classification of waves: limb shakers.

It was a dream session. Did I bring Mike out? No way. This session was about pushing our limits. We were surviving, not tube hunting. The moment never felt right.

What about King Kurt? Unfortunately, he had back spasms that forced him to sit out the swell. I wasn't worried. Kurt had and will see bigger and better waves than I can comprehend. He later pulled up to the *hostal* in a forty-foot RV to take Nick back north to Arica, normal.

That afternoon the dry desert winds blew offshore as the swell continued its coastal battering. Thoughts of the backpackers in the Atacama Desert made my chapped lips crack. I smiled about the absurdity of going out of the way to seek out more desert. I looked for shade and climbed the *salvavidas* (lifeguard) tower for the best seat in the house. With the sun plunging into an oil-slicked sea, we returned to our seaward gaze, caught in her powerful spell. As another set layered the golden horizon, the lifeguard broke the silence. "*Todavía, el mar no está en su máxima expresión.*"

The ocean isn't in its maximum expression, yet.

Zona Patagónica-The End of the Road

"Happiness and unhappiness are one, only the
illusion of time separates them."
—Buddha

This trip has not been governed by rigid schedules and seeing-doing everything, but on feel. Mendoza, as beautiful as it is, didn't feel right, so in the *mañana,* I continued onward toward Bariloche and Patagonia. In Mendoza, a Che told me to avoid the old mountainous road running along the Andes. "Stay on the principal highway!" He told me of his friend's near-death experience walking three days in white-out conditions without another person in sight. No thank you.

After nearly two full days of driving, I rounded another blind turn. The vista literally ran me off the road. I had read about the beauty of Patagonia, but to experience it firsthand evoked emotions that words cannot describe. After nearly driving off a cliff, I pulled over on the shoulder. An explosive celestial blue lake mirrored the faint white strokes hanging above. The plateau's reddish clay pastels bled into the waterline. Backed by the snow-covered spine of the Andes, infinite pines layered the landscape. Cars sped around the corner with indifference.

I climbed to the roof of the *Camioneta,* stretched out my wings, and claimed it. The past and future converged in the glory of the present. My emotions erupted outward. The floodgates opened. As my cheeks chilled with tears, I wondered if the surf trip was over. How could it get any better?

I thought about the surf video Wes had sent from the bottom of the world. I had heard reports of hurricane-force winter winds from Antarctica lashing the archipelago of Tierra del Fuego. Winter surfing in Antarctica?

My mind migrated to my happy place, the warm sands of North

Carolina. Hurricane season was coming. What was I doing? I was still clinging to the idea of Southern salvation. When would I ever be in this position again? What inconceivable adventures waited ahead?

After several days among the boundless beauty of Villa Angostura's lakes and mountains, the road called. Onward, over the frozen tundra. As I rounded a sharp curve, a backhoe struggled to pluck a truck from its icy grave, a product of a vicious *vado* (dip). I proceeded with "an abundance of caution." Returning to the Pampas (plains), where "winds own the land," the *Camioneta's* worn-down suspension wobbled in the pummeling gusts.

Dark, industrialized sprawls became my existence. My days consisted of *vados*, *baches* (potholes) and tractor-trailers. The pale sun offered a flicker of hope only to be suffocated by the dreary shades of urban gloom. The dark, dreary days of the Southern Cone clumped together. The lack of waves in my future was beyond dispiriting. What was the objective now?

A billboard for whales in Puerto Madryn answered my query.

Outside of Puerto Madryn stood a man *tirando dedo*. The hitchhiker was from Spain. His name escaped my unfocused attention. Fresh off the plane, his eyes glistened with optimism before the great unknown. He had given up his sedentary life to travel and live free. The Spaniard talked of his plans to hitchhike north, possibly to Central America. I listened with a half-interested ear. My ten-month trip and its thousands of miles astern had taken their toll. Aside from my borrowed funds evaporating[96] and my credit card debt piling high, I missed home.

Where was home?

Ah, my mind flew back to summertime along the Jersey shore. My mother was there on the beach in her chair with her feet buried in the hot sand. She was surrounded by the Shusters, "family friends." I could feel their joy radiating from that little chunk of soft sand. My mental flight was snapped back to reality with another tooth-rattling *bache*.

In the absence of hunting waves, my soul felt tired. The Spaniard questioned my vitality and purposefulness. I struggled to find an answer. We took a short trip around the bend to look for penguins. There were none. I didn't care. The Spaniard and I uneventfully parted ways, and I returned to the cold drabness of my existence.

---

[96] Thanks to my brother Leon and Mariska for loaning me money to continue on from Peru.

Where was this fifty-hour drive to the end of the world heading? For what, a photo? To say I did the Americas? To get Mike pitted? Fifty mph winds in subzero temperatures cutting through icebergs didn't seem like a good resting place for Mike. It seemed like hell, an icy one.

Tierra del Fuego translates to "land of fire." Why? Because of volcanic activity? No. When Magellan and the early explorers arrived in the region, the night skies were torched with coastal fires. The locals were known as *Fueguinos*. I tried to imagine the warmth of a raging bonfire. I couldn't. The cold had its icy grip around my soul.

An abandoned boat lay heeled on the edge of the frost-bitten highway. Icicles hung from its keel. The quick diversion of attention on a slight *curva* gave way to a slide. I helplessly gripped the wheel as the *Camioneta's* back tires slung across the road at high speed. I wondered if I was going to be crushed and put out of my frozen misery. I held on for the ride. Luck would have it that the ice worked to my benefit, and the *Camioneta* executed a perfect 360. The tires finally grabbed the road and shot me forward. I let the *Camioneta* slow to a stop and sat there, panting. The *Camioneta* shuddered under the wailing winter winds of Earth's bottom, *el culo del mundo*.

I took a breath and looked over my left shoulder, *gwanakos* (similar to a llama) filled with curious fear bunched behind a wooden fence. I couldn't help but think of El Salvador, and the unfortunate factory workers laboring like beasts to provide us, *"First World"* consumers, with cheap clothing[97]. Inhaling another cold breath, I stomped on the gas pedal. My eyes were glued to the road, which was buried under snow and ice.

The end was near.

Empty parked cars lined up before a sign reading, "Estrecho de Magellan." I stepped out to take a look at the historic Strait of Magellan. The waterway looked like white horses galloping upon tormented death. My body quivered in the biting wind. The conductor swayed his rigid body back and forth.

"Cerrado. Cachai?"

---

[97] El Salvadorians got the name Gwanakos from the Peruvians who operated a hydro-plant in San Salvador. After working them extremely hard, the Peruvians applied the name Gwanako to the population. It still is used throughout Central America. Not all El Salvadorians like this term, so use with caution.

Chileno?

Yes, there was another border crossing to Chile; there would be one final crossing into Argentina and Ushuia, "The end of the world." I found a restaurant and hoped for the best. My frozen bones tentatively began to thaw. I kept my mind busy by thinking about my middle school social studies class with Mrs. Mucci. In the sixteenth century, Magellan discovered the strait, which made for a much quicker passage between the two oceans, avoiding the treacherous Cape Horn. I imagined that Magellan and his men weren't dumb enough to be in this region during winter. Would I be stranded at the strait for the season? No way was I turning around.

Just as my spirits were dropping into oblivion, hope battered across the whitecapped horizon. Salt sprays flew through the frosty air as the afternoon ferry ploughed across the savage sea. The ferry conductor motioned us to our cars for loading. People bundled up and waddled like stiff penguins over black ice.

Entering Argentina for the last time thrust me into another blizzard of paperwork, insurance, and pesos. I was told that I needed snowchains. I let the official know that the *Camioneta* and my Tacna tires could handle it. After a sneering stare, his furrowed brows loosened, and I got a gruff "pásale."

The final border crossing; I felt relieved, tired, and fucking cold. After twenty-six crossings on expired tags, I was *done*.

Once a place of exile for prisoners, Usuhia marks the end of the Andes mountain range, which abruptly plummets into Beagle Bay. The average temperature for winter months (June, July, and August) is 0 degrees Celsius with wind chills well below. Sunset saw the sky blush a vivid shade of pink and orange upon the towering spires, a divine vista. Bathing in the sunset's glory, the end, a surreal setting frozen like a block of ice, I exited the *Camioneta* to experience it. My peace was short-lived as a taxi hammered his horn. The *Camioneta* was protruding out on the road. OK, OK *tranquilo*.

Usuhia, the edge of Earth's rim, is a great marketing scheme for tourism. As they say along the tourist trail, "Time to DO Ushuia." Thousands of people come each year to boast that they have traveled to the end of the world, but have they driven? Many have. This trip has been done before.

There is always someone who has done it faster, more extreme, and better than you. I even met an Indian guy who was cycling down, and he didn't even know Spanish[98]. Then there are the cup drinkers: overlanders who put a mug in Prudhoe Bay, Alaska, and drink from the Bay. Then they run the gauntlet of the Americas and drink again in Beagle Bay.

Every now and then we have to follow. Honoring the touristic nature of the place, I slid down the road to the icy bay. From the sheet of ice stood the picturesque sign that read, "Ushuia-*Fin del Mundo*."

I figured it would be a nice way to commemorate the end to my ten-month American odyssey. Gliding over the ice, phone in hand, I stopped a family and asked, "Excuse me, could you please take a photo?"

"No, estamos por salir."

What? After 26 *aduanas*, 12 countries, and 35,000 kilometers (around 22,000 miles), she couldn't spare 10 seconds of her time?

I didn't argue.

"Very nice, thanks."

After a prolonged glare, I unleashed an uncivilized laugh from the pit of my stomach. An embarrassed Argentinian offered to take the photo. I extracted Mike and put him up on the sign like he was looking down on me.

The picture earned eighty-three electronic validations.

I later found out that there was an outpost twelve miles farther south-the OFFICIAL southern-most point. Did it matter? What would that do?

No más sur. I was done.

---

[98] A guy recently just walked the entire continent. Maybe someone will crawl it or walk it backward?

Hasta Luego, Chelandia

"Try something different. Surrender."
−Rumi

At the end of the road, people asked, *"Y la Camioneta?"*

Everyone had a different opinion about the *Camioneta*: gift it, scrap it, abandon it, sell it, drive her back to where she came from.

Most people suggested that I just abandon her.

"No problema, no pasa nada."

It was easy for them to say no problem; their names weren't linked to the title and registration, nor had they spent the last 10 months with such a loyal travel companion. I checked with *aduanas* to see if maybe I could donate it to a worthy Che or organization.

NO, was the response.

I circled back to the first mechanic who offered me cash, *abajo de la mesa*. He said he would trailer the *Camioneta* to the *campo* where she could roam free in the open fields. His name was Eduardo, owner of a stout moustache and a pair of cold eyes. At the very least, he represented the working-class Latino who liked to operate outside the system. My kind of a guy. It felt like I had sold my child to a doctor. I gifted a great deal of camping gear and cooking supplies to Eduardo. What remained, I crammed into my board bag and headed for the hotel. It was sad to leave her, but the sun had set on our story. *Hecho. Chau, Camioneta.*

That night I celebrated the end of the journey with a good *Bife (steak)* and a few glasses of red wine. My thoughts returned to what I had just done. DONE. With my flight the next day, the image of home grew warmer.

Three hours prior to my flight to Buenos Aires, I began searching

199

for a taxi. The receptionist wagged her finger and said, *"Hoy hay una manifestación de los taxistas."* Taxis on strike.

What were the chances?

She informed me that they were blocking the streets to show their disapproval of the local government and its inability to maintain the roads. After driving the suspension-busting roads, I had to agree. But why start today?

I had to chuckle. Of all the hurdles, this was nothing, right? Surely someone would continue working. She shook her head, "Everyone strikes. If they don't, the others will damage and vandalize their cars."

There had to be a way. Maybe I could hitchhike or flash a few bills? An hour later, there was a lull in the action. A few taxis broke free. There was no way this taxi was getting past me. Like a *policía,* I blocked the road and *Latinoed* him to pull over. The driver maintained a stressful grip on the wheel. His radio roared with static and frantic voices. The street closures blared over the speaker. There were blockades on Nueve de Julio and hostile marches on Avenida San Martin. It felt like the end of the movie, *Gangs of New York* where civil war and riots were breaking out all over the city. After ten minutes of riot-protest dodging, the *taxista* pulled over. He slammed the wheel in frustration and said, *"Lo siento. No hay una manera llegar al aeropuerto."*

No way to the airport?

"No. There has to be."

I wasn't getting out of the taxi. I had gone too far. I explained what I had been through to get to this point. The miles, the strife, the defeat, the glory. He nodded and dropped the cab back into gear. Thirty minutes later, after exploring the underworld of Ushuia, *los caminos escondidos,* we arrived at Aeropuerto Malvinas de Argentinas.

I knew we would. Mike was still with me.

Wes seemed disappointed about the end of the surf adventure. He wrote, "I thought you and Mike would keep going." I wish I could, but the reality was that I was physically, emotionally, spiritually, and financially drained. I felt fortunate to have tasted the *tierra* and sea of the Americas, but the Pathfinder and I had run our course.

Surely, after driving to the end of the world, I would feel some sort of resolution, right?

Wrong.

I still had a profound sense of incompletion. Mike's remains still rested in my hands.

Departing from Ushuaia felt like the trip was over; I had no idea that it marked the beginning of the end.

September Sessions

*"You didn't come to the world. You came out
of it like a wave from the ocean."*
–Alan Watts

Hurricane season is always a roll of the dice. Who will cop the wrath of Mother Nature? Everyone who lives along the Eastern Seaboard and the Caribbean knows that it is part of our existence. Storms will forever be, and surfers will forever sea. When I was a teenager, hurricanes filled my soul with a wild and exhilarating trepidation. My summer clock revolved around tropical updates and surf checks. This is what I live for.

Moving back East to work an office job in Pennsylvania brought internal conflict. Sure, I had clawed my way out of debt. Sure, I had a steady paycheck. Sure, I was making my family and society happy. But in my heart, I was suffering. I found myself going through the motions, pretending to care. Binge drinking was my escape. The seasons, like the swells, rolled by. My soul withered under the fluorescent lights; the smell of hot plastic and coffee made me nauseous. As I sat at my desk watching the squirrels frolicking in the setting summer sun, the same question returned: How could I focus on material wealth and acquisitions while Mike's ashes collected cobwebs? I couldn't. Something needed to change or my dreams would be buried under obligations and the endless pursuit of possessions and personal power, *money*.

After cutting the chord of comfort, quitting my office job, it was time to return to what I knew, the ocean and chasing storms. Despite my enlightenment and being rooted in the present, I dreamed of the future. Which storm would be Mike's session? I looked at all the hurricane names: would it be Nate or Jose? Of course, Mike would like to have his day with a swell produced by a hurricane with a male name. Indigo blue cylinders spun within.

With September rounding the corner, the tropics flicked a switch. Oceanic combustion, three tropical systems churned across the Atlantic. My mind fluttered. Patience. Like they say in Hawaii for the contest in honor of Eddie Aikai, "Eddie calls the day." For them, this means twenty to twenty-five foot Hawaii swells, which translates to thirty to forty-plus-foot faces. Based on that spiritual logic, I concluded that Mike would call the day. Despite all of those glorious sessions down the Americas, Mike's moment never came. Oliver, from Salina Cruz, consoled me at the end of the trip. "It would make sense to get Mike barreled where he came from, North Carolina, with his people." He was right.

The barrier islands of Cape Hatteras seemed like a good place to start.

Super storm Irma broke records in 2017, maxing out with wind speeds of 160 mph before demolishing Florida. The swell charts looked gigantic. I had my eyes fixed on Hatteras. The internet was loaded with shots from the previous Gert swell. Thousands of surfers gawked at the images of dredging, aquamarine barrels. For the Irma swell, Jason Brant was already there. Everyone else in our crew bailed.

Five in the afternoon. The wheels of my Silverado, *the Camioneta II*, screeched out of the parking lot. I had liberated Mike from his cobwebbed tombstone in an office space and got him back on the road. I knew this trip south, three years after his passing, was a one-way trip for Mike. I felt it.

Three in the morning. Buxton, North Carolina arrival.

The next day saw north winds that led us to southern-facing beaches. I remained calm. Climbing the berm at Frisco, it was clear there was no "Frisco inferno dance" to be had. Brant's barrels would have to wait. Mike clearly called the day OFF.

Not to worry, there was plenty more swell on tap with Jose following on Irma's heels. My internal compass had led me to this moment, so why question it? We considered heading to meet Vic and Adam in Emerald Isle. Brounion?

Jason wanted to keep hunting, but the ocean and conditions had other ideas. As Gerry Lopez's book indicated, *"Surf is where you find it,"* and it was in Emerald Isle, Bo. Jumping back in the car for another extended drive, I reminded myself to keep the faith.

Emerald Isle saw clean, fun, head-high conditions. Barreling? No way. The backside of the swell looked to be the call for tubes in Hatteras. Returning north to New Jersey was not an option. I was committed to see the vision through.

Jason headed back to Wilmington, and once again, I was left alone to dream of Mike's pit. The emotions poured out of me as I found myself circling back up to Hatteras. I knew I couldn't sustain this emotional rollercoaster much longer. It wasn't healthy. **The end is where you find it.** Liquid grenades bombed the roadways with heavy, tropical energy. Squirting through the flooded streets, I made my way to an abandoned house and parked for a few hours of shut eye.

I felt relaxed and confident walking up the cool, damp sand dunes. The sea oats gently brushed my arms along the narrow path. Looking at the Atlantic, golden sunrays flickered upon emerald water. There was one guy out in a seasick ocean. Like Gerry Lopez once said, "When in doubt, paddle out."

Paddling out (water temp a refreshing seventy-eight degrees), I saw a sign flashed in the form of a square barrel that piped its way down the beach—an oceanic wink. I tried to corral my firing nerves. I engaged the dude, a sponger. "Any fun ones out here?"

"Ahh, it's alright."

He looked disappointed. Maybe his expectations needed an alignment?

After a drift, I decided to head south. As they say in North Carolina, "It's always better down the beach, Bo!" Walking along the shore, a sweet Southern lady greeted me and said, "Aren't ya 'fraid of sharks[99]?"

I stopped. We smiled at each other. Looking into her sun-wrinkled face, I responded, "No. Humans scare me much more than sharks."

"Some dude almost ran me over crossing the street, probably a damn Yankee."

We both let out a hearty laugh. I wondered if she knew I was a Yankee.

"Yup, prolly. Those guys r always ruuushin."

Were them damn Yankees heading in the right direction? I knew I was. Sea oats waving toward the water indicated one thing: the wind had

---

[99] Isn't that a lovely thing to ask someone before they paddle out Alone?

clocked offshore. I entered the ocean. I felt the warmth of glowing embers in the pit of my stomach. Something special was going to happen.

A wave peaked from the bosom of the sea. Hurling me up through the air, I made the drop, looked for the exit, and got puffed out onto the shoulder. Not a super deep barrel, but the wave was definitely hollow. It was enough to make me dart back for another. Just south of me, a thick blonde mop of hair and a fluorescent green foam board disappeared and got spat out of a deep tube. He snapped his blonde mane hard against his neck before paddling back out.

That was Mike's specialty—flipping his hair. My mind raced. *Was this it? Was it big enough?* I started to think about the logistics of paddling Mike out. I looked over and saw a kid with a GoPro snarling from his mouth as he scoured the coast for clips.

I sat there for a moment, contemplating, *should I go get Mike out of the car? Maybe bring him closer to the action?* I looked to the horizon with my heart thudding. A rogue wave, the biggest of the day, lumbered across the sea. I tore at the water to escape its carnage. This big aqua-green cathedral of perfection went unridden. What was I doing? I looked over at a pair of kids hooting each other into the waves of their lives, not a care in the world.

Looking at the beauty around me, the truth struck me like a lightning bolt.

For the longest time, I thought that maybe getting Mike barreled would bring validation to his life and spin a positive from something negative. But looking back at his life, I realized it never needed validation. What happened was the way it was meant to be. I thought back to the beginning, my belief that Mike's day of redemption would come. Mike lived his life the way he wanted to, and his stories now reside in the hearts of many across the *Americas*-and now you.

The quest had taken me away from the purity of the moment, the purity of surfing. I know Mike, a pure and considerate soul, wouldn't have wanted to burden anyone. It was in this moment that I knew that my dream, which had taken me down the Americas, was a fallacy-a mere fantasy. A fantasy that would forever keep me running into the future, away from what I wanted, the present. No barrel would ever be good enough for Mike.

I needed to let go.

I thought about the essence of my friend. Did I see him standing tall in gaping barrels? No, Mike wasn't concerned about the glory of the pipe. He just wanted to make his bros happy. **The truth was that Mike was at his best when the ocean was at her worst.** Most dudes would be negative and bummed out, yet Mike reveled in those moments. The vision of his stretched-out smile, riding crappy boards across crappy, blown-out waves and having the time of his life, streaked before me.

When I let go of the pipe dream, the present came flooding in.

A fluorescent yellow butterfly fluttered in the warm, salty breeze while three pelicans banked over an unbroken swell line. Spanish mackerel busted the surface of the emerald-turquoise waters, sending menhaden flying through the air. The ocean began to fully express herself, and waves magnetized to my presence.

The present had never felt so good!

After the session, I called Jason and told him of my epiphany. He was confused.

"So you are saying you are going to drive away from perfect surf to come back to Wilmington? I don't get it. Why would you drive five hours?"

"I drove for ten months searching for this moment. What's another five hours?"

And so it ended where it all began: in sloppy surf down at Carolina Beach.

Of course, I stopped and checked one more spot on the way out. The universe spoke, a sun blazing down upon perfectly sculpted peaks throwing out left and right barrels. The ocean-sea sparkled. I dove into the tropical water feeling an ecstatic weightlessness.

The ocean had taught me invaluable lessons about myself, the present, and the fluidity of dreams.

It was true, Mike's flame burned twice as bright, and as I made the drive back down to Carolina Beach, his candle was still burning. That afternoon, and on into the evening, Mike's spirit shined upon us as he found his place in her brown waters. Mike loved the sea and inevitably became part of it. I felt comforted knowing he would be there, and the other watery regions of the globe, to watch over us, his seafaring family.

Epilogue

"Faith is knowing there is an ocean because you have seen a brook."
–William Arthur Ward

All rivers eventually return to the sea.

The river snaked its way along lush green landscape immersed in a tropical mountain dream. The river flowed from the sacred valley through the palm-shaded lagoon bending along a cobblestone cove. The ocean was near. Cobalt blue water rose up from the smooth sea. Adrenaline electrified my veins. Pelicans arched over the rocky coast, stretching their wings for the optimal glide, waiting. Waiting for that perfect moment to take their Pacific plunge. The water below boiled black with sardines. Green season, the rainy season, had begun.

Dark clouds loomed over the rolling, tree-covered peaks.

Surfers sat waiting. Waiting for that moment, that moment where anticipation and imagination become reality. A moment, like a wave, never to return.

Yet something in the moment didn't feel right. Tension built in my stomach with the sound of a fiberglass hull slamming into the sea. A *solo panguero* approached with the throttle pinned, carving inside the swell lines like a skilled surgeon.

His body taught; eyes hidden below a sun-bleached *Soberana* hat.

"La policía va a venir."

My gut squeezed.

Warning delivered. Task complete.

The *panguero* grabbed the throttle, knifed a quick turn and sped off for the port.

His words lingered in his wake like a sugar and *Seco(Rum)* hangover in the tropical heat.

Dark thoughts clouded the hot day. My mind returned to the known, the past. It had been five years since Mike's shapeshift, now surfing was outlawed, and the police were coming. As a foreigner, this could translate to jail. The combination of jail and gringo resulted in fear, mental terrorism.

Jail? Dingy dungeon and shackles.

Gringo? I already felt violated.

NO.

ESCAPE!

Maybe head up stream and hide in the jungle?

The river held fish. The ocean, *mariscos*. And crabs! *Dios mío!* The Chachili, florescent orange and purple crabs, had emerged with the rains, and hermit crabs swarmed the beach by the thousands. But raw? My drifting mental landscape settled on fallen fruit, MANGOS.

I will SURVIVE.

"Fuera del agua!" a local screamed pointing shoreward.

Time to go.

The brackish, blue water churned as we scrambled to shore. I wondered how long we had till the *policía* arrived. The once funny, phallic-shaped rock in the cove now seemed menacing and repugnant. I longed for the safe comforts of the *casa*. My hands ripped through the water. FASTER. My breath failed to bring tranquility to my world.

My mind still processing the absurdity....

Since when was surfing a crime? What happened to surfing being a respected "mainstream" sport? An Olympic sport? Since when did this divine connection with Mother Nature serve as a justification for imprisonment?

What the fuck happened?

Coronavirus, COVID-19, a global pandemic.

I paddled for a crappy closeout, thinking about how quickly our world had changed from a virus 1,000 times smaller than a speck of sand.

In a matter of weeks, our world had been capsized and was now drowning in vulnerability. Fueled by misinformation. Mistrust. Violence. Hate. Manipulation. Corruption. Control. Chaos.

Whatever the perception, the reality was, our world, as we knew it, had been ground to a halt. Locked Down. Commerce stood still. *Tiendas cerradas.* The streets empty.

And this world, like a wave or a moment, will never be the same. The EVENT quarantined in time.

For surfers, this time translated to surf. We had taken a risk for what we love, and now we would pay. Surfers sprinted down the beach, stashing their boards behind palm trees and driftwood. No one wanted to be caught with a surfboard, *contrabanda*. Others jumped on *motos* and sped off to the mountains.

I was left holding my board flat-footed waiting for my ride at the end of the road. *The police would show up at any minute. I'm screwed.* Cooling tropical water dripped down my bare legs, erupting goose bumps all over my skin. I felt a gentle nudge on my leg. I looked down. Jack, a local mutt/car protector/chicken bone eater, stared up at me. He wanted answers. My decisions, LIFE, had brought me to the present, surely there was an answer. The answer opened behind me as my friends lowered their gate to their *finca*, REFUGE. There was still love and trust in our world. These small actions drive hope for humanity. We crouched behind the thick, tangled foliage and waited. Then we waited some more. Silence fell over the jungle below.

After receiving a message from town, *"Police never came."* we concluded our jungle scare was pure fiction. When I exhaled RELIEF and inhaled GRATITUDE, the present returned.

The sinking sun glittered upon unfurling lines rolling down the point. My heart danced upon the watery walls. Looking down at the beach below, life's brilliance beamed back at me. White cranes. Cormorants. Humming birds. Plumerias, white mountain flowers, ignited the seascape with divine beauty and fragrance. Nature, in the absence of man, was flourishing like never before. My body filled with awe and hope, a smile on my face. I returned my gaze to the phallic-shaped rock at the bottom of the cove. It glowed in the golden light, rocketing out of the water with glee. Had the rock changed? No, my perception had.

In a matter of minutes, my perception had changed my reality. *Collectively can we alter our perceptions to see that the Coronavirus is happening FOR our world?* The virus has given Pachamama, Mother Earth, time to recover. Clear skies. Deserted beaches. Open oceans. Some believe

Pachamama sent us this EVENT as a warning: change our systems and our perception of life, OR there will be no life. As author John Perkin's writes in *Touching The Jaguar*, "It's time to transform our world from a death economy to a life (sustaining) economy."

You might be asking, *what can I do?*

Follow your heart. Follow your heart to a life of passion and service for the greater good of our planet. Leverage your skills to sustain this passionate pursuit. Happiness, excitement and fulfilment wait for you in an infinite ocean of opportunity.

In surfing, a spiritual dance with nature, we let the ocean take the lead and believe in our instinctive adaptability to respond. Do we know how the wave is going to end? No. Do we know if we are going to make it? No. Rumi once wrote, "Let the beauty we love be what we do."

What is it that burns the embers of your soul?

Find it and fight for it. If you follow your heart, your passions, the universe will reward you.

The time has come to believe. I had pushed myself over the Latin American ledge in pursuit of a new dream. I was exactly where I needed to be, surrounded by the right people in this volatile time in history. All that was missing from my story was FAITH. I had to BELIEVE in the dream. The dream of giving back, breaking down borders, and bridging cultural gaps towards a better world for coming generations LIVES.

What happens next? That's another story.

What's your STORY?

Por Qué No Poetry

An Ode to Our Watery World

Wave is Me
Nature is FREE
World is BE

See the Sea

We sweat under the same sun
Breathe the same air
But our eyes
Fill us with lies
About who we are
Let us not look far
What do we see?
You, me, and the sea

Life

A life is a mountain range with summits and valleys
A tide with ebbs and flows
A swell with peaks and troughs
A journey
En-JOY!

Acknowledgements

*"No one steps into the same river twice because it is not
the same river, and you are not the same person."*
–Heraclitus

This is why we pick the pen, to bridge the gap of who we once were with who we are and lay the foundation for who we will become. We are a collage of everything that has come before us. I wouldn't be who I am, and these stories wouldn't exist, if it weren't for my friends, family, and all the CHARACTERS in these stories. Time, energy, and attention is the best thing you can give to someone, and Matt Munz deserves some sort of trophy for always lending an ear for my overactive mouth. And talk about talent, from the map of the Americas for this book to the video slideshow for Mike to the countless epic clips of nature and life. Gracias por la inspiración @rickyplace!

Special thanks to the Brant family for the trust and support to honor Mike. Wes without your endless encouragement this trip wouldn't have been possible. The Endless Summer lives on!

My parents for their continuous support on this wild ride. Mom for passing on her adventurous, compassionate spirit and for cheering me on when I was a kid from those fly-infested beaches while my friends and I surfed west winds. Grandma Renee, whom I never met, who talked my grandfather Lee into buying a house on Long Beach Island(LBI, Life's Best Investment). This investment birthed my love for surfing and this book. All the credit goes to the ocean for kicking my ass and opening my heart. Her perpetual pull sculpted these tales; I was merely a conduit #seaservant. And of course my dad, the sheriff, who showed me how to have a heart of gold, unwavering optimism, and the gift of gab to relentlessly pursue dreams.

Chris and Lori for your time, love, and support when I needed it most. May the seas of karma be kind to your beautiful vessel, *The Mandolin*. Nate Graham, Crystal Carothers, and Ryan Brower for giving me feedback in the early stages. GRACIAS AMIGOS!

Latin America for all the loving hospitality that changed my life. I will forever be indebted and filled with gratitude. *Mi amor para América Latina comenzó con Aura en Pimentel, Perú. Ella me cuidó cuando yo estaba enfermo. La amistad y amor de ella y sus hijos Brunela, Carlos, Camila y su familia (Nano, Mauricio y por supuesto Chato Beto) cambió mi vida! Gracias a Pache y su papá, Leiter. Uds. son mis héroes. Gracias a Galápagos y sus leyendas y Los Chingones Mexicanos. Y al final gracias a todos en el camino por cuidar este gringito y compartir sus olas, comidas, y culturas ricas. Jamás olvidaré esta amistad y ayuda que me dieron. Que vengan pronto a visitarnos en Panamá.*

Laurie Gibson for her extraordinary edits.

Pachamama for giving us air to breathe, food to eat and still loving us despite our abusive behavior. We will change.

Spirit Quest for opening my soul to the powers much bigger than the self and exposing me to the life-changing lessons from "Mother."

John Perkins for his writing workshop, "Writing in a Time of Crisis," as well as all his inspirational and consciousness-activating books.

Much love to my friends and family who have passed on: Grandaddy, Mormor, Brian Tanner, Uncle Mike and Fred Edwards, Kurt Gotwals, forty-three Normalistas in Mexico and the thousands of other people who have disappeared following their courageous path fighting oppression and corruption. It's better to die for something than to live for nothing.

Jackie Brant left us just before this book was published. We know she is in a better, more loving place with Mike.

And lastly, you. Yes, you. By reading this, you brought life to these characters and stories.

Consciousness is spreading one seed, one journey, one story, one day at a time. Let us all keep climbing to BE the person the world needs us to BE.

A portion of the proceeds will go toward the development of Escuela Sin Fronteras, a cross-cultural language school based in rural Panama focused on: outdoor-oceanic education, expansive arts, language, culture, and building the wave of human potential.

Con Mucho Amor,
Cory
June, 2020

Come visit and share your talent(s).
Web: www.escuelasinfronteras-mundo.com

Readings

Mexico
"Zapatsita Comunique: May the Earth Tremble at its Core."
November 4, 2016. Upside Down World. Zapatistas.

"Zapatista and Indigenous Mexicans Create Parallel Government for Indigenous Autonomy." Jan. 10, 2017. Upside Down World. Ryan Mallet-Outrim.

"The Latin American Disappeared and Repeating History in Mexico." October 22, 2014. Truth Out. Jeff Abbott.

"Organic Consumers Association, "Nafta: Truth and Consequences of Corn Dumping." http://www.organicconsumers.org/chiapas/nafta040504.cfm

Deep: Freediving, Renegade Science, and What the Ocean Tells Us about Ourselves. 2014. Profile Books. James Nester.

Guatemala
"US Policy Driving Militarization in Guatemala."
July 5, 2015. Truth out. Jeff Abbott.

"Guatemala's Indigenous Water Protectors Organize to Challenge Hydroelectric Projects." Waging NONVIOLENCE-People-Powered News & Analysis. November 30, 2016. Truth Out. Jeff Abbott.

Panama

"America's Prisoner, Noreiga: The Memoirs of Manuel Noriega. 1997. Random House. Manuel Noriega and Peter Eisner."
"Getting to Know the General." 1984. Bodley Head. Graham Greene.
"Confessions of an Economic Hitman." 2004. Barrett-Koehler Publishers. John Perkins.

Reading List from 2017-2018

Book List	Author	Genre
Getting to know the General	Graham Greene	Nonfiction
The Power and Glory		Fiction
Confessions of an Economic Hitman	John Perkins	Nonfiction
Hoodwinked		
Shapeshifting		
Psychonavigation		
Spirit of the Shuar		
The World is As you Dream it		
This is how you Lose Her	Junot Diaz	Fiction
Brief and Wondrous		
Life of Oscar Wao		
Drown		
Breath	Tim Winton	Fiction
In Search Of Captain Zero	Alan Weisbecker	Nonfiction
Can't you Get along with Anyone		
Road Fever	Tim Cahill	Nonfiction
Two Wheels Through Terror	Glenn Hegsstad	
NoFX	Jeff Alulis	Nonfiction
Teachings of Don Juan	Carlos Castenada	Nonfiction
The Active Side of Infinity		
The Art of Dreaming		
Alchemist	Paul Coelho	Fiction
The Pilgrimage		
Travels with Charley	John Steinbeck	Nonfiction
Secret Seas	Carlos Eyles	Nonfiction
The Sea Around Us	Rachael Carson	Nonfiction
Silent Spring		

Book List	Author	Genre
Motorcycle Diaries Otra Vez	Ernesto Che Guevara	Nonfiction
Che	Fidel Castro	Nonfiction
Far Tortuga	Peter Matthiessen	Fiction
Tell My Horse	Zora Hurston	Nonfiction
Kite Runner	Khaled Hosseni	Fiction
Water for Elephants	Sara Greun	Fiction
Old Souls	Tom Shroder	Nonfiction
Bones of My Master: A Journey to Secret Mongolia	George Crane	Nonfiction
Blue Mind	Wallace Nichols	Nonfiction
The Power of Now A New Earth	Eckhardt Tolle	Nonfiction
All Our Wavers are Water Saltwater Buddha	Jamal Yogis	Nonfiction
Moby Dick	Herman Melville	Fiction
Siddhartha	Herman Hesse	Fiction
Jesus	Deepak Chopra	Fiction
Memories, Dreams, Reflections	Carl Jung	Nonfiction
Getting Stoned with Savages The Sex Lives of Cannibals	J Maarten Troost	Nonfiction
The Old Man and the Sea A Moveable Feast	Ernest Hemmingway	Fiction Nonfiction
King of the Moon	Gene Kira	Fiction
Following the Equator: A Journey Around the World	Mark Twain	Nonfiction
Long Way	Bernard Moitessier	Nonfiction
Deep	James Nester	Nonfiction
A Walk in the Woods	Bill Bryson	Nonfiction
Dark Alliance	Gary Webb	Nonfiction
Americas Prisoner: Memoirs of Manuel Noriega	Manuel Noriega and Peter Eisner	Nonfiction
Happy Teachers Change the World Fragrant Palms The Heart of Buddha's Teachings	Thich Hanh	Nonfiction

Book List	Author	Genre
The Book	Allan Watts	Nonfiction
Heart of Darkness	Joseph Conrad	Nonfiction
Barbarian Days: A Surfing Life	William Finnegan	Nonfiction
Sapiens: A Brief History of Humankind	Yuval Harari	Nonfiction
The Ultimate Gift	Mitch Albom	Fiction
5 People You Will Meet in Heaven	Mitch Albom	Fiction
Life of Pi	Yann Martel	Fiction
Feast of the Goat	Mario Llosa	Fiction
The Voyage of the Cormorant	Christian Beamish	Nonfiction
A Strangeness in my Mind	Orhan Panuk	Fiction
The Code	Sean Thompson	Nonfiction
The Mountain School The Way Finders: Why Ancient Wisdom Matters in the Modern World	Greg Alder Wade Davis	Nonfiction
All for a Few Perfect Waves: Audacious Life and Legend of Micky Dora	David Rensin	Nonfiction
Genealogy of Morals	Fredric Neitzsche	Nonfiction
Meditation of John Muir	John Muir	Nonfiction
When Dreams Become Reality: Why I went and Never Came Back	Crystal Carothers	Nonfiction
Safari as a Way of Life	Dan Eldon	Nonfiction
The Essential Rumi	Translated by Coleman Barks	Fiction
Swell	Liz Clark	Nonfiction
Ines Del Alma Mía	Isabel Allende	Fiction

Belyea dares to dream beyond what his eyes can see. His writing reflects his passionate pursuit of life and purpose. He writes with thought-provoking and poignant prose. Belyea currently resides in Panamá, where he runs Escuela Sin Fronteras, a language school(Spanish-English) aimed at breaking down cross-cultural barriers and giving back to the local community. For more information visit: www.escuelasinfronteras-mundo. com. Belyea remains an avid reader and writer. A direct result of his commitment to the craft of writing is reflected in his online creative writing classes he teaches through UCSD Extension. Finding Our Voices, Telling Our Stories continues to encourage aspiring writers to tell their stories that will inspire global change and higher consciousness.